Teaching the Early Modern Period

W9-ADH-352

Teaching the Early Modern Period

Edited by

Derval Conroy

Danielle Clarke

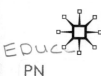
First published 2011 by
PALGRAVE MACMILLAN

Palgrave Macmillan in the UK is an imprint of Macmillan Publishers Limited,
registered in England, company number 785998, of Houndmills, Basingstoke,
Hampshire RG21 6XS.

Palgrave Macmillan in the US is a division of St Martin's Press LLC,
175 Fifth Avenue, New York, NY 10010.

Palgrave Macmillan is the global academic imprint of the above companies
and has companies and representatives throughout the world.

Palgrave® and Macmillan® are registered trademarks in the United States,
the United Kingdom, Europe and other countries.

ISBN 978–0–230–28450–0   hardback
ISBN 978–0–230–28451–7   paperback

This book is printed on paper suitable for recycling and made from fully
managed and sustained forest sources. Logging, pulping and manufacturing
processes are expected to conform to the environmental regulations of the
country of origin.

A catalogue record for this book is available from the British Library.

A catalog record for this book is available from the Library of Congress.

10   9   8   7   6   5   4   3   2   1
20   19   18   17   16   15   14   13   12   11

Printed and bound in Great Britain by
CPI Antony Rowe, Chippenham and Eastbourne

Contents

Acknowledgements

The editors would like to gratefully acknowledge the support of the Early Modern Research Strand of University College Dublin, whose financial support made possible both the initial 2008 conference that sowed the seed for this volume, and the translation of foreign-language material for publication. We extend our warm thanks to all those scholar-teachers who enthusiastically accepted our invitation to contribute, in addition to all those who proffered encouragement and support. In the nascent stages of this project, it was incredibly heartening that so many of those renowned for their research were enthusiastic about a scholarly volume devoted to pedagogical questions. We are particularly grateful to our six specialist readers who gave very generously of their time and expertise, as well as to our contributors for their patience, commitment to the project and gracious acceptance of suggestions for revision. Thank you also to the Palgrave Macmillan anonymous reviewers whose guidance was most helpful. A special thank you to Teresa Bridgeman for her professionalism and linguistic gymnastics, to Christabel Scaife who welcomed the proposal initially at Palgrave Macmillan and to Catherine Mitchell who has facilitated its completion, with tremendous patience and precision.

A volume such as this would not exist without the inspiration and commitment of generations of teachers. We would like to acknowledge our former teachers and current colleagues for their role as inspiring mentors: at Prendergast School, Jean Cran, Patricia Hayes, Valerie Maclean and Mary Passande; at Plumcroft School, Mrs Jewel; in Oxford, Jeri Johnson, Don Mackenzie, David Norbrook and Ann Wordsworth; at St Catherine's School, Miss O' Flaherty; at Mount Mercy College, Janet Browne-Dale and Patricia O'Shea; at Trinity College, Ruth Whelan, and at the École Normale Supérieure in Fontenay-Saint-Cloud, Christian Biet. We would also like to pay particular tribute to those colleagues in the School of English, Drama and Film, and the School of Languages and Literatures at UCD whose dedication to teaching and support in all matters pedagogical is perpetually uplifting.

Finally, the editors would like to thank each other for the mutual support and encouragement that ensured this project reached fruition. Danielle would like to thank Róisín for all her help and support, on and off the page; Derval would like to thank Nicolas for making her work possible and Alex for providing the most exhilarating pedagogical challenge of all!

Notes on Contributors

Christian Biet is Professor of Theatre Studies, Université de Paris Ouest-Nanterre, Professor at the Institut Universitaire de France since 2006, and visiting professor at New York University. His research focuses on French and English seventeenth- and eighteenth-century theatre, and more broadly on culture, literature, theatre and law in the early modern period. He is the author of over a hundred articles and book chapters, and of numerous monographs and critical editions including *Les Miroirs du soleil* (1989 and 2000), *Œdipe en monarchie: tragédie et théorie juridique à l'âge classique* (1994), *Racine ou la passion des larmes* (1996), *La Tragédie* (1997 and 2010), *Droit et littérature sous l'Ancien Régime* (2002) and, with Christophe Triau, *Qu'est-ce que le théâtre?* (2006). Recent editions include *Théâtre de la cruauté et récits sanglants en France (XVIe–XVIIe siècles)* (2006) and *Tragédies et récits de martyres en France (fin XVIe–début XVIIe siècle)* with Marie-Madeleine Fragonard (2009).

Susan Broomhall is Winthrop Professor of History at the University of Western Australia. Her research focuses on late medieval and early modern European history, specifically the history of women and gender, science, medicine and technologies, religious change, poverty and work. Recent publications include *Women and Religion in Sixteenth-Century France* (2005), *Early Modern Women in the Low Countries: Feminising Sources and Interpretations of the Past* (co-authored with Jennifer Spinks, forthcoming in 2011), as well as a collection of essays, *Emotions in the Household, 1200–1900* (2008), and *Women, Identities and Communities in Early Modern Europe* (2008), co-edited with Stephanie Tarbin.

Mark Thornton Burnett is Professor of Renaissance Studies at Queen's University, Belfast and author of *Filming Shakespeare in the Global Marketplace* (2007), *Constructing Monsters in Shakespearean Drama and Early Modern Culture* (2002) and *Masters and Servants in English Renaissance Drama and Culture: Authority and Obedience* (1997). He is also co-editor of numerous collections including *Shakespeare and Ireland: History, Politics, Culture* (1997) and *Screening Shakespeare in the Twenty-First Century* (2006).

Patrick Cheney is Distinguished Professor of English and Comparative Literature, Penn State and the author of *Reading Sixteenth-Century Poetry* (2011), *Marlowe's Republican Authorship: Lucan, Liberty, and the Sublime*

(2009), *Shakespeare's Literary Authorship* (2008), *Shakespeare, National Poet-Playwright* (2004), *Marlowe's Counterfeit Profession: Ovid, Spenser, Counter-Nationhood* (1997) and *Spenser's Famous Flight: A Renaissance Idea of a Literary Career* (1993). He is a General Editor for *The Oxford Edition of the Collected Works of Edmund Spenser* (forthcoming).

Danielle Clarke is Associate Professor of English Renaissance Language and Literature in the School of English, Drama and Film, UCD. She has published widely on questions of gender, language and representation in the early modern period, is author of *The Politics of Early Modern Women's Writing* (2001), co-editor of *'This Double Voice': Gendered Writing in Early Modern England* (2000) and is currently completing a monograph provisionally entitled *Articulating the Feminine: Gender, Language and Discourse, 1500–1700*. She was Vice-Principal for Teaching and Learning in the College of Arts and Celtic Studies, UCD, from 2004 to 2007, and is the leader of a 1st-year Enquiry Based Learning project, which was introduced in UCD in September 2008.

Derval Conroy is Lecturer in French at University College Dublin and convenor of the 'Early Modern Research Strand' at UCD since its inception in 2006. Her research interests revolve primarily around early modern women's history and women writers, and the early modern book. She has published numerous articles on both areas, and is co-editor of *Racine: The Power and the Pleasure* (2001) and *L'Œil écrit: études sur des rapports entre texte et image, 1800–1940* (2005). She is currently completing the manuscript of a monograph entitled *Ruling Women: Configuring the Female Prince in Seventeenth-Century France*, and has plans for a second study entitled *Strategies of the Image: Rhetoric, Gender and Iconography in the French Early Modern Book*.

Jonathan Dewald is UB Distinguished Professor of History, State University of New York at Buffalo and author of numerous monographs including *The Formation of a Provincial Nobility: The Magistrates of the Parlement of Rouen, 1499–1610* (1980), *Pont-St-Pierre, 1398–1789: Lordship, Community, and Capitalism in Early Modern France* (1987), *Aristocratic Experience and the Origins of Modern Culture: France, 1570–1715* (1993) (winner of the Leo Gershoy Award of the American Historical Association), *The European Nobility, 1400–1800* (1996) and *Lost Worlds: The Emergence of French Social History, 1815–1970* (2006).

Paul M. Dover is Assistant Professor in the Department of History at Kennesaw State University in Georgia, USA, where he teaches courses on Renaissance and Reformation Europe, historical methodology and historiography. He has published several articles on Renaissance diplomatic and intellectual history and is currently completing a book on ambassadorial praxis and culture in fifteenth-century Italy.

Henriette Goldwyn is Professor of French at New York University. She is co-founder and former vice-president of SIEFAR (Société internationale pour l'étude des femmes de l'ancien régime, http://siefar.org/) and responsible for seventeenth-century entries of the SIEFAR dictionary. Her teaching and research activities focus on literature, history and cultural studies of early modern France. She has published widely on seventeenth-century French women writers, and on early modern political and religious controversy. Recent publications include a critical edition of Madame du Noyer's *Mémoires* (2005). She is also co-editor-in-chief of the five-volume series *Le Théâtre des femmes de l'ancien régime, XVIe–XVIIIe siècles*, of which volumes 1 and 2 have already appeared (2006 and 2008). She is currently working on the Huguenot literary production of the diaspora.

Jane Grogan is Lecturer in Renaissance Literature in the School of English, Drama and Film at University College Dublin. She is the author of *Exemplary Spenser: Visual and Poetic Pedagogy in 'The Faerie Queene'* (2009) and editor of *Celebrating Mutabilitie: Essays on Edmund Spenser's Mutabilitie Cantos* (2009). Her research interests lie in Spenser and Sidney, early modern poetic theory, classicism and reception of the classics, and literary encounters between east and west in the early modern period.

Andrew Hadfield is Professor of English, and Co-Director of the Centre for Early Modern Studies, University of Sussex. His many publications include *Shakespeare and Republicanism* (2005), *Shakespeare and Renaissance Politics* (2004) and *Shakespeare, Spenser and the Matter of Britain* (2004). He is editor of *Renaissance Studies* and previously taught at the University of Leeds, The University of Wales, Aberystwyth, and Columbia University, as a visiting professor (2002–3).

Bernadette Höfer is Assistant Professor in the Department of French and Italian at the Ohio State University. Her research focuses on the intersection of early modern literature, philosophy, history and medicine, as understood through the prism of that era as well as of contemporary neuroscience and psychoanalysis. She is author of *Psychosomatic Disorders in Seventeenth-Century French Literature* (2009), as well as articles on Descartes, Molière, Lafayette, Spinoza, Surin and Michel de Certeau. Her teaching interests focus particularly on interdisciplinarity and on foreign-language pedagogy.

Carole Levin is Willer Cather Professor of History and Director of the Medieval and Renaissance Studies Program at the University of Lincoln-Nebraska. She has published very widely on women, gender and early modern history; her books include *The Heart and Stomach of a King: Elizabeth I and the Politics of Power* (1994), *The Reign of Elizabeth I* (2002), *Dreaming the English Renaissance: Politics and Desire in Court and Culture* (2008) and, with John Watkins, *Shakespeare's Foreign Worlds* (2009). With Diana Robin and Anne Larsen she edited *The Encyclopedia of Women in the Renaissance* (2007), which received book awards from the Sixteenth Century Studies Conference and Society as well as the Society for the Study of Early Modern Women. She was the Senior Historical Consultant on the exhibit, 'Elizabeth I: Ruler and Legend' at the Newberry Library in 2003 and the curator, with Garrett Sullivan, of the exhibit, 'To Sleep, Perchance to Dream' at the Folger Shakespeare Library in 2009.

Henry Phillips is Emeritus Professor of French at the University of Manchester, former Head of School of Modern Languages, former Research Director of the School of Languages, Linguistics and Cultures and a former chair of the UK Society for Seventeenth-Century French Studies. He is author of *The Theatre and its Critics in Seventeenth-Century France* (1980), *Racine: Mithridate* (1990), *Racine: Language and Theatre* (1994), *Church and Culture in Seventeenth-Century France* (1997) and *Le Théâtre catholique en France au XXe siècle* (2007).

Deborah Seddon is Senior Lecturer in the English Department at Rhodes University, Grahamstown, South Africa, where her teaching includes early modern, American and post-colonial literatures. She has published a number of articles in journals such as *Scrutiny2*, *English in Africa* and *English Studies in Africa*. A major area of her research is the work of the South African scholar and politician Sol Plaatje (1876–1932), the first translator of Shakespeare into an African language. She is currently involved, with a number of other Southern African scholars and the Sol Plaatje Educational Trust, in a collaborative project to publish bilingual editions of all Plaatje's Setswana writings.

Guy Spielmann is Associate Professor of French at Georgetown University in Washington, DC. He has also held visiting positions at the Université Marc Bloch/Strasbourg II (2001–3), and at the Université Paris X-Nanterre (2001). His scholarly interests cover early modern European performing arts, with a particular focus on stagecraft and non-literary genres. He has published widely in *Revue d'histoire littéraire de la France*, *Revue d'histoire du théâtre*, *Dix-septième siècle*, *Les Cahiers du dix-septième*,

Papers on Seventeenth-Century French Literature, Littératures classiques, Studies on Voltaire and the Eighteenth Century, Texte and *L'Esprit créateur*, has contributed to numerous collected volumes and is author of *Le Jeu de l'ordre et du chaos: comédie et pouvoirs à la fin de règne, 1673–1715* (2002). Professor Spielmann has also created a virtual resource on early modern European performing arts, 'OPSIS: Spectacles du Grand Siècle' (http://opsis.georgetown.edu).

Siep Stuurman is Professor of the History of Ideas in the Center for the Humanities at Utrecht University. His many publications include books on the history of Dutch nineteenth-century liberalism, *Wacht op onze Daden* (1992), on European state formation from the medieval period to the present, *Staatsvorming en Politieke Theorie* (1995), a study of a seventeenth-century marriage scandal, *Het Tragische Lot van de Gravin van Isenburg* (1999), and *François Poulain de la Barre and the Invention of Modern Equality* (2004), which was awarded the George Mosse Prize by the American Historical Association. He has also edited *Les Libéralismes: la théorie politique et l'histoire* (1994) and co-edited *Perspectives on Feminist Political Thought in European History* (1998) as well as *Beyond the Canon: History for the Twenty-First Century* (2007). His most recent book is a concise world history of discourses of common humanity, equality and cultural difference (*De Uitvinding van de Mensheid*, 2009). He is now working on a revised and expanded version in English.

Ceri Sullivan is Professor of English, Bangor University. She is author of *The Rhetoric of the Conscience in Donne, Herbert and Vaughan* (2008), *The Rhetoric of Credit: Merchants in Early Modern Writing* (2002) and *Dismembered Rhetoric: English Recusant Writing, 1580–1603* (1995); and co-editor of *Writing and Fantasy* (1998) and *Authors at Work: The Creative Environment* (2009).

Alain Viala is Professor of French Literature, University of Oxford and Emeritus Professor at the Université de Paris III – Sorbonne Nouvelle. He is author of *La France galante* (2008), *Lettre à Rousseau sur l'intérêt littéraire* (2006), *Racine: la stratégie du caméléon* (1990) and *Naissance de l'écrivain: sociologie de la littérature à l'âge classique* (1985), and co-editor of *Le Dictionnaire du littéraire* (2002). He is director of the collection 'Les Littéraires' at the Presses Universitaires de France and is co-founder of the 'Groupe de recherches interdisciplinaires sur l'histoire du littéraire' (EHESS-Paris III).

Karolyn Waterson was a professor in Dalhousie University's Department of French in Halifax, Nova Scotia, Canada from 1970 until retirement in 2009. Her primary research interests continue to address the theatre and moralist writing of seventeenth-century France, Acadian literature, censorship and intercultural education. She is author of *Molière et l'autorité: structures sociales, structures comiques* (1976) and has published widely on La Bruyère and Molière (in periodicals such as *Dix-septième siècle, Neophilologus, Studies in Early Modern France* and *Papers on Seventeenth-Century French Literature*) as well as on language and literature pedagogy.

Ruth Whelan is Professor of French, National University of Ireland, Maynooth and author of *The Anatomy of Superstition: A Study of the Historical Theory and Practice of Pierre Bayle* (1989). She is also a joint editor of *De l'humanisme aux Lumières: Bayle et le protestantisme* (1996), co-editor of *Toleration and Religious Identity: The Edict of Nantes and its Implications in France, Britain and Ireland* (2003) and co-editor of *Narrating the Self in Early Modern Europe* (2007). She has written some 80 articles and book chapters on the religious and intellectual culture of seventeenth-century France and is currently writing a book on the religious culture of the Huguenots in Ireland. She was elected a member of the Royal Irish Academy in 2000, and a *Chevalier dans l'Ordre des Palmes Académiques* in 2007.

Merry E. Wiesner-Hanks is Distinguished Professor of History at the University of Wisconsin-Milwaukee, and a leading authority on early modern Europe, women's history and gender. She is the author of many books, essay collections and articles, many of which have been translated into several languages. Key publications include *Women and Gender in Early Modern Europe* (1993, 2nd edn 2000), *Gender in History* (2001), *Early Modern Europe, 1450–1789* (Cambridge History of Europe, vol. II, 2006), as well as scholarly articles and essays. She has a particular interest in editing and producing materials for classroom use, and in the relationship between research and teaching.

Amy Wygant is Senior Lecturer in French at the University of Glasgow and editor of the journal *Seventeenth-Century French Studies*. She publishes on witchcraft, tragedy and psychoanalysis, is author of *Towards a Cultural Philology: Phèdre and the Construction of 'Racine'* (1999) and *Medea, Magic and Modernity in France: Stages and Histories, 1553–1797* (2007), and editor of *The Meanings of Magic from the Bible to Buffalo Bill* (2006), as well as a special issue of the *Forum for Modern Language Studies* on 'Stagecraft and Witchcraft'. Her current book-length project is 'Food and Fantasy in Early Modern France'. Dr Wygant is a co-founder of Women in French in Scotland (WIFIS), convenor of 1100+, the medieval and early modern research cluster of the University of Glasgow, and a co-founder of the 'Groupe de recherche sur l'histoire du français en Angleterre' (GRHIFA).

Introduction

Danielle Clarke and Derval Conroy

Teachers and scholars of early modern texts and histories have more reason than many academics to be grateful to, and frustrated by, mass media and popular culture. The 'Renaissance', a prepackaged Renaissance, a post-modern gallimaufry of doublets and hose, hot extramarital sex, power intrigues and tear-jerking execution scenes, is everywhere. *The Tudors*, first aired in 2007, and now in its fourth and final series – its event-driven narrative inevitably precluding further series – has brought in audiences more likely to be hooked by *The Wire* or *The Sopranos*, and whose interest was only partially or secondarily historical. It is perhaps to miss the point spectacularly to complain about the liberties that *The Tudors* takes with period specificity or historical fact – indeed, the real strength of the series is precisely that it captures convincingly what one imagines to be the atmosphere of intense intrigue, clashing egos and unconstrained masculine ambition that pertained at court. Other box-office successes like the flurry of films based on the life of Elizabeth I, or those retelling the story of the Boleyn sisters, or Vermeer's models, all play their part in making the early modern seem both modern and 'authentic', full of ideas and issues that hook modern and highly visually literate viewers into a world burnished with pleasing period details and settings which shape and form our contemporary ideas of the 'early modern'.

Of course, the sense of familiarity engendered by the presence of the Renaissance in popular culture presents as many challenges as solutions. In fact, the greatest obstacle that early modern teachers face is that their period is already known, always already familiar. The challenge therefore is to create a dialogue with the past that can accommodate this dialectic of familiarity and difference, and that can facilitate engagement with the specificities of a particular historical moment. And it is

1

precisely this pedagogical challenge presented by our simultaneous intimacy with, and estrangement from, the contours of the early modern that the essays in *Teaching the Early Modern Period* set out to address.[1] Equally, however, the essays in this volume address the diversity of the early modern, responding to and reflecting on how the narrowly based 'Renaissance' of Burckhardt and his followers is extended and challenged by questions of culture, location and perspective. The fractures between a Renaissance focused on ideals of civilization and civility and the consequences of those ideals form the framing context for several essays in this collection which outline the particular calibrations of the 'early modern' as it migrates across continents and through different educational systems.

So, if the doublets and hose seem familiar, what is different? More to the point, what is specific? To such an open-ended question, we will limit ourselves here to a few suggestions. In the first instance, the materials and artefacts that we attempt to explore and situate often straddle the nineteenth-century disciplinary boundaries that still largely structure our universities, and determine the expectations and ideologies that we bring to bear on students. The interdisciplinary nature of Renaissance Studies has been to the fore in recent years, although specific epistemes still strongly govern particular areas: historians and literary critics frequently use the same sources, but tend to read them in radically different ways. Scholars of English literature have a great deal in common with those who work on the literatures of Europe, but frequently their focus tends to be narrower and more defined by national traditions. Art historians are committed to the decoding and reading of images, but literary scholars are highly conscious of the fact that the written represents only one medium in the early modern period and frequently venture into territory that lies outside their own disciplinary grounding. The point is, that however interdisciplinary we attempt to be, we are still caught up on the 'inter' of interdisciplinary – attempting to make links and connections between spheres that have become distinct from one another, and reading materials that derive from and speak to an entirely different epistemological system. To take but the crudest example, 'literature' in the *belles-lettres* sense that configures the teaching of literature from school through to university is, at worse, an anachronism in the early period, and, at best, is in the complex process of formation. A series of other profound differences mark the discontinuity between the early modern and the contemporary moment in ways that are not true for the study of later historical periods: the evolving complexities of the relationship between print and manuscript, the profound upheavals in belief and subjectivity that mark the Reformation, the relationship of the body to other modes of being prior to Descartes, the fluid and relatively unfixed nature of the vernaculars, the relative marginality of all but masculine subjectivity to key discourses, the tendency to homogenize an enormously diverse and complex process of historical change. The list is infinitely expandable ...

The paradigms that traditionally structured the teaching of the early modern have come under significant pressure in recent years, and are, at the very least, in need of reconsideration. Notions relating to the rise of the individual, the development of a proto-capitalist economic model, the establishment of the nuclear family and the inauguration of the nation state have all undergone revision in the light of new evidence, new methodologies and new theories. The reinvigoration of the field, spearheaded by the twin forces of new historicism and feminism, started some time ago to give way to new challenges and imperatives, and the explorations in this volume both outline and respond to these. It is worth noting, however, that whilst many contributors in this volume describe and analyse in detail their own particular methods for helping students bridge the divide between the modern and the early modern (or even to make them aware that the divide is there), they are all broadly committed to the historicist project. This principle crosses the various disciplines represented here, as well as the quite distinctive national traditions. In particular, the contributors set out to examine the theory and practice behind a number of innovative and productive ways of teaching the early modern, some of which are specific to the period (that is, which exploit its own underlying principles, and interrogate how these can be applied in the twenty-first century), others of which are informed by principles of teaching literature and history which transcend the period (from intercultural and interdisciplinary challenges to the use of film in the classroom). The work represented here attempts to continue the move away from debates concerning canonicity and coverage to larger questions of pedagogy by concentrating on the interface between teaching and research, and by considering the broader implications of how and why we teach. One of the key issues to emerge from this cross-section of critical reflections on practice in the field is the plurality and diversity of early modern teaching within a framework of shared assumptions. Unlike many volumes dedicated to teaching, *Teaching the Early Modern Period* makes a virtue of difference, ranging through several disciplines (English, French Studies, History, Film, Drama) and a number of national contexts (Irish, British, French, Dutch, North American, South African, Australian).

Frequently, volumes on teaching tend to focus on methods for teaching specific texts, or break down a more general subject area into topics and author studies. This volume sets out to do something rather different by bringing together a wide range of perspectives all of which are unified by one central concern, that of dialogic engagement with the past. A word on the genesis of the volume may explain its structure, comprised as it is of eight essays and 14 shorter pieces, in addition to a type of literature review. This last, which directly follows this Introduction, sets out to examine some of the recent publications concerning the scholarship of teaching, and aims to point implicitly to some of the lacunae which the current volume strives to fill. Moving on from that, the eight core essays provide in-depth reflective examples on how the early modern is appropriated and negotiated in today's universities, focusing on four key areas: the digital classroom, the dialectic between familiarity and difference, classroom praxis and, finally, performance. For the 14 shorter pieces, eminent scholars renowned for their contribution to research were invited to comment on an aspect of their early modern teaching – what was fundamentally important or challenging or rewarding for them; what had changed most over the course of their careers; an approach they particularly upheld; a course or an assessment strategy that worked well. The result is a diverse and colourful insight into classroom practice and pedagogical reflection across a wide range of teaching environments on four continents – from leading research-led universities to smaller institutions where pre-1800 courses are rare – in which are highlighted a number of methodological and theoretical principles equally applicable to graduate as well as undergraduate teaching. Despite the diversity of approach and of teaching environments, a number of recurrent constants emerged which married harmoniously with the eight core essays. The retrospective ordering of these 14 pieces around the eight core essays aimed to underline the associations and shared concerns of our contributors. There is no doubt, however, that some essays would fit equally well into other subsections, and it is hoped that different synergies will suggest themselves to readers as they peruse the volume.

In Part 1 on the digital classroom, the focus is on the dialogue between the specificities of the early modern historical moment and the current technological age. Danielle Clarke concentrates on epistemological parallels, analysing how the configuration of knowledge in the modern electronic classroom owes much to its Renaissance forbears, while Paul Dover examines the parallels between the information revolutions of Renaissance Europe and those of today, underlining the role of resonances in the generation of historical empathy and historical understanding. In Part 2, the core essays examine issues of alterity and multiculturalism. Deborah Seddon analyses how student engagement with the complex associations between culture, politics, gender and representation can hugely benefit from an approach to early modern drama (*King Lear*) that draws on the complex cultural heritage of the students. For Jane Grogan, the central pedagogical issue is the necessity of unpacking the disparate heterogeneous discourses of the prepackaged familiar 'Renaissance' through curricular choices that exploit the specific multicultural moment that was the Renaissance in order to engender greater understanding of today's multicultural society. Once again, it is the creation of a dialogue between past and present that underpins both these approaches. Grouped around these essays are reflections on alterity and difference (Dewald, Stuurman, Whelan), on the pedagogical and ethical reward of what Whelan calls *dépaysement*, a constructive unsettling, on the importance of a global perspective (Wiesner-Hanks) and on the curriculum (Hadfield), while Susan Broomhall provides an overview of the diverse teaching approaches to the early modern in today's multicultural Australia.

Part 3 focuses on a range of classroom approaches that aim to foster student engagement with the past, and analyses the pedagogical issues behind certain 'in-roads' (to use Patrick Cheney's phrase). Karolyn Waterson examines the pedagogical benefit of an analysis of early modern censorship, while Bernadette Höfer focuses on the dialogue between the early modern mind/body debate and current neurobiology, and convincingly presents the case for interdisciplinarity. The shorter contributions in this section give lively insight into other specific courses, from Versailles (Henriette Goldwyn) to Shakespeare (Cheney and Burnett), into particular assessment strategies (Carole Levin), and into the principles that inform particular approaches (Viala and Sullivan). The focus of Part 4 is also on classroom approaches but more specifically this time on the appropriation of the early modern through performance (filmic or theatrical). Guy Spielmann's essay proposes a number of methodological guidelines, informed by an analytical stance on theories of representation, on how to place filmic representation of spectacle in a critical and pedagogical framework, through analysis of a wide range of examples from France and England. Wygant's focus, on the other hand, is on the bugbear of 'relevance', a pedagogical buzzword that, as she argues, is all too often unquestioned. Her essay analyses the dilemma faced in trying to encourage students to develop a resistance to unexamined relevance and argues that a pedagogical strategy informed by psychoanalytic theory provides a useful way of fostering such resistance. Juxtaposed with these essays is Henry Phillips' reflection on the pedagogical benefits of an approach that prioritizes performance and reading aloud in the classroom. The volume ends with Christian Biet's broad-ranging overview of what, for him, are the fundamental prerequisites of engagement with the past, both in the classroom and in research. To the extent that an analysis of the interface between research and teaching was one of the central ideas behind the genesis of this volume, this celebration of the overlap between the two provides a fitting conclusion to the collection.

A number of other key concerns link the contributions throughout the collection. Vital for many is the engagement with the primary text (Phillips, Cheney, Stuurman, Dewald, Sullivan), literary or historical. In fact, interestingly – and fittingly in a volume devoted to a period which was blithely unaware of ulterior disciplinary separations – the apparent differences between the approaches of historians and literary scholars seem to dissipate here, as historians advocate the use of 'literary' texts (Wiesner-Hanks, Levin, Stuurman) and literary scholars emphasize the importance of a historical perspective (Viala, Biet, Burnett). This is no doubt complemented by the fact that many early modernists, irrespective of their institutional disciplinary alignment, work in fact on the history of ideas, broadly construed. Also repeatedly raised are the fundamental changes wrought by the development of gender as a theoretical category of analysis, not only in the pieces written by scholars for whom women's history and women writers are an important research interest (Levin, Wiesner-Hanks, Broomhall, Goldwyn) but for others for whom it is now part and parcel of early modern work (Biet, Stuurman, Cheney, Whelan). Moreover, it is interesting that no one (in the shorter or longer pieces) chose to focus specifically on the use of 'theory' in the classroom as a particular challenge, although almost all the contributions are framed within one framework or another (feminist, psychoanalytical, performance-oriented, historicist, comparative). Although Alain Viala does warn against the use of post-modernist theoretical frameworks to the detriment of the historical/endogenous, many contributors do not mention theory overtly at all, while others take the use of a theoretical framework for granted: it would appear that, for most, 'Theory' has been assimilated, and is no longer a flashpoint for discussion. Another recurrent concern is the research/teaching dichotomy, which is implicit in many essays and explicit in some: Ceri Sullivan advocates abandoning 'the distinction between research and teaching, in favour of the Renaissance term "learning"'; for Andrew Hadfield, '[e]stablishing a symbiotic relationship between teaching and research [...] does not mean simply teaching our research', while Christian Biet provides an example of how the same methodological principles can inform both. Finally, and happily, a number of our contributors (Sullivan, Whelan, Biet) evoke the idea of pleasure, pleasure derived from the text, pleasure derived from teaching, pleasure derived from the mutual endeavour of teachers and students to fully comprehend materials that are both familiar and strange.

When Princeton luminary Elaine Showalter published *Teaching Literature* in 2003, she did more than provide an invaluable pedagogical tool for teachers: she implicitly demonstrated by example the possible existence of a dual commitment to research and teaching. What has made this project exhilarating has been the encounter with the energy, enthusiasm and commitment of 21 other teacher-scholar early modernists, together with their absence of cynicism, despite the increasingly depressing gradual metamorphosis of universities into businesses. Teaching, as it emerges in these pages, is not only a source of pleasure and reflection, it is also often the driving force behind innovation in research, as individual teachers respond to issues and problems initially raised in the classroom. Teaching often returns a highly specialized researcher to basic and fundamental questions that can be highly productive avenues of inquiry. Most university environments assume that the teaching–research traffic is one way: researchers accumulate knowledge that they then transmit to students. These essays suggest, in manifold ways, the shortcomings of this model, and highlight how the relationship is symbiotic. It is our hope that this volume will serve as a reminder that there need not be incompatibility between a high-powered successful research career and a profound commitment to the classroom.

Note

1. This is not the place to enter into the debate about the relative merits of the terms *early modern* or *Renaissance*. Suffice to say that the terms have subtly different valences in different countries, different traditions and different disciplines, as is reflected in the diverse usage of the terms throughout the volume.

1
The Scholarship of Teaching the Early Modern: An Overview

Derval Conroy

The original objective of this overview was rather simple. I would read a body of material devoted to teaching the early modern period, primarily as it pertained to English and French courses in higher education, with two aims in mind: firstly, to provide useful bibliographical information on the topic, and secondly, to present a synthesis of the key ideas in circulation concerning the perceived challenges involved in teaching the early modern period and the proposed solutions to those challenges. This would then serve implicitly to contextualize the approaches and principles highlighted in the contributions brought together in the current volume. The first aim proved realizable: various bibliographical searches brought to my attention a considerable body of literature (albeit certainly not a vast one, particularly if one excludes the studies devoted to the teaching of Shakespeare) that I was able to sift through, and attempt to evaluate. The second aim proved more illusory as it became quickly apparent that while much material was devoted to theorizing approaches (pedagogical and interpretative) to specific works published in the early modern period, very little came to my attention that analysed the broader concerns raised by teaching the period from the fifteenth to the eighteenth centuries. The reasons for this are probably twofold: on the one hand, not even the least historicist approach to the teaching of a particular early modern author or text can entirely ignore its historical context, and so such studies are by implication already rooted in the specifics of the period. On the other hand, it is understandable that the specificities of any one time period are less important than the broader issues involved in fostering engagement with the past, with texts and with the texts of the past. So, while it is left to some of the contributors in this volume to try to examine the particularities of the early modern in the classroom, the modified aim of this essay is, firstly, to outline what literature exists concerning the teaching of early modern printed texts and, secondly, to focus on a number of articles that raise issues of broad concern for all teachers of the period or that provide particularly useful examples of innovative and creative teaching. My selection is precisely that – a subjective selection mainly of articles directly relevant to English and French sources but I hope indirectly relevant to a wider readership of early modernists. While all attempts have been made to be as inclusive as possible (which has meant drawing on the usual suspects of JSTOR, Project Muse, the MLA International Bibliography, in addition to subject searches in the catalogues of major research copyright libraries on both sides of the Atlantic and requests for suggestions circulated to academic discussion lists), nonetheless this overview does not claim any exhaustivity. If it brings to a wider readership titles that may be new to some readers, then it will have fulfilled its aim.[1]

* * *

An obvious first port of call, for the teaching of literature at least, is the MLA 'Approaches to Teaching World Literature' series. Since its inception in 1982, the series has grown to 112 volumes, 31 of which concern the period from the fifteenth to the eighteenth centuries. The series, particularly in its early decades, appears primarily devoted to the stalwarts of the canon: *The Divine Comedy, Don Quixote, Paradise Lost, King Lear, Candide, Faust, Gulliver's Travels, Tristram Shandy* in the 1980s; volumes on the metaphysical poets, Samuel Johnson, Pope, Montaigne as well as *The Tempest* and other late romances of Shakespeare, *The Faerie Queen, Tartuffe* and *La Princesse de Clèves* in the 1990s; *Romeo and Juliet, Hamlet, Othello, Robinson Crusoe*, Milton's shorter poetry and prose, Rousseau, Richardson and Marguerite de Navarre since 2000. However, four of the most recent volumes – devoted to Sor Juana Inés de la Cruz (2007), *Lazarillo de Tormes* and the picaresque tradition (2008), the sixteenth-century Dominican missionary Bartolomé de Las Casas (2008) and Teresa of Ávila and the Spanish mystics (2009) – together with the volume in preparation on Inca Garcilaso de la Vega, suggest a move towards examining a broader intellectual and geographical landscape.[2] In addition to the volume on metaphysical poets, three further volumes are devoted to genre rather than to a single author or single text, namely shorter Elizabethan poetry (2000), English Renaissance drama (2002) and early modern Spanish drama (2006).[3] It is perhaps not surprising that it is precisely in these volumes of broader scope that a number of articles appear, as we will see below, which raise issues of more general concern to teachers of the early modern. Also genre-focused are *Teaching Early Modern English Prose* (2010), which makes its appearance in the MLA 'Options for Teaching' series, *Teaching with the Records of Early English Drama* (2006), part of the 'Studies in Early English Drama' Toronto series, *Teaching Eighteenth-Century Poetry* (1990), and the earlier discrete volume *Approaches to Teaching Spanish Golden Age Drama* (1989), the latter very clearly focusing on different critical/interpretative approaches to the material.[4]

As anyone reading these pages will know, the format of an MLA 'Approaches' volume has remained unchanged since the beginning of the series: Part One, entitled 'Materials', provides an overview of available materials – editions, translations, background studies, critical and pedagogical studies, bibliographies and so on – as well as aids to teaching (visual, audio-visual and, more recently, electronic resources). Since recommendations here are drawn from responses to a survey circulated to academics involved in teaching the field concerned, these sections benefit from a considerable amount of cumulative experience. For the most part, the articles in Part Two, entitled 'Approaches', reflect the profound changes that have marked the past decades in the way scholars and teachers approach and think about these texts. While focus in earlier volumes is on critical/interpretative approaches, or historical and intellectual context and background, later volumes include articles on comparative and interdisciplinary approaches, and, more recently, classroom practice or 'pedagogical strategies'. Although the overall thrust of the series may remain on ways of reading rather than ways of teaching[5] – the value of which in itself cannot be underestimated for specialist and non-specialist teachers, and indeed undergraduates, in highlighting some of the diversity in possible perspectives – numerous examples abound of more recent articles which focus on pedagogical process rather than critical interpretation. Of which, more anon.

Readers outside the United States may not be familiar (as I was not) with the peer-reviewed journal *Pedagogy: Critical Approaches to Teaching Literature, Language, Composition, and Culture*, published by Duke University Press since 2001, and devoted to English-language literature. Of interest to Spenser specialists may be the five articles in the subsection entitled 'Teach *The Faerie Queene* in a Week? Spenser in Today's Curriculum' (*Pedagogy*, 3.2, Spring 2003). This journal has also published six articles devoted to Shakespeare but nothing else specifically early modern that I could find. Also potentially of interest is *Studies in Medieval and Renaissance Teaching (SMART)*, currently published by Wichita State

University, although its emphasis seems to be primarily medieval. Articles concerning the teaching of literature can equally be found in journals more associated with literary criticism, such as *English, English Record, New Literary History* and the *French Review*, as well as those associated more broadly with foreign-language teaching such as the *Modern Language Journal* and the *ADFL Bulletin*.[6] The UK-based English Subject Centre, part of the Higher Education Academy, maintains a very useful website with a wide-ranging section on resources, while the online journal *Literature Compass*, produced by Blackwell, regularly publishes 'Teaching and Learning Guides'.[7] In seventeenth-century French studies, the inclusion of a panel on teaching at the annual SE17 conference has resulted in the regular inclusion of an article on teaching in the *Cahiers du dix-septième: An Interdisciplinary Journal*.[8] Other relevant articles that have come to light focus on Molière, Racine and the fairy-tale genre.[9]

Unsurprisingly, the literature concerning the teaching of Shakespeare is too considerable to do justice to here. The following texts are merely pointers. A warmly received recent collective volume with a number of informal yet inspirational essays (13 in total) is *Teaching Shakespeare: Passing it On* (2009). Seven essays are devoted to 'Teaching: Technology, Pedagogy and Ideology' in *Shakespeare Matters: History, Teaching, Performance* (2003), while *Teaching Shakespeare and Early Modern Dramatists* (2007) includes essays which examine Shakespeare's plays by genre (tragedies, comedies, histories), and a number which focus on his contemporaries and on other genres (city comedy and revenge tragedy). The format for these last essays is appealing in its concision: almost all include a section on chronology, a critical overview that outlines the interpretative approaches the work/author has provoked in recent critical history and a practical section on pedagogic strategies, including precise questions for classroom discussion and suggestions for workshop activities.[10] On performance, readers can consult *Teaching Shakespeare through Performance* (1999) as well as *Performance Approaches to Teaching Shakespeare* (2005), while for the issues involved in teaching Shakespeare through film, good starting points can be found in *Shakespeare on Film* (2005) and the collective volume *Screening Shakespeare in the Twenty-First Century* (2006).[11]

Part of the awareness that material on critical interpretation and content is not sufficient to set about answering the challenges of teaching literature is reflected by the appearance in recent years of books which focus on the pedagogical processes of teaching the discipline: these raise concerns which are relevant to any literature classroom, including evidently the early modern one. Well known by now, and greeted some years ago by this reader at least with an enormous sigh of relief, is Elaine Showalter's *Teaching Literature* (Oxford: Blackwell, 2003), a wonderfully refreshing and uplifting guide, inspired by a desire to re-evaluate the role of teaching, and an underlying belief that 'we should reconceive our pedagogy to make it as intellectually challenging as our research'.[12] Three chapters are devoted to genre (Teaching Drama/Poetry/Fiction), while others focus on 'The Anxiety of Teaching', 'Theories of Teaching Literature', 'Methods of Teaching Literature', 'Teaching Theory' and 'Teaching Teachers'. In each of these, Showalter addresses the question of *why* and *how* we teach literature rather than *what* we teach.[13] The volume is filled with both observations concerning the philosophy of teaching and numerous pieces of advice concerning the activity of teaching, from issues of student engagement and motivation, to the use of humour and entertainment. Two particularly useful chapters are devoted to 'Teaching Dangerous Subjects' (such as suicide) and 'Teaching Literature in Dark Times', both of which serve as reminders of the ethical dimension to our work. As she comments in this last chapter:

> In dark times, moments of personal or collective anguish, literature professors have to think about the abstractions of professional ethics in a much more urgent and existential way. At these moments, the clichés of our field suddenly take on startling life, and the platitudes of the humanities become credos that confront us with real choices and decisions on how to act.[14]

In the discussion that follows, Showalter is highly engaging, informal, personal and sensitive. This is a tremendous book that is both informative and witty, thought-provoking and utterly enjoyable.

Another useful volume is the collection *Teaching Literature: A Companion* (2003), whose first part 'Fields of Study in the Twenty-First Century' theorizes approaches to a range of genres and study areas, while the second part 'Classroom Rituals, Old and New' provides an insight into a number of practical pedagogical strategies used in the classroom. These latter essays in particular raise issues that go beyond the specific contexts described and suggest solutions that are adaptable to many teaching situations.[15] Taking a different tack, and marked by an engaging conversational tone, is *Teaching Literature: Writers and Teachers Talking* (1995) which brings together 23 interviews of 'teachers who write, writers who teach, writers who don't teach, writers whose books are taught', drawn from Ireland, England and the USA. Numerous contributions are specifically relevant to higher education and the book as a whole is underpinned by a resounding insistence on the fundamental importance of both literature and teaching in today's world. For writer and university teacher Judy Kravis, editor of this collection: 'We can, we may, we should teach literature as the breath of life – or at any rate the breath of virtual reality. Once upon a time we discovered we couldn't live without it. We should remember that.'[16] At the other end of the spectrum is *Teaching and Learning English Literature* (2006), firmly rooted in pedagogic theory and full of much practical advice, with chapters on curriculum and course design, specific teaching methods, assessment and the evaluation of teaching, in addition to chapters entitled 'What is Good Teaching?' and 'Teaching Literary Theory and Teaching Writing'.[17] Finally, teachers of French, or indeed other foreign-language literatures, would find of great benefit *Modern French Literary Studies in the Classroom* (2004).[18] Although this volume is devoted to nineteenth-century literature, many of the lively and reflective essays could easily be transferred to other historical periods. Particularly inspired is the simple yet brilliant idea behind Michael Garval's 'Teaching Tours de France', a whirlwind pedagogical tour around France which provides an introduction to both nineteenth-century and present-day France by requiring students to compare the content and implicit ideologies of the old school book *Le Tour de la France par deux enfants* (1877) with present-day materials. It is very easy to envisage how a modified version of this could work as a first-year undergraduate introduction to the early modern.

Corresponding volumes which focus on pedagogical process in history teaching include *Teaching History at University: Enhancing Learning and Understanding* (2003), *Teaching and Learning History* (2005) as well as the earlier collective volume *The Practice of University History Teaching* (2000).[19] All of these volumes contain practical advice useful to the early modern history instructor. Furthermore, the journal *The History Teacher*, published by the US Society for History Education, has been publishing articles on history pedagogy since 1967.

* * *

So much for the titles that my various bibliographical searches brought to light. I would now like to bring attention to a number of articles which I found thought-provoking either because of a creative student-centred approach or because they raise issues relevant to broad elements of the early modernist teaching community. Three disparate but specific challenges frequently evoked resonated particularly with me: the exploitation of a sense of alienation in dealing with the past; the integration of women writers into curricula; and the use of technology in the early modern classroom. What follows are some suggestions for reading concerning these three challenges.

The dynamic between familiarity and difference that encounters with the past engender is a constant that appears in much of the literature on teaching the early modern, and indeed in the essays of Part 2 of this volume. There is widespread agreement that emphasizing only the familiar is not in students' best interests, and the pedagogical value of keeping 'a sense of strangeness' or resisting 'the lure of too easy familiarity or too facile relevance' is repeatedly lauded.[20] In answer to his question, 'What can a teacher and director do who is committed to teaching historical and cultural difference and to showing students how their intellectual labor in the theater is grounded in a specific historical and cultural site?', Ric Knowles gives as one suggestion '[shaping] a research exercise as a process in translation among cultures rather than as an exegesis of canonical texts with universalist meaning'.[21] For Melveena McKendrick, writing about the Spanish *comedia*, the issue is about maintaining 'the delicate balance between cultural invisibility (failing to see the present in the past because the social circumstances and moral vocabulary are different) and anachronism (treating the past as if it were no different from the present)'.[22] Her solution to maintaining this balance between diachronic and synchronic readings is

> not to ignore the diachronic perspective but to embrace it, mapping connections and differences between then and now in order to create a more sophisticated degree of historical understanding. Even at the simplest and most obvious level, demonstrating what links us to and separates us from the past can contibute to the processes of historicization and humanization that bring a text alive.[23]

Another way of exploiting a sense of alienation is outlined by John Hunter who very wisely points out that frequently the cultural representations of the present are no less alien to students than those of the past, and that historical distance alone cannot be held responsible for incomprehension or alienation. Hunter recommends a class discussion of 'the kinds of resistance that most art mounts against easy interpretation' which can allow lecturers 'to begin to suggest that the difficulties of historical drama [and by extension, this reader would add, of any early modern text] are not history's fault but simply one manifestation of the dialectical nature of any encounter between an object of interpretation and an interpreter'.[24] Ultimately, as he summarizes,

Once students realize that difference is a mutable and contingent condition of all reading and not the exclusive property of the past, the act of reading itself can be historicized and analyzed. With this recognition of difference in place one can investigate the specificities of the early modern period and the ways in which we construct relations between it and the present. The complex interactions between history and literature can thus become the crucial subjects of a course rather than just the unspoken assumptions behind it.[25]

Issues of alienation and alterity take on a different resonance in the context of women writers. The development of interest in women writers and gender as a category of analysis over the past 30 years is reflected (if somewhat belatedly) in two volumes from the MLA 'Options for Teaching' series, *Teaching Tudor and Stuart Women Writers* (2001) and *Conversations with Seventeenth- and Eighteenth-Century French Women Writers* (in press) in addition to *Teaching Other Voices: Women and Religion in Early Modern Europe*.[26] Published to mark the tenth anniversary of the Chicago University Press 'Other Voice in Early Modern Europe' series, the 14 essays of this last volume, which focus on the religious writings of women, vary in their emphasis on course content or classroom practice, addressing a dual readership of both students and specialists. Particularly helpful are the suggestions for courses and modules which precede the essays and the later appendix that provides a summary of the suggestions for course design or approach made in the essays themselves.[27] While this volume focuses on continental European women, *Teaching Tudor and Stuart Women Writers* focuses on England. The first part of this book is devoted to the historical contextualization of women writers and readers, and the second to a biographical introduction of ten women writers from Elizabeth I to Aphra Behn. These sections provide succinct introductions that advanced undergraduates or non-specialists could find useful.[28] The three essays that make up the fourth section 'Resources for Further Study' together provide an impressively rich bibliography of primary and secondary sources relevant to women writers.[29] But for the early modern lecturer, at least this one, most appealing is Part III entitled 'Models for Teaching' which amidst its 16 essays includes three short essays on the use of theory in the early modern classroom as well as six which provide insight into concrete pedagogical strategies used. Particularly engaging is Paula Loscocco's account of how theory helped her combat, among other issues, the all-too-common nightmare in courses on women writers of the 'wave of distorting essentialism [which] would sweep the class, committing all male writers to the dustbin of sexist history and making prescient saints out of [...] pro-woman writers'.[30] In other articles, Ramona Wray describes how students in Belfast were led to question issues of canonicity, Betty S. Travitsky and Anne Lake Prescott examine the possibilities of paired readings of early modern male and female writers, while Ann Hurley provides a fascinating account of a course where students develop the skills of descriptive bibliography as well as a greater understanding of the humanist model and its marginalizing effect on women writers.[31] Elsewhere, in a volume on teaching Shakespeare and other dramatists, Karen Raber provides a concise overview of the issues involved in integrating fully the work of women dramatists into course programmes – in sum, how does one strike a balance between situating women writers within a broad literary tradition and yet doing justice to the specificities of a distinct female literary tradition? – and suggests a number of classroom strategies which go towards addressing these challenges.[32] Faith Beasley's answer to that question, it would seem, would be to focus on conversation: the forthcoming collection of 32 essays centres on the theme of conversation (and hence dialogue) – conversations between male and female writers of the (mainstream) early modern period, conversations between past and present. As Beasley puts it: 'Reconstructing the conversations between women and men of the Ancien Régime changes our view of the period as a whole, offers new interpretations of the canonical men's texts so celebrated in Western culture, and changes the very questions we ask as scholars and teachers.'[33]

And finally to the digital classroom. While the influence of technology and the teaching of the humanities is a subject that has spawned much debate and given rise to numerous publications over the past ten years,[34] articles devoted to the integration of technologies into early modern courses can be particularly useful. Immediately striking is Clark Hulse's 'Elizabethan Poetry in the Postmodern Classroom' that, as Clarke and Dover do in this volume, examines the parallels between the early modern and the current digital age. Hulse describes how in class he aims to

> use Elizabethan poetry as a way of understanding cultural transformations in the early modern period – indeed to see Elizabethan poetry as itself a product of and shaper of those transformations – and reciprocally, to use the study of Elizabethan poetry as a way of understanding the equally large transformations in which we and our students are caught in the postmodern period.[35]

He does this by organizing his course around the three concepts of 'reproductive technology, authorship, and the literary market', and uses as one of the student assignments the creation of online commonplace books.[36] Requiring students to create online annotated editions is an ingenious strategy that has clear appeal for both students and lecturers. Sheila T. Cavanagh describes in 'Editing an Elizabethan Poem: A Course Assignment' how editing a poem obliges students to delve into the historical, philosophical and religious context as well as considering issues of poetics (depending on the level of the class).[37] A similar approach is described by Matthew D. Stroud in 'The Closest Reading: Creating Annotated Online Editions', although here the author does point out how time-consuming for the lecturer the creation of electronic editions of six *comedias* by a small group of students (17 in this instance) proved to be.[38] Food for thought on time-effective assignments, conversely, can be found in John Webster's account of how the use of writing portfolios provides a way of using 'daily writing as a primary means by which to help [...] students become active readers'.[39] Likewise, Frances Teague provides a very interesting example of the pedagogical value of writing itself in her account of how student response papers, posted online, gradually bring the students themselves to question their received ideas about Renaissance drama.[40]

Another assignment option frequently mentioned involves the creation of websites. In 'Webbing Webster', C.E. McGee describes his experience of having students 'prepare 8–10 pages of educational material on John Webster's *The Duchess of Malfi* as if for inclusion on the Stratford Festival Web site' – a type of enquiry-based-learning approach.[41] A useful account of course website design, from the lecturer's point of view, can be found in Mark Aune, 'Always a Work in Progress: Creating a Course Website for Introduction to Shakespeare',[42] which describes in considerable detail the process(es) involved in establishing from scratch a course website and outlines some of the difficulties and pitfalls one may encounter. Elsewhere, Guy Spielmann provides a very interesting insight into the rationale behind the design of his site 'Spectacles du grand siècle' for the teaching of French seventeenth-century spectacle.[43] Finally, for an example of whole-hearted embracing of technology-use in the early modern classroom, readers could consult Diane E. Sieber's highly impressive account of how technologies, in the form of hypertext syllabi, immediacy rooms, Flash animations and three-dimensional modelling for example, transformed her teaching practice of seventeenth-century Spanish theatre.[44]

If articles on how technology has changed the dynamics of authority in the classroom are thought-provoking as well as practical, as scholars reflect on how the relationship between teacher/text/student is altered, such reflection long predates the digital age. A final mention here should go to an article by the late Barbara Johnson, 'Teaching Ignorance', written nearly 30 years ago (1982), but widely cited ever since.[45] The article focuses on the character of Arnolphe in Molière's *L'École des femmes* (*School for Women* or *School for Wives*) and falls primarily into the category of literary analysis. However, since the analysis examines Arnolphe's role as a mentor of his future wife, it provides a basis to comment on the teacher/student dynamic in a general way. The entire article, therefore, is underpinned by an interrogation concerning the pedagogic process, since the play, Johnson maintains, could be 'aptly re-named "the portrait of an anti-teacher"'.[46] Through her examination of a character usually associated with satire and ridicule, she is led to ask some uncomfortable truths about the relationship between teaching, authority and knowledge. As she puts it:

> Could it be that the pedagogical enterprise as such is always consti-tutively a project of teaching ignorance? Are our ways of teaching students to ask *some* questions always correlative with our ways of teaching them *not to ask* – indeed, to be unconscious of – others? Does the educational system exist in order to promulgate knowledge, or is its main function rather to universalize a society's tacit agree-ment about what it has decided it does not and cannot know?[47]

Her conclusion is unequivocal:

> The question of education, in both Molière and Plato, is the question not of how to transmit but of how to *suspend* knowledge. That question can be understood in both a positive and a negative sense. In a nega-tive sense, not knowing results from repression, whether conscious or unconscious. Such negative ignorance may be the necessary by-product – or even the precondition – of any education whatsoever. But positive ignorance, the pursuit of what is forever in the act of escaping, the inhabiting of that space where knowledge becomes the obstacle to knowing – *that* is the pedagogical imperative we can neither fulfill nor disobey.[48]

Wise words.

* * *

At the end of my brief excursion into the scholarship of teaching the early modern, I am left with two very distinct impressions. On the one hand, it is hard not to be struck by the repeated sense of dedication and enthusiasm, the novel ideas, the relishing of a challenge that emanate from the writings of those scholar-teachers consulted here. It has been a fruitful and enjoyable investigation from which I walk away with ideas for at least five new courses and an infinite number of assessment strategies in mind. On the other hand, the paucity of scholarship concerning the activity that is supposed to be, and certainly perceived by many to be, the primary role of university academic staff in the humanities appears at best anomalous, at worst a cause for concern, certainly when compared with the vast publication machine which is part and parcel of literary scholarship. This is not in any way to detract from the latter, but quite simply to point out that the imbalance is striking. This bibliographical overview confirms, if confirmation were needed, that there is an urgent need for volumes, such as this one, which aim to play a role in filling the gap. Let the redressing of the imbalance continue.

Notes

1. Throughout the research for this essay, I have been forcefully reminded of the power of the Internet to render visible and therefore also to occult, and the extent to which, in searching for recent publications, one is entirely at the mercy of the vagaries of various databases which not only tend to index journal articles rather than book chapters, but where the variation in the keyword used ('teaching' as opposed to 'pedagogy' for example) will frequently produce very different results. I am conscious therefore of the workings of a type of inverse serendipity which has made of this research an interesting learning experience in itself. However, it must be admitted, to the credit of the databases, that enquiries made to human beings (via, of course, Internet discussion lists) led to the discovery of the grand total of two new articles that I had not come across listed electronically.
2. A volume is also in preparation on Ariosto's *Orlando furioso*, and a second edition on *Paradise Lost*. It is not the aim of this essay to examine the role of this series, certainly in its early decades, in the reproduction, and continued institutionalization, of the traditional canon. On this issue, and for a critique of other aspects of the series, see Sheree Meyer, '"Broadly Representative"? The MLA's Approaches to Teaching World Literature Series', *Pedagogy*, 3.1 (2003), 21–51. For Meyer, '[t]he series reproduces not only a pedagogical canon of works but the often veiled ideological contradictions embedded in the institutional structures of schools, departments, and courses' (p. 25).
3. *Approaches to Teaching Shorter Elizabethan Poetry*, ed. Patrick Cheney and Anne Lake Prescott (New York: MLA, 2000); *Approaches to Teaching English Renaissance Drama*, ed. Karen Bamford and Alexander Leggatt (New York: MLA, 2002); *Approaches to Teaching Early Modern Spanish Drama*, ed. Laura R. Bass and Margaret R. Greer (New York: MLA, 2006).

4. *Teaching Early Modern English Prose*, ed. Susannah Brietz Monta and Margaret W. Ferguson (New York: MLA, 2010); *Teaching with the Records of Early English Drama*, ed. Elza Tiner (University of Toronto Press, 2006); *Teaching Eighteenth-Century Poetry*, ed. Christopher Fox (New York: AMS Press, 1990); *Approaches to Teaching Spanish Golden Age Drama*, ed. Everett W. Hesse and Catherine Larson (York, SC: Spanish Literature Publications Company, 1989). Also in the 'Options for Teaching' series are two volumes on women writers (see below, n. 26), a volume on Shakespeare in performance (see n. 10) and a volume entitled *Teaching the Literatures of Early America*, ed. Carla Mulford with Angela Vietto and Amy E. Winans (2000). Furthermore, in press in this series is a volume on *Teaching Literature and Law*, co-edited by A. Sarat, C. Frank and M. Anderson, which contains a number of contributions relevant to early modern teaching, while another volume is in preparation entitled *Teaching Early Modern English Literature from the Archives*, co-edited by Ian Moulton and Heidi Brayman Hackel. I would like to thank Peter Herman for bringing these last two volumes to my attention.

5. For a general comment on this issue, unrelated to the MLA series, see Elizabeth B. Bernhardt, 'Teaching Literature or Teaching Students?' *ADFL Bulletin*, 26.2 (1995), 5–6.

6. See, for example, Bill Overton, 'Teaching Eighteenth Century English Poetry: An Experiment', *English*, 40.167 (1991), 137–44.

7. See http://www.english.heacademy.ac.uk/ [accessed 10 September 2010]. For *Literature Compass*, see, for example, Andy Mousley, 'Teaching & Learning Guide for: Renaissance Literary Studies after Theory: Aesthetics, History and the Human' (June 2007); Jennifer C. Vaught, 'Teaching & Learning Guide for: Men Who Weep and Wail: Masculinity and Emotion in Sidney's *New Arcadia*' (August 2008); Evi Mitsi, 'Teaching & Learning Guide for: "Nowhere is a Place": Travel Writing in Sixteenth-Century England' (July 2008). These guides provide very useful advice on textual and electronic resources, possible course outlines, topics for classroom discussion and suggestions for assessments. See http://www.blackwell-compass.com/subject/literature/ [accessed 10 September 2010]. I would like to thank Jane Grogan for bringing this journal to my attention.

8. To date, the following have appeared: Jean-Marc Poisson, 'Pour une approche interactive de l'enseignement des textes littéraires au niveau intermédiaire: Les *Contes* de Perrault', 8.2 (2003), 77–82; Katherine Dauge-Roth, 'Crossing Lines, Encouraging Ownership: Teaching the Occult Early Modern', 10.2 (2006), 107–41; Allison Stedman, 'Teaching the Interdisciplinary Seventeenth Century to Undergraduates: A Literary Historian's Perspective', 11.1 (2006), 171–92; Stella Spriet, 'Enseigner *quel* XVIIe siècle?' 11.1 (2006), 121–36; and Larry Riggs, 'Teaching the Seventeenth Century: Modernity, Motives, and Further Reflections on Critical Literacy', 12.2 (2009), 71–86.

9. See Jean-Denis Marzi, 'An Introduction to Teaching Molière: *La Jalousie du Barbouille*', *Modern Language Journal*, 68 (1984), 125–9; Charlotte Trinquet and Benjamin Balak, 'Teaching Early Modern Fairy Tales to Disney Princesses: Or, If Only Mme d'Aulnoy Had a Wiki', in *Origines*, ed. Russell Ganim and Tom Clark, coll. Biblio 17, No 180 (Tübingen: Gunter Narr Verlag, 2009), pp. 311–24; John Campbell, '"Enseigner Racine": mission impossible?', in *Racine et/ou le classicisme*, ed. Ronald W. Tobin, coll. Biblio 17, No 129 (Tübingen: Gunter Narr

Verlag, 2001), pp. 249–60 and in the same volume, Michael S. Koppisch, '"Tout fuit, tout se refuse à mes embrassements": Can We Continue to Teach Racine?' pp. 309–19. More historically oriented is Julia Douthwaite's 'Making History from Fictions? The Dilemma of Historicism in the French Revolution Classroom', *EMF: Studies on Early Modern France*, 7 (2001), 201–25.

10. *Teaching Shakespeare: Passing it On*, ed. G.B. Shand (Chichester, West Sussex and Malden, MA: Wiley-Blackwell, 2009); *Shakespeare Matters: History, Teaching, Performance*, ed. Lloyd Davis (Cranbury, NJ and London: Associated University Presses, 2003); *Teaching Shakespeare and Early Modern Dramatists*, ed. Andrew Hiscock and Lisa Hopkins (Basingstoke and New York: Palgrave Macmillan, 2007).

11. *Teaching Shakespeare through Performance*, ed. Milla Cozart Riggio (New York: MLA, 1999); Edward L. Rocklin, *Performance Approaches to Teaching Shakespeare* (Urbana, IL: National Council of Teachers of English, 2005); Judith Buchanan, *Shakespeare on Film* (Harlow and London: Pearson Education, 2005); *Screening Shakespeare in the Twenty-First Century*, ed. Mark Thornton Burnett and Ramona Wray (Edinburgh University Press, 2006). See also the older volume by H.R. Coursen, *Teaching Shakespeare with Film and Television* (Westport, CT: Greenwood Press, 1997).

12. Elaine Showalter, *Teaching Literature* (Oxford: Blackwell, 2003), p. 11. On this important volume, see the Round Table articles devoted to it in *Pedagogy*, 4.1 (2004): Martin Bickman, 'Moving from the Margins', 141–50; Beth Kalikoff, 'Not Your Father's Literature Classroom', 150–4; and Christine Cheney, 'Sweet Dreams', 155–60.

13. Showalter, *Teaching Literature*, p. vii.

14. *Ibid.*, p. 131.

15. *Teaching Literature: A Companion*, ed. Tanya Agathocleous and Ann C. Dean (Basingstoke: Palgrave Macmillan, 2003). This volume also contains two short but very useful appendices on 'Web Resources for Teaching Literature', pp. 186–8 and a 'Bibliography of Resources on Teaching Literature', pp. 189–92.

16. *Teaching Literature: Writers and Teachers Talking*, ed. Judy Kravis (Cork University Press, 1995), 'Introduction', p. 8.

17. Ellie Chambers and Marshall Gregory, *Teaching and Learning English Literature* (London: SAGE, 2006).

18. *Modern French Literary Studies in the Classroom: Pedagogical Strategies*, ed. Charles J. Stivale (New York: MLA, 2004).

19. Alan Booth, *Teaching History at University: Enhancing Learning and Understanding* (London: Routledge, 2003); Geoff Timmins, Keith Vernon and Christine Kinealy, *Teaching and Learning History* (London: SAGE, 2005); *The Practice of University History Teaching*, ed. Alan Booth and Paul Hyland (Manchester University Press, 2000).

20. Alexander Leggatt, 'Introduction: The Strangeness of Renaissance Drama', and Ric Knowles, 'Teaching History, Teaching Difference, Teaching by Directing Heywood's *A Woman Killed with Kindness*', both in *Approaches to Teaching English Renaissance Drama*, pp. 23–8 (p. 23) and pp. 99–105 (p. 105).

21. Knowles, 'Teaching History, Teaching Difference', p. 100.

22. Melveena McKendrick, 'Communicating the Past', in *Approaches to Teaching Spanish Drama*, pp. 29–38. One of the concrete examples she gives of countering 'cultural invisibility' involves presenting the fundamental preoccupation

with honour in Spanish drama, which can seem archaic to students, in terms of 'self-worth, self-respect, self-image and public image, good name and reputation', or with reference to the laws of slander and libel (p. 31).

23. *Ibid.*, p. 38.

24. John Hunter 'How Much History Is Enough? Overcoming the Alienation of Early Modern Drama', in *Approaches to Teaching English Renaissance Drama*, pp. 165–71 (p. 168).

25. *Ibid.*, p. 171.

26. *Teaching Tudor and Stuart Women Writers*, ed. Susanne Woods and Margaret P. Hannay (New York: MLA, 2001); *Conversations with Seventeenth- and Eighteenth-Century French Women Writers*, ed. Faith Beasley (New York: MLA, in press); *Teaching Other Voices: Women and Religion in Early Modern Europe*, ed. Margaret L. King and Albert Rabil, Jr (Chicago University Press, 2007).

27. *Teaching Other Voices*, pp. 25–8 and 203–15.

28. The volume introduction in itself provides a concise overview of the socio-cultural situation of English women at the time (pp. 1–20).

29. Particularly comprehensive is Georgiana Ziegler's lengthy 'Lost in the Archives? Searching for Records of Early Modern Women', pp. 315–47.

30. Paula Loscocco, 'Theory in the Teaching of Early Modern Women Writers', pp. 227–34 (p. 228). See also Gary F. Waller, 'Teaching the Writings of Early Modern Women from a Theoretical Perspective', pp. 221–6.

31. Ramona Wray, 'Canons and Course Packs: Teaching Seventeenth-Century Women's Writing in Belfast', pp. 271–6; Betty S. Travitsky and Anne Lake Prescott, 'Juxtaposing Genders: Jane Lead and John Milton', pp. 243–7; Ann Hurley, 'Archival Studies: Retrieving the "Nonexistent" Women Writers of the English Renaissance', pp. 253–7. As someone whose research interests are in both the history of the book and early modern women writers, this last course is one I envy the students.

32. Karen Raber, 'Early Modern Women Dramatists', in *Teaching Shakespeare and Early Modern Dramatists*, pp. 218–34. Also of interest on the same question is Regina M. Buccola's '"These So-called Early Modern Women Writers": Strategies for Integrating Women Writers into English Department Curriculum', *Sixteenth-Century Journal*, 34.1 (2003), 147–54.

33. Faith Beasley, 'Introduction', in *Conversations with Seventeenth- and Eighteenth-Century French Women Writers*. I would like to thank Faith Beasley for sharing this material with me prior to its publication.

34. See, for example, Gilly Salmon, *E-moderating: The Key to Teaching and Learning Online* (London: Kogan Page, 2000); *Teaching and Learning Online*, ed. J. Stephenson (London: Kogan Page, 2001); *Teaching Literature and Language Online*, ed. Ian Lancashire (New York: MLA, 2009) and *Teaching Literature at a Distance: Open, Online and Blended Learning*, ed. Takis Kayalis and Anastasia Natsina (London: Continuum, 2010).

35. Clark Hulse, 'Elizabethan Poetry in the Postmodern Classroom', in *Approaches to Teaching Shorter Elizabethan Poetry*, pp. 66–74 (p. 67).

36. *Ibid.*, p. 68.

37. Sheila T. Cavanagh, 'Editing an Elizabethan Poem: A Course Assignment', in *Approaches to Teaching Shorter Elizabethan Poetry*, pp. 141–4.

38. Matthew D. Stroud, 'The Closest Reading: Creating Annotated Online Editions', in *Approaches to Teaching Early Modern Spanish Drama*, pp. 214–19.

39. John Webster, 'The Elizabethan Age Portfolio: Using Writing to Teach Shorter Elizabethan Poetry', in *Approaches to Teaching Shorter Elizabethan Poetry*, pp. 145–9 (p. 147).

40. Frances Teague, 'Responding to Renaissance Drama: One Way of Guiding Students', in *Approaches to Teaching English Renaissance Drama*, pp. 65–72. See also Katherine Dauge-Roth's account (n. 8 above) of the use of online learning journals and other learner-centred pedagogical strategies in her teaching of seventeenth-century France.

41. C.E. McGee, 'Webbing Webster', in *Approaches to Teaching English Renaissance Drama*, pp. 106–12 (p. 106).

42. Mark Aune, 'Always a Work in Progress: Creating a Course Website for Introduction to Shakespeare', *Sixteenth-Century Journal*, 32.1 (2001), 127–33. On an earlier text, see Massimo Riva, 'The *Decameron* Web: Teaching a Classic as Hypertext at Brown University', in *Approaches to Teaching Boccaccio's 'Decameron'*, ed. James H. McGregor (New York: MLA, 2000), pp. 172–82.

43. Guy Spielmann, 'Spectacles du grand siècle': du projet épistémologique au projet éducatif', in *French 'Classical' Theatre Today: Teaching, Research, Performance*, ed. Philip Tomlinson (Amsterdam and Atlanta: Rodopi, 2001), pp. 285–303. The course outline is included in an appendix (pp. 301–2).

44. Diane E. Sieber, 'The Digital *Comedia*: Teaching Golden Age Theater with New and Emerging Technologies', in *Approaches to Teaching Early Modern Spanish Drama*, pp. 206–13.

45. Barbara Johnson, 'Teaching Ignorance: *L'École des femmes*', *Yale French Studies*, 63 (1982), 165–82. I would like to thank Katherine Ibbett for bringing this article to my attention some years ago.

46. *Ibid.*, p. 166.

47. *Ibid.*, p. 173.

48. *Ibid.*, p. 182.

Part 1

The Early Modern in the Digital Age

2

Renaissance Teaching and Learning: Humanist Pedagogy in the Digital Age and What it Might Teach Us[1]

Danielle Clarke

On the surface, there would appear to be a yawning gulf between the modern seminar room and the Renaissance classroom. Materially, at least, they are poles apart. A modestly endowed university in the first world will have at least some teaching rooms with movable furniture, whiteboards, wireless Internet connectivity, a data projector, as well as more basic audio-visual equipment and a blackboard – or, failing this, aspirations to acquire these pedagogical prosthetics. The typical Renaissance schoolroom, on the other hand, would most likely have fixed (or no) seating, with a teacher's desk or lectern at the front of the class, and may have been located in a space dedicated to other uses. While the modern classroom typically houses a group of students at roughly the same stage of academic development (although potentially diverse in other respects – age, background, ethnicity), that of the Renaissance combined students from different stages of development (from the mastery of basic English and arithmetic through to proficiency in more complex exercises in imitation and composition) but with a relatively high degree of social cohesion. The Renaissance classroom was also an all-male space, although schoolrooms in the home were often mixed-sex at least until the boys moved onto more formal schooling.[2] The configuration of the learning space in each instance both reflects and constructs the dynamics of the educational experience, and encodes the hierarchy of teacher and pupil. In the case of the modern classroom, teacher and student are engaged (ideally) in mutual endeavour, where the teacher is the locus of information and guidance. In the early modern classroom, pedagogical authority is ideally wholly vested in the teacher, reinforced by whatever means necessary, including the use of physical force.[3] Early modern texts on pedagogy are barely concerned with the material at all, beyond the basic necessities – books, slates, pens, ink, paper – and these are viewed as shared and reusable commodities.[4] This stress on the collective and the communal, on the enduring and the reusable, as opposed to the constantly renewed, disposable and refreshed Virtual Learning Environments (VLEs) of contemporary universities provides a pivotal distinction between two forms of pedagogy which, nevertheless, as I hope to show, have more in common than critical discourses on these topics often care to admit. The modern classroom (and a host of other debates in higher education), by contrast, is fixated on questions of resources – the furnishings of the room, the purchasing power of students; indeed, an entire area of thinking on pedagogy is concerned with the learning environment.

I want to concentrate on the similarities between early modern pedagogical practices and what happens in the modern classroom, and to suggest that, in many ways, modern teaching is closer to its early modern roots than we often acknowledge (not least in its social effects), and that the post-Enlightenment focus on aesthetics and evolutionary models is implicitly challenged by these practices. The authority of the teacher is also challenged, and starts to reside in operations and skills that go beyond his or her supreme mastery of materials, just as the early modern concept of the teacher (in theory) at least shifted from authoritarian (usually symbolized by the pedagogue's fondness for beating the knowledge in) to sympathetic, gentle, exemplary. The basic format of contemporary humanities' teaching is surprisingly similar to its Renaissance forbear, despite fundamental distinctions in social configuration and cultural context. Thinkers on both teaching and Renaissance literature have been preoccupied by the parallels potentially offered by the new technologies for the transmission of text – print in the case of the Renaissance, electronic media in the contemporary context.[5] More predictably, historians of the book have been fascinated by analogies between the transition to print and the transition to electronic media.[6] This essay examines our indebtedness to the Renaissance and its ideas of knowledge and ideals of teaching, and considers the electronic revolution in Renaissance studies as a kind of simulacrum of some key early modern intellectual and material debates about epistemology, authority, textuality and literacy. As Neil Rhodes and Jonathan Sawday have suggested, '[t]he experience of our own new technology has enabled us to re-imagine the impact of new technologies in the past'.[7] I argue that we might find more productive ground for arguments about the value and applicability of literary study if we attend more carefully to the early modern legacy, and try to unpeel the layers of accumulated myth about the kinds of ideals, notions such as the transcendent mind, supposedly embodied and transmitted by humanities teaching. I want to suggest that careful attention to the practical and worldly orientation of early modern pedagogy might help us be more open-minded and thoughtful about the huge potential offered by our own information revolution, and to reintroduce the orientation of the humanities *towards* the world (as opposed to being in *retreat* from it) with less rancour than has been characteristic of these debates in the recent past.[8] As Richard Lanham remarked with great perspicacity back in 1989, the information revolution challenges as much as it facilitates, and the default response is often that of retreat, rather than embrace: 'We may expect a deal of commentary greeting the electronic modification of print literacy as the death of the Western self.'[9] Along with other scholars, I want to suggest that this identification of self with text is itself a historical phenomenon, and that it is a product of a technological revolution that enabled individuals to own (literally and metaphorically) the texts that they read, and to shape them to their own desires and purposes through active interventions – annotation, underlining, the use of manicules, pointers and indexes.[10]

Underlying debates about the future direction of the humanities – contrarian and passionately felt as they are – is a fundamentally philosophical question about the purpose, function and application of the humanities (by and large, funded from the public purse). This essay argues that the information revolution reveals our indebtedness to the early modern anew, defamiliarizes our teaching of it and enables us to see beyond the assumptions of disciplinary boundaries that are the product of Enlightenment thought. We can then, I suggest, see humanities education as a mode of thought, an approach to the world, and new media as a way of freeing ourselves from the dichotomies that currently structure our education systems, sequester certain kinds of knowledge and place unequal values on them. As Sawday suggests, print enabled a particular kind of epistemological development, the opening up of a potential that was then in effect limited by the time-bound physicality of the printed text, but which may finally be realized in the age of hypertext 3.0.[11]

Before teasing these issues out in a little more detail, I want to put one key concept – implicit in all that follows – on the table, namely John Guillory's interpretation of 'cultural capital' (in turn heavily dependent on Guillory's reading of Bourdieu).[12] Simply and crudely summarized, this is the notion that social and cultural position, future status and economic position, are derived not from ownership or property (although it might lead to these, and that material wealth enables certain social groups to access cultural capital more efficiently, even ruthlessly), but from the knowledge, skills and educational norms that guarantee success in the labour market. Recent debates about the advantages conferred by internships (particularly in the UK in recent months) focus this issue nicely – where contacts and connections are effectively achieved through parental advantage (and subsidy). Guillory applies the notion to the acquisition of skills and values through the learning of literature, most notably in his nuanced discussion of the literary canon, and the modern heir to the rhetorical education of the sixteenth and seventeenth centuries, literary criticism. Humanist education has always been profoundly concerned with questions of cultural capital, leaving the more direct relationship to economic capital to other fields (trades and crafts, merchants, and, increasingly, science, management and business), and the Renaissance both acknowledged this and obscured it in ideas of social service, moral improvement and spiritual growth. In the contemporary climate, this equates broadly to skills transfer, knowledge rollout and commercial application. Debates over the value and direction of humanities education – born out of a frequently overstated sense of crisis – tend to envisage the education of the past as being in some way innocent of these worldly intentions.[13] Since the rise of science as an academic subject with economic application (a process that began in the nineteenth century), the humanities response to more overt relationships between education and the marketplace has been, by and large, to adopt the mantle of retreat, opposition and denial. Differing demographic, economic and cultural conditions require terminologies and forms of analysis that move beyond the early modern model, but this paradox (or self-deception) is still at the heart of debates about the future and purpose of humanities education (study for its own sake vs transferable skills; true intellectual enquiry vs 'dumbing down', independence of thought vs economic utility).[14] In other words, for cultural capital to function *as capital* in the marketplace, its economic substructure must be obscured, or disguised. Contemporary educational policy has done away with the disguise, thus – in the view of many – fatally undermining the abstracted and esoteric value of humanities scholarship. Yet in the Renaissance, education is less concerned with the production of knowledge, than with its careful and delimited *re*production, a process that entails a careful balance between the notion of the individual as a textual locus and that individual's future social role. Education is far more concerned with the status quo than with notions of freedom, liberty or self-fulfilment, and its effects are self-consciously *social* rather than individual, a point that is easily missed because our narrative of Renaissance literary output focuses so heavily upon exceptional individuals. As Jonathan Goldberg asserts, education's intended role in the

Renaissance was 'not to disturb social relations and hierarchies, but to maintain them'.[15]

The knowledge that the Renaissance schoolboy acquires is rarely of any direct practical use, but it does enable him to demonstrate that he is in possession of the cultural capital that defines his role – that he can summon an appropriate saying or precedent from Roman history, that he can argue by analogy, and he knows how to fillet a text for materials, examples, style, and rhetorical tropes and figures. As Grafton and Jardine suggest, the Renaissance was interested primarily in the programmatic mastery of a stable body of texts, which viewed 'culture as something given, absolute, to be mastered, not questioned – and thus fostered in all its initiates a properly docile attitude towards authority'.[16] Then, as now, some students were better at it than others, as the topos of the slow-witted schoolboy in a range of early modern texts illustrates (William in *Merry Wives* comes immediately to mind). These moments, where the redundancy of the method is revealed at the same time as its creative and powerfully transformative potential is fulsomely demonstrated, are a notable feature of early modern English drama. Later attempts to obscure or redirect the essential inapplicability of humanities training focused on two key things: the process of moral reform that the learner underwent (what Lanham refers to as '[t]his "great text + right reading = moral truth" equation'), and the notion of the humanities as a training for the mind that then formed a platform for further learning.[17] But 'content' is not readily separable from the form in which that content is delivered, whether that be the *progymnasmata* or the detailed syllabi of modern courses (and the idea of the 'course' as a self-contained unit of knowledge within a larger discipline is quite distinct from the Renaissance understanding that what was being learned was a system, a way for organizing knowledge). Teaching methodologies and technologies also encode ideologies, key assumptions about what knowledge is, how it is compartmentalized and accessed, represented and circulated.[18] Increasingly, users and learners are alienated from these ideologies, which are mostly invisible to us, and certainly beyond our individual control – we might manipulate them, or populate them in particular ways, but we are just as in thrall to the categories created for us in a VLE as the Renaissance schoolboy was to the five parts of rhetoric.

Most VLEs are commercial applications, are strongly user-orientated and can only be customized within parameters that have already been decided. In the modern university, intellectual endeavour is arguably ever more programmatic and externally directed, less concerned with what the student can think/do/discover than with ensuring that the student attain preordained goals in the form of learning outcomes which are articulated at all levels, from individual assignments up to degree programmes in their entirety.[19] This is not in any sense an argument against the use of learning outcomes which in my view have done a great deal to improve the overall standards of attainment of a diverse student body. But this means that cultural capital is seen to reside in skills and operations rather than in the texts or curriculum studied. It cannot be denied that, for all the rhetoric of student-centred learning and independent research skills, learning outcomes essentially define a preordained set of conclusions – even when framed carefully in terms of skills – that students are expected to arrive at. Teacherly authority is no longer effectively asserted over what students read and access, but is displaced onto the control of what does and does not conform to the aims and objectives of the given module which are set in advance by the teacher. This is very different from a traditional model of 'reading' a humanities subject over the course of three years with only very broadly based structure or outcomes. Thus the exercise of authority takes place primarily in the form of assessment, not in text selection or interpretation. Paradoxically, the Socratic method depended fundamentally upon the pre-eminent and unassailable authority of the teacher, and generally adopted a restrictive approach to *what* was studied, yet ultimately permitted a high degree of autonomy to students in terms of the conclusions that they might draw. Modern university teaching, by contrast, frequently encourages students to range widely through non-canonical materials (particularly for longer pieces of written work), yet attempts to predetermine what benefits students will derive from studying them – once a set of goals has been articulated and defined for what constitutes success or failure in a given assignment, only very reckless students will attempt to buck the trend.[20] Process and product are increasingly hard to distinguish, and cultural capital tends to be located rather less in terms of the kinds of material that have been mastered, and more in terms of the reputation, status or ranking of the degree-awarding institution.

* * *

The early modern period itself was one that witnessed a profound revolution in education. Not only did the number of individuals in education increase markedly, but in England education largely moved from the domain of the religious orders into primarily secular institutions. Whilst the provision of basic skills (literacy, arithmetic, catechizing) was often rather loosely the responsibility of the parish, the period also witnessed a significant growth in more formal, but local institutions – grammar schools.[21] Curricular development was significant, but patchy, focused rather narrowly on one area of education (grammar and rhetoric) and drew on a highly circumscribed selection of texts (Lily's grammar, Terence, expurgated Ovid, some Erasmian texts). Yet such an education ensured that the willing student encountered knowledge in forms quite unthinkable to us – predigested and often rather arbitrary, but ranging freely across a number of what subsequently became distinct discursive fields or disciplines. As Höfer's essay in this volume illustrates, one of the things that early modern teachers have to help their students do is to question, reimagine and sometimes shelve their notions of disciplinary identity. A rhetorical inflection to the use and analysis of electronic resources and epistemologies is, I suggest, one way that this might be done, by placing early modern texts in their proper historical context, and by focusing students' attention on how knowledge is produced, packaged, parcelled and circulated.

That modern classroom practice in the university should be indebted to its sixteenth-century roots is perhaps no surprise; but what is intriguing is the extent to which this has been enhanced by the advent of new technologies, and by the more overtly market-driven models and imperatives that now structure higher education in the Western world. The longevity of these methods is also quite astonishing, when one considers that Renaissance pedagogical habits were, in their turn, indebted to the classical and medieval periods. What this suggests though, is that our nostalgia for purer times is perhaps misplaced, and that humanities education has always been concerned with utility of one kind or another, the acquisition of economically productive skills within an ideology that purports to advance 'pure' knowledge, or to produce morally and civically minded citizens. A couple of brief examples will illustrate this point. The most obvious pedagogic debt we owe to the Renaissance (and indeed to classical and medieval culture) is the lecture – still valued in most institutions as a highly efficient way to communicate ideas to large groups of students. The lecture, of course, is a technology (in Walter Ong's sense) designed to allow the passage of complex ideas in a setting without the capacity to reproduce multiple copies of text.[22] Its effectiveness depends crucially on two skills which have fallen victim to circumstance – the art of listening, and the ability to take notes, or more specifically, to analyse and dissect a text (whether extempore or not) that is delivered orally by a single voice in a single setting. The student encounter with texts in the electronic age is anything but linear or unidirectional, and tends not to deal with a single argument unfolding via example and counter-example; rather it is both 'malleable and self-conscious':

> The textual surface has become permanently bi-stable. We are always looking first AT it and then THROUGH it, and this oscillation created a different implied ideal of decorum, both stylistic and behavioural.[23]

Yet the human voice and embodied presence remain important to the teaching process because teaching is fundamentally a relationship between teacher and student – a relationship that may take many forms. A skilled teacher, however, is adept at balancing the needs of her students, and the demands of her discipline, and, ideally, puts them into creative and ongoing dialogue, enabling both mediated and unmediated encounters with primary and secondary sources. Thus the teacher is, structurally at least, a kind of locus where meaning and knowledge are traded, created and questioned. In many instances, particularly where time and numbers limit the development of a relationship between a teacher and his students, however, the teacher's role is fundamentally altered – s/he becomes firstly a guide to the proliferation of resources, and secondly an individual who takes final responsibility for what the student has (or has not) learned. The teacher, in effect, becomes a disembodied authority, whose traffic with students is only one way. This is to an extent an effect of the impact of electronic media on both the learning process and the ways in which information is accessed, yet it recapitulates in interesting ways the sense of displacement noted by Renaissance thinkers and writers when they considered the primacy and intimacy of the spoken word, versus the alienation and disembodiment of the printed text. But, as Lanham (and others) have argued, the very malleability of the electronic textual surface, the ways in which it can be continually and simultaneously co-opted to new ends, holds out the promise of reinstating a rhetorical understanding of the world as 'an information *system*':[24]

> I have come to conceive the intellectual history of this period [1969–89] as the return, after a long Newtonian interlude, of the rhetorical paideia as our dominant theory of knowledge and education. [...] [O]ne element in the mixture did not exist to dazzle prophecy – the digitized word displayed on a personal computer screen. Even now it is not easy to survey this extension of rhetoric's domain, to envision how rhetoric is again functioning *systemically* as a way of thinking.[25]

Richard Lanham's work is unusual in its prescience, but also in its benign and productive view of the potential impact of electronic text on the humanities, seeing it as a powerful and much-needed force for radical change, rather than the last nail in the coffin.

The second key area of indebtedness exhibited in the modern university classroom lies in annotation. Once more, electronic media, word-processing packages, blogs and wikis all demonstrate a powerful destabilization of the integrity of textual boundaries, and enable students to traverse the boundary between self and text in powerful ways. Once again, our notions of what constitute academic value depend heavily on romantic and post-Enlightenment ideals about originality and aesthetic integrity, and this is frequently and problematically at odds with undergraduates' actual textual practice. Bill Sherman's recent work demonstrates that early moderns were – to our minds – bibliographic vandals: ripping out pages, doodling in margins, underlining texts, writing comments (and in some cases commentary) in all of the available blank space, in apparent defiance of our strongly held convictions that the space of the page is somehow sacrosanct, inviolate. Later bibliophiles were so committed to the aesthetic integrity of the virgin page that they often cropped early modern books in order to expunge the scribbles and scratchings of previous owners. What the practice of annotation reveals is another dimension to the notion of active reading, the orientation of textual interaction towards production, rather than towards reception, which has dominated literary study since the Romantics. Many of the functions of annotation reflect the kind of systematic training in the organization of textual information that was a standard element of early modern grammar school education – the keeping of notebooks, the taking of notes from sermons or orations, the selective recording and citation of one's reading. One might venture that the use of the learning journal in modern teaching might start to return students to the *activity* of learning (after all, it was the Renaissance that orientated education away from the unthinking inculcation of values to the notion that the individual needed to be drawn out and shaped). As Rebecca Bushnell argues:

A respect for the often productive tension in sixteenth-century scholarly discourse between rhetoric and logic, history and philosophy, interpretation and disputation, suggests that in our own literary pedagogy we might re-examine the relationship between the scholastic emphasis on the 'forms' of thought articulated in language (rather than the forms of whole books) and the humanists' awareness of language's historicity and social function.[26]

Annotation represents the movement of classroom practices into private spaces, the continuation of a method for dealing with texts in non-institutional sites. What this suggests seems to me to have important implications for our own early modern classroom practice; namely that such skills and competencies have the potential to transcend the space of the classroom. For the early moderns, this was often predicated on a notion that textual formation was inseparable from character forma-tion, a notion in turn that depends upon the close relationship between self and text. Many Renaissance theorists and rhetoricians present this relationship through metaphors of digestion and incorporation, in turn drawing heavily on their classical forbears. One of the lessons that we might derive from Renaissance annotation is the importance of facilitat-ing the student's own analysis of the text within established disciplinary norms (self-directed learning, if you will); one of the others is the need for the student to engage productively with the difference of the past.

As a final example of the early modern roots of modern pedagogy, I want to turn to the classroom technology that symbolizes what tradi-tionalists most dislike. As a direct consequence of the loss of aural skills, many humanities academics use the software package PowerPoint centrally in their teaching. It is much hated by academics and often blamed for all sorts of things, but much loved by students, as Edward Tufte has argued in relation to the secondary school sector:

> Particularly disturbing is the adoption of the PowerPoint cognitive style in our schools. Rather than learning to write a report using sentences, children are being taught how to formulate client pitches and infomercials. Elementary school PowerPoint exercises (as seen in teacher guides and in student work posted on the Internet) typi-cally consist of 10 to 20 words and a piece of clip art on each slide in a presentation of three to six slides – a total of perhaps 80 words (15 seconds of silent reading) for a week of work. Students would be better off if the schools simply closed down on those days and everyone went to the Exploratorium or wrote an illustrated essay explaining something.[27]

PowerPoint forms part of a range of products that are classified as 'persuasion technologies', primarily intended to promote sales and to facilitate managerialism. Yet PowerPoint, particularly its custom slide layouts, mimics the approach to argument of Renaissance rhetoric quite closely. In the first instance, the process of communication depends heavily on inductive logic, where information and evidence is marshalled to a preordained end, rather than deploying the deductive logic that post-Baconian thought associates with the creation of knowledge (survey evidence, draw conclusions). This recalls the Renaissance habit of division (one of the topics), where the organization of the exposition or argument is laid out in advance.[28] Secondly, bullet points recall the Renaissance habit of gathering arguments around topics or headings fixed largely by practice and convention, and indeed, early modern rhetorical treatises are inordinately fond of *brachia* based around headings and distinctions. In other words, rather like much Renaissance rhetoric, PowerPoint is largely conservative, concentrating on the communication of what is already known, rather than upon the development of new knowledge.[29] It is, like rhetoric, a closed system, which exceeds the input of any given user, and one where authority is vested primarily in the technology (one might say that rhetoric is simply a technology of language) or method, rather than in the practitioner who gestures impotently towards what he or she has created, and whose authority is simply ancillary to the linear and successional logic of the presentational form. It undoubtedly subordinates something that we might designate as content to method or process, much as rhetoric does. Debates about how PowerPoint 'dumbs down' the humanities echo rather neatly the early modern period's anxieties about true versus false knowledge, between the superficial acquisition of stylistic competence and real learning, and between Ciceronian concentration on style and surface versus Senecanism's belief that plain language embodied truth and knowledge (Bacon again). For the vast majority of Renaissance pupils, education was entirely instrumental, superficial and fixated upon the consolidation of a given social status signalled by the capacity to repeat and recycle a fixed set of examples according to relatively rigid *formulae*. The potential of rhetoric to persuade and move depends fundamentally upon a mastery of the key principles, the ability to dissect syllogisms and proofs, and to understand the foundations upon which an argument is based (*ethos, pathos, logos*). It also depends upon the capacity of some highly skilled users to exploit its potential – yet such power depends in turn on the ability of the readership/audience to recognize which model has been modified, and how.

The renewal of the Renaissance: or, the contemporary early modern

Despite the high-profile attention paid to the new historicism, in recent years early modern studies has, in actuality, been marked by two quite specific trends. The first is a renewed interest in the materiality of texts (I say renewed because this was actually an important preoccupation of the first wave of professional academic bibliographers, such as Greg and McKerrow), with a range of scholars not only analysing the *content* of texts, but their physical form, their orientation in space and their use. This is undoubtedly a direct response to the development of electronic text and hypertext, which, as Rhodes and Sawday assert, finally encode what editors have always known, namely that textual stability is an illusion. Writing of the 'varorium' edition, they say that it is 'in some measure, an admission of failure, a recognition that there is no last word in textual matters'.[30] The extension of this concern with what happens on the page (whether of printed or manuscript texts) can be found in exhilarating work on the intellectual and pragmatic habits of literate folk in early modern England – the work of Ann Moss (commonplace books), Ann Blair (note-taking and transmission), Alison Wiggins (annotation of books, likewise Heidi Hackel), Bill Sherman, in *Used Books*, Alan Stewart (composition; the role of carriers), Grafton and Jardine, Steven Zwicker and Jane Stevenson.[31] Other work in this emergent field focuses on the use of paratexts, bindings and so on.[32] It is safe to say that whilst this work is often ambiguous about the hold that electronic media now has over the field, it is also heavily indebted to that same media. Equally, such work implicitly acknowledges, even as it often fetishizes the materiality of text (a sort of nostalgic retro-fitting, not dissimilar to the ideological underpinnings of Renaissance pastoral, or the early modern's own interest in manipulating print to render a simulacrum of the manuscript text[33]), that the fixity of text is a fiction, and that the humanistic impulse 'to nail it down forever and then finally explain it' is a paradigm that is in the process of a complex re-formation as the physical text is in retreat.[34] Most crucially, the text moves out of the corral of the specialist academic library and is multiply and simultaneously available to a potentially infinite number of users, none of whom will necessarily access that text in precisely the same way. This is in stark contrast to the coming of print, where the distinguishing feature, compared to manuscript transmission, is the simultaneous availability of a text that is virtually *identical* in most particulars.[35]

A series of arguments are mobilized in order to make sense of the complex relationships between increased access to the primary data of Renaissance literary study, and the consequences (positive and negative) of the fact that students, many of whom will never have encountered a Renaissance text other than one by Shakespeare before (and many of whom will not have studied Shakespeare in any sense as a Renaissance author), are able to access raw data without necessarily having the skills or knowledge to interpret what they see.[36] These arguments fall into two main camps: those who see the hold that electronic media now has over the field as an unmitigated force for good (openness, democracy, engagement with the material basis of early modern texts) and those who view resources such as EEBO and LION as having a restricting effect on the kinds of research that are possible, and further alienating students from fully understanding the artefacts that they think they are handling.[37] In other words, this argument runs, the potential complexities of the materials far outrun students' capacity to manage and discriminate the information that they can uncover.[38] Resources like EEBO create a levelling effect between institutions, and enable unprecedented access to editorially unmediated materials on the part of students who in the past would never have encountered them.[39] The widespread availability of search terms and, increasingly, searchable text, means that even quite sophisticated academic work can be very narrowly based, deriving from pre-existing categories of analysis rather than from a rigorous survey of the relevant material. Student research, facilitated by such tools, is often intensive rather than extensive, based upon inductive rather than deductive logic. This perhaps unanticipated consequence of the digitization of early modern materials (aided and abetted by the fact that the texts fall outside copyright law) interestingly returns us to pre-Baconian, pre-modern modalities, but in a context where a given concept or idea or term can be pursued over a dizzying range of material – material that is itself effectively selected in advance according to criteria that are often less than transparent. Again, this enables some kinds of work, and stymies others, yet recapitulates a powerful binary in the history of ideas, as Richard Foster Jones states:

> It is hard to say who makes the greater mistake, the one who painfully collects an abundance of data over a wide field and then leaves them an unanalyzed, undigested mass, or the one who seizes upon a few random opinions and constructs a beautiful pattern logically sound but historically dubious.[40]

The texts represented by EEBO, for example, provide a sample of Renaissance texts determined by the willingness of libraries to allow them to be scanned, not a sample shaped by expertise about what is, and is not, important.[41] The ways in which such databases are underwritten by questions of ownership and accessibility is a topic for another essay, but the point here is that, like the early modern period, access to such texts is primarily based upon economic status/institutional position, but unlike the early modern period, texts can be connected by links far more myriad than the extent of one individual's reading, recall and memory.[42] Arguably, then, the capacity of the originating term to generate material is in excess of the individual's ability to sift, sort or order the resulting evidence in a discriminating way. Where the commonplace tradition, for example, repeatedly mined and rehearsed the same topoi drawn from a largely agreed canon of texts, the modern search engine juxtaposes materials brought together through the occurrence of key, preselected, terms, which is often not at all the same thing as similarity, parallelism or actual relationship.[43] Thus, the search engine provides merely a sample of literary strata, raw data that requires careful contextualization, a sample that is intensive rather than extensive. Central here is a profound distinction, at one level, between early modern pedagogy's insistence upon the moral and stylistic utility of texts (albeit within a historicizing impulse) and contemporary attempts to understand texts both in themselves and in context, to respect the integrity – historical and textual – of the verbal artefact, and to see its utility less in the lessons it might teach, and rather more in the skills that it forces us to learn. The loss of the moral imperative in humanities teaching is a relatively recent phenomenon, and is considerably more far-reaching in its effects than the reconstituting of the canon (namely, the displacement of certain authors and texts by authors and texts selected – partially, at least – by identity-based criteria). Selection according to algorithm may be highly efficient, interesting and productive, but it cannot teach us how to read or organize what we find – unlike the early modern period which had an evolving and complex understanding of how materials from the distant past might be understood, and how they might usefully function as examples in the contemporary setting.

The second key trend is a not entirely unselfconscious interest in Renaissance pedagogy. Again, this has older roots (Baldwin's *Smal Latine and Lesse Greeke*; Richard A. Lanham, *The Motives of Eloquence*; histories of education), but has been reinvigorated both by theory (Jonathan Goldberg, *Writing Matter*; Richard Halpern, *The Poetics of Primitive Accumulation*) and by the changing conditions governing pedagogy in the contemporary classroom, both institutional and technological. This strand of scholarship can be subdivided into works that focus on Renaissance pedagogical theory and practice (Stewart's *Close Readers*; Rebecca Bushnell's *Culture of Teaching*), and those that attempt to bridge the divide between ancient theory and modern practice (e.g. Corbett and Connors, *Classical Rhetoric for the Modern Student*; Lanham's

Handlist of Rhetorical Terms; An Introduction to Classical Rhetoric: Essential Readings; A Companion to Rhetoric and Rhetorical Criticism). Whilst these accounts are inevitably framed by the experience of teaching the Renaissance, it is rare to find overt commentary on the relationship between Renaissance pedagogy and the contemporary early modern classroom, although parallels between the electronic revolution and the coming of print have become commonplace if still rather superficial. Rebecca Bushnell, writing in 1996, astutely notes the continuities and distinctions between modern and early modern teaching, or what she calls 'the paradoxical relationship between masters and students and [...] the ambivalence concerning freedom and control'.[44] Teacherly authority is tempered by its nurturing role, a development central to early modern thought on pedagogy, discourse that echoes the Renaissance's interest in education as a tool of social reproduction, and still structures our understanding of teaching today, as both rigorous and benign: 'We still combine the authoritarian image of a teacher with those of the playmate and foster-mother, who lure the pupil into the pleasant retreat of learning.'[45] Much current thinking on teaching and learning either implicitly or explicitly acknowledges the increasing role taken by new media and visual technologies in enticing students to engage with historically based materials. Yet Bushnell rightly notes the development of a far more (apparently) student-centred model of pedagogy – a mode of delivery that has become entrenched in the decade or so since *A Culture of Teaching* was published in 1996 – and one which replaces the idea of students as vessels with the notion of students as consumers, thus endowing them with the authority of the market, free to pick and choose what it is they do, and do not, learn. Such thinking underlies the wholesale shift in the discourses used about pedagogy in the higher education sector, where 'choice' and 'flexibility' are the bywords of modular systems. The logical outcome of such a shift is that the authority of the teacher is dispersed and rendered contingent, and that the teacher is ultimately subservient to the pupil, who symbolizes the inflow of cash to the institution. As Bushnell notes, analysing one case study, the instructor's role is 'not to teach at all'.[46] In what she terms 'a post-modern pedagogy', Bushnell argues that 'the teacher recedes and the class focuses on the students' needs, rights, and experience'.[47] The model is, at time of writing, more capitalist than post-modern, at least in terms of the assumed 'contract' between teacher and student (and the term 'contract' is itself revealing). Much of the language of contemporary pedagogy owes a good deal to the language of the market, with its discussion of 'skills' and 'transfer' and 'innovation' and 'creativity'.

Yet whilst this model is widely accepted within higher education and is strongly encouraged both by government rhetoric and by policies, it still runs counter to some very deep-seated ideas about what university education in the humanities is for.

The remainder of this essay sketches, in broad outline, the potential that these radical changes have for the teaching of early modern texts in the contemporary classroom. The operations that we encourage students to undertake upon texts fundamentally alter the character of those texts, their status, purpose and authority. Interpretive activity is a two-way street, and the kinds of tasks that we set our students to do inevitably *produce* texts as much as they do readings or contextualizations of those texts. Acts of reading and writing are themselves framed by cultural and ideological imperatives that *produce* core ideas: whilst the Renaissance viewed the reader as a textual locus, a clearing house between textual consumption and production, contemporary students of the humanities focus heavily on the experiential, the ways in which they might empathize with the text, on how it resonates or speaks to them. This concept of the text, as something in which one's own experience might be validated and reflected back, is apparently radically different from the early modern student's humble supplication to the authority of the text. Yet in both cases, the act of reading is seen to be, in some sense, constitutive of the self, and as something that hovers uncertainly on the border between public and private: for both eras, the text is an interface. And for both eras, radical changes to that interface are coterminous with a series of perceived threats to the relationship between self and society. In turn, electronic preservation and delivery facilitates an approach that partially overturns the post-Victorian focus on the text as a closed aesthetic artefact, mastery of which remains the (more or less) exclusive domain of the professor, untrammelled by considerations of the social or the functional. For instance:

- the texts (both manuscript and print) that are available reproduce within a reasonable margin, their original material form – size, shape, layout, typeface. Texts are thus unmediated and can be seen to be 'other', thus helping students to grasp the otherness of the past, and the ways in which the spatial and physical properties of a text shape meaning;
- the sophistication of search terms means that, for the first time, activities that we might more usually define as 'research' activities can be brought into the classroom – for example, an Enquiry Based Learning project for final-year students producing a student edition

of the *Tragedy of Mariam*, or selecting, editing and annotating texts for a student anthology of Renaissance poetry;

- the text is presented as being in need of interpretation, criticism, annotation, rather than this work being done for the student by a critical apparatus that sometimes carries overwhelming authority;
- rather than being a 'closed' artefact whose interpretations and meanings the student has to master, the text becomes an 'open' artefact where key issues can be debated (e.g. old spelling vs new; the meaning of black letter).

Arguments about the necessarily selective nature of EEBO's database (although this is improving rapidly) and the loss of the hands-on concrete contact with the material book seem to me to be of limited relevance to the undergraduate experience of the early modern period; very few undergraduates have the privilege that I had, of being able to order up pre-1700 material in Duke Humphrey's library, and EEBO allows them into what was formerly a closed world.

Rather than the comprehensive, holistic approach to texts favoured by the Romantics, and subsequently by the New Critics and others, where the literary text (a category that was more or less assumed) was defined by its aesthetic integrity, the early modern text (not necessarily 'literary', although always amenable to rhetorical analysis) was a resource to be mined. The commonplace tradition, on the other hand, involved the reader in identifying those parts of the text that should be stored up for future use (thus the idea of both storehouse/repository, and utility), whether this was on the basis of theme, precedent, analogy, or the exemplification of some aspect of style.[48] It was this activity that enabled the able student to exhibit *copia* in his writing (and to a lesser extent, in his speech), that most valued sign of cultural capital. In turn, this involves breaking the text apart, reducing it down to a series of topics (topoi) which are effectively situated spatially as well as intellectually, as the student gathers together relevant authorities, apothegms, aphorisms and so on under a series of headings. Thus the linear model of narrative – and of text – is utterly overthrown. In effect, the commonplace book was not directed towards interpretation or reception, but was entirely focused on production, on textual fragments as sources for further invention, and as authoritative anchors for what the individual wanted to say. Such an approach implies that knowledge is, within certain socially and functionally defined limits, the free property of any individual equipped to access it. The text is thus open, a resource, common property, to be adapted and reworked as the reader sees fit. Indeed, such reuse is the purpose of this kind of reading. The development of the index was the next logical step within such a textual economy, enabling the reader to circumvent the troublesome and tedious process of actually sifting through the text for himself, and helping him to find what he was looking for. Like students in the contemporary classroom, such an individual relied on a mediating scholarly tool (an index is a textual technology) to help him identify specific textual loci for the task at hand. Teaching the early modern requires a careful awareness of these kinds of practices, and an understanding of the intervening history that views the free appropriation of others' words as negative, illegal even – and the more that you think about knowledge in these terms, the more peculiar our modern obsession with plagiarism in the academy seems.[49] The commonplace tradition, it should be said, relies on a set of shared values, a field of knowledge which is by definition limited (that is what increases its cultural capital), and thus upon a set of key references within a surprisingly narrow curriculum that mostly do not have to be acknowledged or identified, because *everybody KNOWS* that the image of the bee that you have just used to illustrate nature's bounty and the productivity that results from tight social organization and mutual helpfulness has come from Virgil, and that, in turn, he lifted it from Aristotle. In theory, Internet searches allow this kind of activity on a much grander scale – after all, what is cut-and-paste but a different means of accessing key texts?

The notion of reading for utility that is inherent in the commonplace tradition is implicit in our inherited notion of academic work in the humanities, where the essay remains the gold standard, a form invented, of course, in the early modern period, as one effect of the transition of the oratorical tradition of *suasoriae* into the realm of print, and as a direct output (as we like to say these days) of the commonplace book itself. Yet the forms of analysis that underlie such processes (in particular, an understanding of invention, proof and arrangement) are largely absent from the early modern classroom in our own time. I should add here, that this is less true of the USA, where, albeit in altered form, the teaching of rhetoric lives on in the form of composition.[50] I would suggest that modern students could learn a great deal from an acquaintance with the key outlines of rhetoric, as well as from learning about how Renaissance writers actually used their texts. The *progymnasmata* are easily adapted to modern contexts, and students can be encouraged to apply their newly acquired rhetorical precepts in a range of contexts (ads, media). In turn, such activities can be usefully contextualized by encouraging students to think more deeply about what the tools that they take for granted (search engines in particular) are actually *doing*. Whilst the commonplace 'book' has had something of a revival in cyberspace, it is revealing that most examples are indebted to a nineteenth-century notion of commonplaces which is rather more concerned with preserving fragments that are particularly pleasing to the reader (although there are exceptions, such as Coleridge). Whilst we may not wish to replicate early modern practice in the classroom, it does seem to me to be worthy of investigation, because at the very least it requires students to deal with the texts they read as being constituted of language, as having a material form and as artefacts that are *produced* rather than viewing texts as repositories of themes and plots.

In both Renaissance and modern contexts, information, skills and knowledge are, at one level, a commodity, things of value to be exchanged (usually) inter-generationally, which either directly or indirectly involves economic exchange. Yet the tendency to encourage student-centred learning, to promote research from the earliest stages of the undergraduate programme and to focus on skills rather than content, almost inevitably entails the student learner applying skills learned in non-institutional settings to specialized and dedicated electronic resources that do not necessarily respond to the same techniques and protocols. A good deal of criticism on questions of pedagogy focuses either on the historical moment or on contemporary challenges, or reflects (often negatively) on the contrast between the exclusivity of early modern education and the inclusive rhetoric of the twenty-first-century academy. Although some critics acknowledge the clear continuity between humanism and the humanities (to paraphrase a key title in the field), the task of unearthing the epistemological roots of our current situation in the medieval/early modern periods is still only in its infancy.

Notes

1. I would like to thank Derval Conroy and Niamh Pattwell for their helpful comments on earlier versions of this essay.
2. For a useful example, see Margaret P. Hannay, *Philip's Phoenix: Mary Sidney, Countess of Pembroke* (Oxford University Press, 1990), ch. 1.
3. Much of Renaissance pedagogical theory is concerned with the transition from an educational regime based upon brutality and physical force to one rooted in the character and wisdom of the teacher (see Rebecca Bushnell, *A Culture of Teaching: Early Modern Humanism in Theory and Practice* (Ithaca: Cornell University Press, 1996)); despite this, the prevalent stereotype of both teachers and of learning was one of ignorance, stupidity, concupiscence and violence, as for example Shakespeare's Holofernes in *Love's Labour's Lost*, and Sir Hugh Evans in *The Merry Wives of Windsor*.

4. See John Brinsley, *Ludus literarius: or the grammar schoole* (London, 1612); Roger Ascham, *The scholemaster or plaine and perfite way of teaching children* (London, 1579); Richard Mulcaster, *Positions ... necessarie for the training up of children* (London, 1561). For discussion see Bushnell, *A Culture of Teaching*; Richard Halpern, *The Poetics of Primitive Accumulation: English Renaissance Culture and the Genealogy of Capital* (Ithaca: Cornell University Press, 1991); and Alan Stewart, *Close Readers: Humanism and Sodomy in Early Modern England* (Princeton University Press, 1997).

5. As far back as 1989, Richard A. Lanham was asking searching questions about the potential of computer-generated text (and texts) to transform our understanding of both reading and writing: 'If we are not in the codex book business, what business are we really in?' Lanham, 'The Electronic Word: Literary Study and the Digital Revolution', in *The Electronic Word: Democracy, Technology and the Arts* (University of Chicago Press, 1993), pp. 3–28 (p. 8).

6. See Robert Darnton, *The Case for Books: Past, Present, and Future* (New York: Public Affairs, 2009) for a recent example.

7. *The Renaissance Computer: Knowledge Technology in the First Age of Print*, ed. Neil Rhodes and Jonathan Sawday (London: Routledge, 2000), 'Introduction', p. 2.

8. Roger Schmidt, 'Thirteen Ways of Looking at a Blackboard', *Raritan*, 25.3 (2006), 47–69.

9. Lanham, 'The Electronic Word', p. 25.

10. See William Sherman, *Used Books: Marking Readers in Renaissance England* (Philadelphia: University of Pennsylvania Press, 2007).

11. Sawday, 'Towards the Renaissance Computer', in *The Renaissance Computer*, pp. 29–44. In the same volume, see Leah Marcus, 'The Silence of the Archive and the Noise of Cyberspace', pp. 18–28.

12. See Pierre Bourdieu, *Language and Symbolic Power*, ed. John B. Thompson, trans. Gino Raymond and Matthew Adamson (Cambridge: Polity, 1991) and Bourdieu, *The State Nobility: Elite Schools in the Field of Power*, trans. Lauretta C. Clough (Oxford: Polity, 1996).

13. See, for recent examples, Clive Bloom, 'Money for Antique Rope', *THES*, 13 May 2010, http://www.timeshighereducation.co.uk/story.asp?sectioncode= 26&storycode=411536&c=1 [accessed 12 August 2010], and Tom Garvin, 'Grey Philistines Taking over our Universities', *Irish Times*, 1 May 2010, http:// www.irishtimes.com/newspaper/opinion/2010/0501/1224269475580.html [accessed 12 August 2010].

14. These oppositions have taken a particularly telling turn since the 'downturn' in Ireland, where the arts and humanities are repeatedly presented as one means by which economic capital might be generated. See, for one version of this argument, Declan Kiberd, 'Artists Set Good Example for Wider Economy', *Irish Times*, 7 August 2010, http://www.irishtimes.com/newspaper/ opinion/2010/0807/1224276378817.html [accessed 12 August 2010].

15. Jonathan Goldberg, *Writing Matter: From the Hands of the English Renaissance* (Stanford University Press, 1990), p. 141. This ideological imperative is particularly stark when considering the education of girls and women, which, as A.J. Fletcher argues, is 'a discourse of containment', *Gender, Sex and Subordination in England, 1500–1800* (New Haven: Yale University Press, 1995), p. 375.

16. Anthony Grafton and Lisa Jardine, *From Humanism to the Humanities: Education and the Liberal Arts in Fifteenth- and Sixteenth-Century Europe* (Cambridge, MA: Harvard University Press, 1986), p. xiv.

17. Richard A. Lanham, 'The "Q" Question', in *The Electronic Word*, pp. 155–94 (p. 164). See also Sister Miriam Joseph, *The Trivium: The Liberal Arts of Logic, Grammar, and Rhetoric* (Philadelphia: Paul Dry Books, 2002).

18. Sawday, 'Towards the Renaissance Computer', pp. 40–1.

19. For an extended (and often overstated) critique of this turn in university study, see Duke Maskell and Ian Robinson, *The New Idea of a University* (Thorverton: Imprint Academic, 2002), esp. ch. 6.

20. In addition, the widespread use of continuous assessment in most degree programmes discourages any kind of risk-taking in terms of content or interpretation. See also Maskell and Robinson (*ibid.*, p. 91), who observe, '[a]t the end of the ideal course you will ideally know and be tested on just what the course has taught you, no more and no less'.

21. For a still useful overview, see Lawrence Stone, 'Literacy and Education in England, 1640–1900', *Past and Present*, 42.1 (1969), 69–139.

22. See Walter Ong, *Ramus, Method, and the Decay of Dialogue: From the Art of Discourse to the Art of Reason* (Cambridge, MA: Harvard University Press, 1958); Ong, *Rhetoric, Romance and Technology* (Ithaca: Cornell University Press, 1971), and Ong, *Interfaces of the Word: Studies in the Evolution of Consciousness and Culture* (Ithaca: Cornell University Press, 1977). The point would seem to be confirmed by students' constant demands for lecture notes/PowerPoint slides and their unwillingness to attend when these are provided. Lecture attendance in my own institution has fallen off markedly since the advent of these technologies, and the lecture's pre-eminent position as the primary mode of teaching delivery has been repeatedly challenged.

23. Lanham, 'The Electronic Word', p. 5.

24. Lanham, 'Twenty Years After: Digital Decorum and Bi-stable Allusions', in *The Electronic Word*, pp. 55–96 (p. 57).

25. *Ibid.*, p. 55.

26. Bushnell, *A Culture of Teaching*, p. 202.

27. http://www.wired.com/wired/archive/11.09/ppt2.html [accessed 18 June 2008].

28. For an accessible outline of the taxonomy of rhetoric, see Richard A. Lanham, *A Handlist of Rhetorical Terms*, 2nd edn (Berkeley: University of California Press, 1991).

29. For a useful account, see Peter Mack, *Elizabethan Rhetoric: Theory and Practice* (Cambridge University Press, 2002).

30. Rhodes and Sawday, 'Introduction', in *The Renaissance Computer*, pp. 1–17 (p. 11).

31. Ann Moss, *Printed Commonplace-Books and the Structuring of Renaissance Thought* (Oxford: Clarendon Press, 1996); Ann Blair, 'Note-Taking as an Art of Transmission', *Critical Inquiry*, 31.1 (2004), 85–107; Alison Wiggins, 'What did Renaissance Readers Write in their Printed Copies of Chaucer?' *The Library*, 7th series, 9.1 (2008), 3–36; Heidi Brayman Hackel, *Reading Material in Early Modern England: Print, Gender, and Literacy* (Cambridge University Press, 2005); Alan Stewart, *Shakespeare's Letters* (Oxford University Press,

2008); Grafton and Jardine, *From Humanism to the Humanities*; Stephen N. Zwicker, '"What Every Literate Man Once Knew": Tracing Readers in Early Modern England', in *Owners, Annotators and the Signs of Reading*, ed. Robin Myers, Michael Harris and Giles Mandelbrote (London: British Library, 2005), pp. 75–90, and Jane Stevenson, 'Women and the Cultural Politics of Printing', *The Seventeenth Century*, 24.2 (2009), 205–37.

32. See *Renaissance Paratexts*, ed. Helen Smith and Louise Wilson (Cambridge University Press, forthcoming).

33. Wendy Wall's appropriation of Lewis Mumford's term 'pseudomorph' is particularly relevant here. See *The Imprint of Gender: Authorship and Publication in the English Renaissance* (Ithaca: Cornell University Press, 1993), ch. 4.

34. Lanham, 'The Electronic Word', p. 7.

35. See Rhodes and Sawday, 'Introduction', in *The Renaissance Computer*, pp. 1–17.

36. See Stefania Crowther, Ethan Jordan, Jacqueline Wernimont and Hillary Nunn, 'New Scholarship, New Pedagogies: Views from the "EEBO Generation"', *Early Modern Literary Studies*, 14.2/Special Issue 17 (September 2008) 3.1–30, http://purl.oclc.org/emls/14-2/crjowenu.html [accessed 23 October 2009].

37. See Stevenson, 'Women and the Cultural Politics of Printing', pp. 206 and 225, on the shortcomings of digitized text as it relates to questions of physical format.

38. See Trudi Jacobson and Beth L. March, 'Separating Wheat from Chaff: Helping First-Year Students Become Information Savvy', *The Journal of General Education*, 49.4 (2000), 256–78, who assert that despite the technical know-how to search the Internet, students typically 'lack the critical-thinking skills and database-searching proficiency necessary for them to fine-tune their information searches' (p. 256). And this is before encountering the challenges posed by old spelling, black letter, multiple editions and the complexities of early modern book production.

39. For an interesting student perspective, see Crowther et al., 'New Scholarship, New Pedagogies', n. 36 above.

40. R. Foster Jones, *The Triumph of the English Language: A Survey of Opinions concerning the Vernacular from the Introduction of Printing to the Reformation* (Stanford University Press, 1953), p. viii.

41. To date 125,000 texts have been scanned, of the 460,000 recorded in the ESTC.

42. The debates and controversies over Google books and its digitization project are symptomatic of a largely unexamined takeover of the raw materials of knowledge by large multinational corporations who then effectively 'own' the ideas contained within these texts. Once more, Reformation debates over the desirability of access to Scripture (and who was permitted to access it) seem uncannily relevant. See James Simpson, *Burning to Read: English Fundamentalism and its Reformation Opponents* (Cambridge, MA: Belknap Press of Harvard University Press, 2007) for a recent, popular, account.

43. For an entertaining account of the value and pleasure of traditional research methods, see Keith Thomas, 'Diary: Working Methods', *London Review of Books*, 32.11 (10 June 2010), 36–7.

44. Bushnell, *A Culture of Teaching*, p. 185.

45. *Ibid.*, p. 187.
46. *Ibid.*, p. 191.
47. *Ibid.*, p. 193. See, for example, the work of Sugata Mitra, http://www.ted.com/talks/sugata_mitra_the_child_driven_education.html [accessed 16 September 2010].
48. See Patricia Fumerton, 'Remembering by Dismembering: Databases, Archiving, and the Recollection of Seventeenth-Century Broadside Ballads', *Early Modern Literary Studies*, 14 (2008) 2.1–29, http://purl.oclc.org/emls/14-2/fumerrem.htm [accessed 16 August 2010].
49. See Biet, this volume, pp. 264–6, who raises a similar issue.
50. For a historical analysis, see Robert Scholes, *The Rise and Fall of English: Reconstructing English as a Discipline* (New Haven: Yale University Press, 1998).

3
Information Revolutions Past and Present, and Teaching the Early Modern Period

Paul M. Dover

In the modern-day university history classroom, we as instructors commit an increasingly large portion of our time with our students to discussing means of information delivery. The subjects of these conversations are familiar and recurring: mysteriously lost e-mail messages, purported difficulties with downloading readings and assignments using course management software, and reports of intermittent Internet access. The great potential of these digital forms of data transmission is accompanied by increased incidence of system breakdown, not to mention multiple new opportunities for excuse-making. As we embrace the digital transformations of our age and introduce them to our classrooms, we are aware of the great potential they offer for our teaching, while grappling with admittedly thorny questions of process, implementation and quality control. As a matter of course, we spend a great deal of time negotiating the promise, pitfalls and challenges of the new avenues of information acquisition and sharing.

Digitization, the advent of the Internet as central to much of what we do, and the great proliferation of formats of interpersonal communication: these realities have wrought profound transformations in the history classroom. We are also teaching students who are laden with a diversity of technologies designed to facilitate instantaneous communication (we all know the fury induced by the cellphone or pager going off in class) and the location and transfer of huge quantities of information. It is by now a prosaic notion that we are amid an information revolution, one that places at our fingertips, often in an instant, a staggering amount of data. It is a revolution that both empowers and paralyses us in our personal and professional tasks, one that occasions celebration and wonderment, but also frustration and befuddlement. It is a paradoxical mixture of outcomes that our students know well – it is also one that finds echoes in the early modern European past that I teach.

For those of us who teach early modern European history, this process of negotiating novelty, I would like to suggest, presents opportunities for cultivating historical understanding among our students. The early modern people who populate our courses may never have dreamed of the vagaries of the digital age, but as teachers of the early modern period we should be aware that in managing such expectations and frustrations, we are not that different from our early modern subjects. This is because the transformations of our own information age offer parallels with the early modern period that are interesting, useful and, most importantly, teachable. Such intersections offer the chance for us to do what is essential when teaching the past: to make the unfamiliar familiar, and to cultivate in our students an appreciation for both similarity and difference in the past. This essay will make the case for exploiting such historical analogues in the teaching of the early modern period to university students. It will identify this period as the locus for important transformations in information processing and describe specific representative episodes and phenomena that offer parallels with the current day, by which we might generate historical empathy and genuine historical understanding.

Information revolutions, past and present

In textbooks and survey courses of early modern European history, there is a familiar basket of themes from the period that appear: the passionate embrace of antiquity spearheaded by Renaissance humanists and its social and cultural implications; the opening up of the New World and its repercussions there and in the Old World; the military revolution and the related growth of the state; the splintering of the Western Church; the slow emergence of an empirical spirit in natural philosophy and the advent of modern science; and the triumph of reason, scepticism and critique in the Enlightenment. In my teaching of the period I choose to emphasize a separate theme that is nonetheless intimately connected to those just mentioned: the information revolution of early modern Europe.

In teaching the early modern age, I stress that one of the key features of this period in European history was the challenge that Europeans faced in processing, storing and putting to use the large quantities of information that new technologies, institutions and practices were producing. In my own research on fifteenth-century diplomacy in Italy, for instance, I have shown how ambassadors, statesmen and chancery officials were overwhelmed by floods of paper produced by changes in praxis that stressed daily dispatches and information gathering.[1] Cicco Simonetta, the first secretary of the Duchy of Milan under Francesco and then Galeazzo Maria Sforza, and the architect of a broadly reaching diplomatic network fed by far-flung envoys writing nearly every day, complained that he found himself swimming in a 'world of paper'.[2] The voluminous diplomatic archives of fifteenth-century Italian states are full of such expressions of dismay, as the practitioners of diplomacy struggled to distinguish reliable and useful news among the sheaves of paper reporting all manner of news, rumour and innuendo.[3]

Scholars of the early modern period have pointed to other areas where similar proliferations of paper were taking place. Among these is the expansion of state bureaucracies, fuelled by a surge in the scope of government activity, and in the volume of its written records. It was 'the Renaissance [that] invented the idea of the state', and the state was notable for the reams of paper that it produced.[4] Starting in the fifteenth century, states like Florence and Venice canvassed their populations in tax censuses in order to co-ordinate their *fisc* in the most rational way. The Florentine *catasto*, first carried out in 1427, is but the most famous example of the many efforts made by Renaissance and early modern governments to construct a picture of their populations. Increasingly, numbers were being used to make sense of territories and populations. By the end of the sixteenth century, governments across the continent were doing quantitative surveys to measure all manner of data: tax bases, property ownership, populations, availability of resources and other defining metrics of the state.[5] The rebellious Dutch Republic embarked on what its historians call a 'financial revolution' that took advantage of its commercial boom to finance its war against the Kingdom of Spain.[6] And for all their inefficiencies, the absolutist states of the seventeenth and eighteenth centuries greatly enhanced the information-gathering capacity of the state in their pursuit of money to feed their insatiable war machines.

Similar evidence of this quantifying spirit can be seen in the areas of business and finance, where early modern European men and women of business became assiduous, almost pathological, record-keepers. 'One should never stop using the pen,' was the mantra of early modern merchants, and the ink flowed like never before. I like to cite for my students the work of Luca Pacioli on double-entry bookkeeping, where he warns readers that if they do not keep accurate and up-to-date records of their transactions, they should expect to see their money fly away like houseflies. That this work was the late fifteenth-century equivalent of a bestseller is an indication of how widely such notions circulated, and represents a cultural indicator that even my most mercenary business majors can appreciate.[7] Indeed, the increased emphasis on numeracy was perhaps the defining feature of the Renaissance and early modern economy. Banking, credit, monetary economies and sophisticated contracting instruments – all of these required not only a literate cadre of practitioners, but a numerate one as well. Karl Appuhn has declared: 'if there is one element that ties together all the components of the Renaissance economy – rural and urban, agrarian, carrying and manufacturing – it is numeracy'.[8]

There were also, of course, the far-reaching impacts of the printing press and the 'preservative power' of print (in the phrase of Elizabeth Eisenstein). Print created a reservoir of information that was accessible as never before, allowing unprecedented levels of cross-referencing and information sharing. Europeans also endeavoured to fit within their intellectual horizons a haul of both 'new' data from the New World and of 'old' data 'recovered' by the humanist revival of the Antique. The extent to which the printing press established fixity, as Eisenstein suggests, has recently been brought into question (as will be discussed below) but the revolutionary impact of the printing press that she lays out still obtains. Particularly appealing is her comparison of the mushrooming printing houses of Venice with the start-ups of Silicon Valley – 'not least because so many of the start-ups (like the dot-coms) rapidly went bankrupt and closed down'.[9] To take this analogy further, one might point out that the absence, in the early days of print, of any central authority and the existence of prolonged rivalries between states and other potential agents of control, which allowed significant freedom of action for printers, can be seen as analogous with the free-wheeling, largely ungoverned space of the Internet.[10]

Finally, practitioners of natural philosophy, as Ann Blair and Brian Ogilvie have recently demonstrated, greatly expanded the data at their disposal. Blair has suggested that between 1550 and 1650 the typical academic library grew fivefold, leading to a widely held perception of an overabundance of books.[11] In the natural sciences, the gradual advent of an empirical spirit, something that Ogilvie calls a 'science of describing', meant a new avalanche of descriptive data about the natural world which had to be managed and sifted.[12] It was, in Ogilvie's formulation, a 'botanical information explosion'.[13] The gradual shift in authority from textual tradition to observed fact, if anything, occasioned considerably more information, information which had to be stored, catalogued and in many cases preserved in print; as Ogilvie puts it: 'the book of nature had become illegible unless it was accompanied by nature's bibliography'.[14]

The early modern struggle to encompass all this information has been the subject of increasing scrutiny by scholars in recent years. Daniel Rosenberg has declared that the early modern period experienced nothing less than an 'information explosion'.[15] One of the resonances that have been emphasized of late by scholars of the early modern period is precisely this notion of information overload, a notion that we have come to consider as emblematic of our own age. As Rosenberg puts it: '[f]rom the point of view of our current "information age", it is strange to confront the urgency of these sixteenth-, seventeenth-, and eighteenth-century projects to contain and to comprehend exploding worlds of knowledge'.[16] Richard Yeo has shown that the efforts made to contain and compartmentalize the increased flow of information served in large part merely to preserve it in yet more books, more files and more ledgers. Yeo cites Leibniz, who spoke of the 'the horrible mass of books which keeps on growing', whereby 'the disorder will become nearly insurmountable'.[17]

Rather than praising the press as a heaven-sent invention, many early modern critics lamented its arrival and pointed in particular to how unmanageable and unreliable the glut of information had become. 'The pen is a virgin, the printing press a whore,' declared the Dominican Filippo de Strata, in his *Polemic against Printing*.[18] Andrien Baillet in 1685 feared that 'the multitude of books which grows every day' might return Europe to the Dark Ages 'unless we try to prevent this danger by separating those books which we must throw away or leave in oblivion from those which one should save and, within the latter, between the parts that are useful and those which are not'.[19]

Historical empathy and the early modern period

If history is indeed an unending dialogue between past and present, as Carr has suggested, it is entirely appropriate, and frequently highly fruitful, to take present-day challenges into consideration when seeking to understand historical experience.[20] Thoughtful contextualization is invariably aided by such self-awareness. It may indeed be the case, as Geoffrey Elton put it, with regret, 'that there is no proof that a knowledge of history, recent or distant, at B.A. level succeeds in giving a man much understanding of his own time', but that does not neces-sarily mean that the reverse must be true.[21] Our students, children of the digital age, can scarcely escape the epistemological challenges and uncertainties brought about by the present information revolution. These broadly analogous circumstances can be a useful vector by which to cultivate an understanding of the circumstances of the early modern period and to generate empathy among them for a period far more removed in time.[22] The relative human capacity for empathy has long been a subject of interest to philosophers.[23] That human understanding could be enhanced by the affective communion of one being with another through the union of object and subject was suggested as early as Plato's treatment of the loved and beloved in *Phaedrus*.[24] There was a noisy Enlightenment debate over natural sympathy. Adam Smith, in his *Theory of Moral Sentiments*, insisted 'that there be some correspondence of sentiments between the spectator and the person principally concerned, the spectator must, first of all, endeavour, as much as he can, to put himself in the situation of the other'.[25] David Hume put forward similar ideas in the *Treatise on Human Nature*, although he was less convinced that by such a process one could become a 'disinterested spectator'.[26] Jean-Jacques Rousseau's treatment of natural sympathy focused instead on the notion of pity, which appears as early as his *Discourse on the Origins of Social Inequality*, and which he felt activates our compassion and ultimately makes possible communion with our fellow human beings.

It is only in the past hundred years or so, however, that empathy has become a central concern of moral philosophy. The term 'empathy' is of very recent vintage, and the philosophical principle is rooted in the German notion of *Einfühlung*, or 'feeling into'.[27] The German psychologist Theodor Lipps was perhaps more responsible than any other figure in shaping modern thinking about empathy. His *Ästhetik* (1903) explored empathy in relation to the visual arts, suggesting that an individual's encounter with, and perceptions of, an image originated both in one's sensory reception and in one's self-activity, the latter rooted in one's own life and experiences.[28] Lipps suggested that application of this principle extended beyond the philosophy of aesthetics and could easily be transferred to other humanistic disciplines. There it is often discussed as 'empathetic understanding', an English rendering of the German *nacherleben* (literally, 're-experiencing'), a term employed in the work of Wilhelm Dilthey.[29] Philosophical explorations of empathy continue apace, in forums as varied as Alasdair MacIntyre's *Dependent Rational Animals*, which suggests that practical, independent reasoning is rooted in empathy and an awareness of human vulnerability and interdependence; and Tzvetan Todorov's *Facing the Extreme*, in which he tests the limits of empathetic understanding in recreating the moral universe of the concentration camps of the Holocaust.[30]

Empathy has been a subject of significant interest to scholars of history education of late. Some post-modernists, most forcefully Keith Jenkins, have questioned whether empathy is even possible, pointing to insurmountable cognitive and practical hurdles.[31] Others have rejected it as 'an act of sorcery' that risks us failing to separate our judgements on history from our own historicized selves.[32] Those risks are certainly real, especially if empathy is taken to be nothing more than crude role-playing or conjured communion. The past is past, and merely retelling it with our students cast in the leading roles is a pedagogical dead end. A remedy is to remind students constantly of the importance of remaining aware of the perspectives assumed in historical reconstruction, and of the limitations of using analogy. Asking students to reconstruct fruitfully the perspective of the historical personages in question requires imagination but also information, evidence and contextualization relevant to the period. At the same time, students should be reminded to take full consideration of the perspective that they are assuming. We must encourage them to assess their own positionality as viewers of the past, and remind them that empathy does not equate with sympathy or appreciative self-identification. Failure to take such precautions runs the risk of making everything look just like everything else. Clearly students must resist the temptation to regard those in the past as being just like us. As John Tosh has warned: 'To dress our forebears in our own clothes – as Medieval artists literally did – not only commits a visual solecism but also denies the historicity of the past.'[33]

Another danger that critics of empathy have pointed to is that, in practice, it tends to emphasize feeling rather than facts. From this perspective, empathy is an affective assessment of the past, with the entire concomitant potential for manipulation and projection of self. The suggestion that one can 'feel' one's way to genuine historical understanding is clearly problematic. Ann Low-Beer is among those who have presented this line of criticism effectively, and she rightly refuses to regard empathy as a skill. Too often, she suggests, 'empathy is contrasted with rote-learnt, dry-as-dust facts, and what is so often referred to as "mere" knowledge. The opposition of these two aspects of understanding the past is profoundly unhelpful.'[34] If empathy becomes the end goal, and the basis for assessment, then its use is ineffective, and necessarily produces fictions. But, as Low-Beer herself acknowledges, empathy can be fruitfully employed as one of many tools in the learning process. That is how I choose to regard it, as but a single means of helping my students span the gulf between the current day and early modern Europe.

V.H. Galbraith has written that '[t]o live in any period of the past is to be so overwhelmed with the sense of difference as to confess oneself unable to conceive how the present has become what it is'.[35] Bridging that gap of incomprehension is what historians and history teachers seek to do. Recognition of analogues in the lived present can accompany the acknowledgement of the reality of historical distance and difference. Indeed, the present can scarcely be separated from any past that we are seeking to represent. As David Lowenthal has stated:

> historical understanding merges past with present as well as differentiating them; we cannot avoid mixing up what goes on now with what went on then. To understand what happened, as distinct from what people in the past thought or wanted others to think was happening. We must introduce our own thoughts. And just as present thoughts shape the known past, awareness of the past suffuses the present.[36]

Lowenthal's invitation to introduce 'our own thoughts' reminds us that we need not attempt the impossible by discarding our own perspectives. Denis Shemilt has suggested three different means of empathizing on the part of the historian – one of these, the historian as 'time-traveller', is particularly useful for our purposes here. In this formulation, historical empathy involves 'projecting his own psyche into the past and mentally reliving events from the situation, though not necessarily from the standpoint, of the other'.[37] Thus the historian (or student) always remains a product of the present throughout their 'time-travelling'. Such an approach takes into account the preconceptions of those seeking to achieve empathy, but also encourages them to take on the perspective of their historical subject.[38]

Such opportunities invite our students to employ what Collingwood termed 'historical imagination'.[39] This type of imagination is distinguished from 'pure imagination' by its localization in time and space and the constraints placed on it by evidence; it is not therefore merely fanciful speculation. Careful contextualization is required to exploit 'historical imagination' fully. The institutions, technologies and attitudes pertaining to information in the early modern period were all very different from those of today, and even to speak of an 'information revolution', one must acknowledge the anachronism that the word 'information' appeared scarcely at all during the early modern period and came to be used in its current sense of denoting abstract and quantifiable data only in the early twentieth century.[40]

John Lewis Gaddis, using Spike Jones' quirky film *Being John Malkovich* as a model, suggests that in order to empathize with our historical subjects, or (in the spirit of Jones' film) imagine ourselves inside their minds, we must be open to their own assumptions and impressions. This more or less compels us to be comparative in our approach; effective empathy becomes 'just another way of saying that something is "like" something else. It comes with being a self-reflective, feedback-generating, information-exchanging (if not always utility-maximizing) entity.'[41] While being sure to pay close attention to the distinctive contexts of our historical subjects, the recognition of the 'likes' (and thus, by extension, the 'unlikes') can be highly fruitful.

Genuine efforts at historical empathy are thus invariably comparative, inviting our students to be on the lookout for the familiar and the unfamiliar. Such instances of recognition can be powerful moments of learning. This represents one of the strongest cases for employing empathy, for historical understanding is forged largely through thoughtful consideration of sameness and difference. Finding analogies in the early modern information revolution with the present day can reveal not only parallels but also departures, and, in addition, generate more sensitive understandings not only of the past but also of our present.

Resonances

The struggle of early modern Europeans to make sense, and then make use, of the great quantity of data with which they were confronted has clear resonances with our own day. It is something that every modern-day student, amid the sea of the data that is the Internet, has grappled with and thus she or he can recognize a kindred spirit when confronted with the likes of the Venetian Senate sifting through contradictory information concerning the advance of the Ottoman Turks; a Swabian artisan seeking to make meaning of the mixture of word and image in printed Lutheran propaganda; the Duke of Medina Sedonia seeking to synchronize his operations before the launching of the Armada; a Renaissance chancery secretary complaining that he cannot keep up with the inflow of paper; or with Francis Bacon calling, in the face of an explosion of new books and described facts, for a 'total reconstruction of all knowledge'.

More data, from more sources, impacting a broad range of activities – in this fashion, we see social phenomena that bear much in common with our own information revolution, episodes that intersect with the experience of our own day and in many cases the experiences of the students themselves. In our current day, one of the most commented upon symptoms is the occurrence of information overload – at which point does the task of distinguishing the useful information overwhelm the task at hand? Countless examples of such conundrums could be cited, but let me offer just a single one, described in the *Guardian* newspaper in June 2008. In an instalment in a series entitled 'Digital Rights, Digital Wrongs', Cory Doctorow addresses the dilemmas facing the legion of personnel collecting and analysing data collected in Britain's burgeoning surveillance society. He discusses in particular the use of CCTV feeds in fighting crime, implicitly questioning its utility in cracking cases. He points out that authorities could cover every square inch of the city of London with video feeds, but the result would be so much information that it would be impossible to make any sense of it. At present, closed-circuit television evidence helps solve only 3 per cent of all crimes. Similar dilemmas arose when considering the prospect of fingerprinting every person in Britain for the proposed new biometric identity cards. Such a database would almost certainly result in vast amounts of extraneous data, generate countless false matches and endanger thousands with potential identity theft. In these cases, as with DNA databases and the records of travel and credit card usage, authorities have access to more 'security' information than ever before. But Doctorow poses the question 'what use is that information if we can't process it fast enough? [...] The sweet spot lies somewhere between gathering too much information and gathering too little – and the secret to hitting that spot is intelligent, discriminating data-acquisition.'[42] Such endeavours come to resemble looking for a needle in a haystack. And in our information-obsessed culture, the answer is all too often to create yet more haystacks.

While there were far fewer haystacks in the early modern period, it is evident that similar dilemmas concerning data production and use faced individuals in a wide spectrum of European society. One particularly provocative case study that I choose to share with my students is that of Philip II, the most powerful man in Europe and yet a leader paralysed by the constipating effects of receiving too much information. An account of this fascinating story of strategic dysfunction is found in Geoffrey Parker's *Grand Strategy of Philip II*.[43] There Parker constructs the 'context of strategic culture', providing a stunningly original and valuable treatment of imperial policy-making. Drawing parallels with individuals and episodes from many different historical eras and locales, and judiciously applying the insights of psychology and management science, Parker addresses the question that occurs to all who examine Philip's reign: 'Why did Philip fail to translate so much knowledge into irresistible power?' An intelligent, hard-working and dedicated monarch proved unable to avoid the pitfalls created by his personality, ideology and institutional setting. Philip's failure, Parker demonstrates, was caused in part by a crippling 'information overload'. The *rey papalero* displayed an insatiable desire for information of every variety. Served by a vast, multi-layered and polyvalent bureaucracy, and fed by a network of ambassadors unmatched in Europe, the king was submerged under an avalanche of paper that frequently left him temporizing or even paralysed with indecision. Philip insisted on having 'all' the information from as many sources as possible, obstinately refusing to delegate decision-making authority, and repeatedly demonstrating a cognitive rigidity rooted in the belief that he was carrying out God's immutable will.

Needless to say, my students independently draw comparisons between Philip II's court and more immediate examples of wayward strategic thinking brought about by similar stresses – the debacle of the Iraq War and the decision-making process of the United States' chief executive are sure to come to mind. A few years ago I discussed with my class the predicament of Philip II at just about the same time the 9/11 Commission released its report, revealing that the information gathering arms of the US government knew that the attacks were coming but did not know that they knew it. The thicket of information confronting the hydra-like American law-enforcement and intelligence communities meant that they simply could not put the disparate dots together.

Such parallels regarding attitudes towards information in the early modern period and the current day are increasingly remarked upon. In an essay in the *New York Review of Books* from June 2008, Robert Darnton, speculating on the future of the library, identified four fundamental changes in information processing that have marked human history since we acquired the ability to speak.[44] First, there was the development of early forms of writing around 4000 BC, followed about 3000 years later by the emergence of the alphabet. Then came the invention of the codex in late antiquity, which transformed the practice and facility of reading.[45] The next leap came with the invention of printing in the 1450s, which greatly expanded the availability of texts and the size of the reading public. Finally, Darnton identifies the advent of electronic communication, specifically the Internet and web browsers, as the most recent transformation. Darnton points out that, when looking at the history of information in this way, one witnesses a steadily increasing pace of change: several thousand years between writing and the codex; a little more than a thousand between the codex and movable type; half a millennium between Gutenberg and the Internet; and less than a decade from rudimentary search engines to the algorithmic ranking of Google and other services.

Darnton, however, in his typically insightful and idiosyncratic style, chooses to de-emphasize the discontinuities that these transformations represent, and instead focus on a continuity that he perceives across the millennia of human information processing. He stresses that every age in question was an age of information and that a unifying feature across these epochs was the inherent instability of information. The increased quantity and accessibility of information that these successive changes effected can be characterized by the volume of uncertain information or outright misinformation that they produced. This is a refrain oft-repeated in relation to an Internet age full of blogs, gossip sites and electronic hoaxes; but Darnton insists that we should not regard such uncertainty as novel, as information has never really been stable. The textual stability that many describe the Internet as undermining is in fact a fiction. Writing, the codex and the printed word: all of these means of presenting information have been uncertain, unstable, shifting and unreliable.

This lack of fixity in the so-called information revolutions is one of the points that I emphasize about the early modern experience with my students. In most of my advanced courses, I arrange for a session with information technology staff at my university's library to ensure that my students are aware of the resources available to them in their own historical research. Some students are left bewildered by the vast range of information available to them, in print and in electronic form. Even for students who tend to exhibit considerably more facility with the electronic milieu than do I, the databases and search engines we encourage them to use often leave them unsure of how to distinguish the wheat from the chaff.

In recent years I have incorporated into these library sessions, and at greater length in my course on historical research methods, an extended unit on using the Internet responsibly. This goes beyond endowing them with a healthy mistrust of Wikipedia but also encourages them not to accept something as gospel simply because it has a URL. I discuss all sorts of guidelines for making such determinations, from the domain name to the appearance of the site to the reputability of the host. And yet all of these admonitions do not relieve us of our unease about the Internet as information provider. Tellingly, much the same can be said about the first age of print. As a number of scholars have recently stressed, and perhaps most emphatically Adrian Johns in his *The Nature of the Book*, 'early modern printing was not joined by any obvious or necessary bond to enhance fidelity, reliability and truth'.[46] As those of us who study the early modern period know, print piracy was a thriving cottage industry. Unauthorized print editions were commonplace, as were unattributed borrowings.

This last point should sound strikingly familiar, perhaps especially to those of us who have been forced by bitter experience to employ anti-plagiarism software such as turnitin.com. The Internet is a 'cut-and-paste' universe, a post-modern bacchanal of imitation, inflection and distortion; so too was the freewheeling early world of print.[47] In both episodes, we are confronted with a challenge that at its core is epistemic. We are still feeling our way to some sort of consensus on how to establish confidence in the stability and reliability of the information we receive from the Internet. As Johns and others have stressed, a similar period of adjustment was required to establish a common feeling of trustworthiness in print – one, if we accept Darnton's insights, that was never complete.

As in the early years of print, the fixity of both information and its authorship are susceptible to considerable uncertainty in our information age. The sources of that uncertainty are manifold. Electronic texts are subject to quick, repeated and difficult-to-detect emendation. The computer and cyberspace facilitate and encourage the fragmentation of texts into smaller and more digestible units, in much the same fashion that medieval scholars collected *sententiae*.[48] The nature of the web is particularly conducive to publication under assumed or anonymous identity. In addition, many of the forums for information sharing on the web, such as blogs, chat rooms and open-source information sources such as Wikipedia, further complicate the question of authorship.[49] Johns points out that when an early modern reader picked up a book, he could not assume the book was what it claimed to be, nor that its proper use would be evident.[50] Ultimately, and only very gradually, the West would establish some broadly accepted conventions and codes of civility that would define textual authority and authorship. The free-for-all of the Internet is once again dissolving those established protocols and, as in the early modern period, we, and our students, are endeavouring to locate the moving goalposts.

Another parallel with early print culture and the world of electronic communication is in the inability to control effectively the use and reception of information once it has been disseminated. Once information has been published to the web, little can be done to guide its use rigorously. I like to cite for my students the example of Luther's revolution in print, as recounted by Mark Edwards. Edwards reiterates the importance of the printing press in spreading Luther's ideas, but adds the important caveat that Luther could not control what about him and which of his ideas were being widely disseminated. In this first large-scale 'media campaign', as Edwards calls it, the supposed fixity of print, stressed by Eisenstein, comes up against the great fluidity of its reception. One of the most striking things about the Reformation narrative is just how quickly things spiralled out of any individual's, or institution's control. Edwards demonstrates that this was in large part because different 'communities of discourse' read Luther differently, emphasizing what they chose to pick out. This led to an inevitable 'divorce between Luther's "intent" and the "meaning" that was appropriated by various readers'.[51] Luther, as an early celebrity, was in large part a media creation. The vast majority of prominent Protestant theologians and opinion makers never met him nor had any correspondence with him. The number of people who actually knew Luther beyond familiarity with his media-generated image was very small indeed. Luther was singularly unable to control the reception of his message, or even which portions of his message received emphasis in print. I like to point out to my students that Luther's seminal German translation of the Bible was actually beaten to print by its first pirated edition![52] And another celebrity of the age and sometime sparring partner of Luther, Desiderius Erasmus, complained about his correspondence that 'inevitably I found that it was in circulation and would infallibly be published by someone else, [so] I preferred to revise it and publish it myself'.[53] So much for the fixity of print!

The early history of Luther in print is clearly reminiscent of our own age, where communities of information consumers can pick and choose what and how to consume. One repercussion of the creation of a vast, instantly accessible bazaar of information is that users can select not only what parcel of data they wish to receive but how they wish to see it represented. Once information enters the public domain, control of it is lost almost immediately. Spin is more or less instantaneous. Web coverage of the 2008 American presidential election provides ample evidence of these dynamics. The same speech by Barack Obama was parsed and reinterpreted in radically different ways in the different ideological recesses of the blogosphere. Similarly, different information providers report or emphasize different stories. A story that might receive a banner headline at the left-leaning *Huffingtonpost* might not even merit an appearance on the right-leaning *Drudge Report*.

The analogue of the information market in the Reformation is interesting for our purposes here for an additional reason. As Robert Scribner has reminded us, the role of print in the dissemination of reformed ideas and doctrine had as much to do with the projection of the visual as it did with the written.[54] These images were designed not only to reinforce the theological and doctrinal messages of Reformation propagandists with which they appeared, but also to appeal to the illiterate and semi-literate portions of the population. Such images, celebrating the virtues of the reformers, the vices of the papacy and the truth of reformed interpretations of the Word, remind us that the information flood of the early modern information revolution was not exclusively one of words. David Staley, among others, has stressed that computers and the Internet are in fact more important as conduits of visual data than they are of written data. The great multiplication of digital means of information delivery, including voice, video and music, as well as static visual images, is likely to reduce the importance of the written word as a delivery vehicle of information. Our students regularly employ these manifold means of data sharing, and many have come to expect that they will be exploited in our pedagogy. As we negotiate this period of flux, we can invite our students to empathize with early modern people seeking to manage novel ways of data exchange in their own day.

As we do today, early modern people expended a great deal of energy and employed considerable inventiveness in seeking to make all this data more accessible and sortable. Such activity was the focus of the *Renaissance Computer* project organized by Neil Rhodes and Jonathan Sawday, in which scholars from a range of disciplines examined the parallels between the modern-day computer and early modern efforts to make sense of what Rhodes and Sawday term a 'paperworld', gener-ated largely by the proliferation of the printing press.[55] Many of the problems associated with the computer-driven information revolution were anticipated in the years after Gutenberg. The printed book and the other media of information storage and delivery helped humans understand their world and yet also paradoxically made it more uncer-tain and unknowable – a tension that our own students know only too well. Thus the fascination of the early modern period with indexes, *scholia* on printed works, and encyclopaediae – these are all attempts to categorize and make manageable an exploding corpus of knowledge. These were the search engines of the early age of print. The emergence of such coping mechanisms in the early modern period constituted a leap forward in the availability and importance of artificial memory – in the form of print, account books, archives and other 'containers' in which to preserve writing and images – at the expense of natural memory. The increased reliance in the subsequent centuries on printed matter and on proliferating reference materials undermined the capacity of natural memory. The emphasis was now less on remembering data, but rather knowing where best to look for it.

I describe these transformations to my students and then suggest to them that they too are living in a period witnessing a radical altera-tion in the nature of human memory. The computer and the Internet may very well represent the ultimate triumph of artificial memory over natural memory. If early modern society was gradually becoming a 'look it up' culture, the availability of Internet search engines has greatly accelerated that process. Today's portals, such as Google, are for our students the entry points for most information retrieval; they are akin to the *florilegia* and commonplace books of the early modern period.[56] In today's education, apparently 'what matters is not knowing the answer but knowing where to look it up'.[57] No wonder our students question the utility of memorizing facts and figures.

It is easy to feel overwhelmed by the oceanic dimensions of today's information culture. Early modern Europeans were already questioning the finitude of information. Alfred Crosby has highlighted the difference in scholarly efforts between the medieval and early modern periods as follows:

> the first was an attempt to save as much as possible from a shrinking body of knowledge – a grasping at straws, as it were – and the second was an attempt to make sense of an expanding body of knowledge as a whole hay mow spilled onto the barn floor.[58]

This may be a bit unfair to the dynamism of the medieval intellectual project, but it does capture the explosive nature of the expansion of data in the latter period. Whatever doubts were seeded in the early modern period about the capacity to encapsulate all information in some sort of *summa* or all-encompassing virtual library, today we tacitly acknowledge that efforts towards totality are exercises in futility. We cannot help but feel helpless before the sheer volume of information we have to sort through – this sense of helplessness is familiar to our students and again offers them points of intersection with their early modern forbears.

The current digital revolution continues to evoke a mixture of embrace and rejection, of wonder and of discontent. It facilitates communication but also breeds miscomprehension. As we have seen, such ambivalence was also evident in reactions to the changes of the early modern period. The surfeit of information in our current age has regularly been linked to a burgeoning sense of alienation, anxiety and *anomie*. But even with these seemingly distinctively modern psychoses, we find parallels in the early modern world. By the seventeenth century something resembling a news industry had emerged in many parts of Europe, and already complaints could be heard about the quantity and reliability of the news, and the anxiety that this caused. A passage from Robert

Burton's oft-cited *Anatomy of Melancholy* (1621) is worth quoting at length:

> I hear new news every day and those ordinary rumours of war, plagues, fires, inundations, thefts, murders, massacres, meteors, comets, spectrums, prodigies, apparitions, of towns taken, cities besieged in France, Germany, Turkey, Persia, Poland, &c [...]. A vast confusion of vows, wishes, actions, edicts, petitions, lawsuits, pleas, laws, proclamations, complaints, grievances, are daily brought to our ears. New books every day, pamphlets, currantoes, stories, whole catalogues of volumes of all sorts, new paradoxes, opinions, schisms, heresies, controversies in philosophy, religion &c [...] Today we hear of new Lords and officers created, tomorrow of some great men deposed, and then again of fresh honours conferred [...]. Thus I daily hear, and such like, both private and publick newes.[59]

Such 'vast confusion' serves as a reminder to me and to my students that the truly important and useful ability both in the seventeenth-century England of Burton and in our own digital age is the capacity to apply a discerning filter in the breach against a raging torrent of information. The cultivation of such a filter aids in the search for wisdom, rather than the mere accumulation and dissemination of information. These are skills that extend well beyond merely the achievement of nuanced historical understanding. They are essential in creating thoughtful and engaged citizens.

Pointing out such early modern epistemological uncertainties to my students and inviting my students to identify with such struggles has been fruitful and, I believe, faithful to our historical subjects. In recognizing the inherent paradoxes of information revolutions, we invite the welcome irony that the past becomes somewhat less of a foreign country, something other than just 'a vast confusion'.

Acknowledgements

The author wishes to thank Ann Blair, Bryan McGovern and Thomas Keene for their assistance in the revision of this essay.

Notes

1. See, for example, Paul Dover, 'Deciphering the Diplomatic Archives of Fifteenth-Century Italy', *Archival Science*, 7.4 (2007), 297–316.

2. See Francesco Senatore, *'Uno mundo di carta': forme e strutture della diplomazia sforzesca* (Naples: Liguori, 1998).

3. See, for example, Paul Dover, '"Saper la mente della soa beatitudine": Pope Paul II and the Ambassadorial Community in Rome (1464–1471)', *Renaissance and Reformation*, 31.3 (2008), 3–34, and Dover, 'Good Information, Bad Information and Misinformation in Fifteenth-Century Italian Diplomacy', in *Shell Games: Studies in Scams, Frauds and Deceits (1300–1650)*, ed. Mark Crane, Richard Raiswell and Margaret Reeves (Toronto: Center for Reformation and Renaissance Studies, 2004), pp. 81–104.

4. Edward Muir, 'Governments and Bureaucracies', in *A Companion to the Worlds of the Renaissance*, ed. Guido Ruggiero (Malden, MA: Blackwell, 2002), pp. 107–23 (p. 107).

5. On the Florentine *catasto*, see the seminal study by David Herlihy and Christiane Klapisch-Zuber, *Tuscans and their Families: A Study of the Florentine catasto of 1427* (New Haven: Yale University Press, 1985).

6. See Marjolein 'T Hart, 'The Merits of a Financial Revolution: Public Finance, 1550–1700', in *A Financial History of the Netherlands*, ed. Marjolein 'T Hart, Joost Jonker and Jan Luiten van Zanden (Cambridge University Press, 1997), pp. 11–36.

7. A recent translation of Pacioli's treatise on accounting is *An Original Translation of the Treatise on Double-entry Book-keeping by Frater Luca Pacioli*, trans. Pietro Crivelli (Osaka: Nihon Shoseki, 1974).

8. Karl Appuhn, 'Tools for the Development of the European Economy', in *Worlds of the Renaissance*, ed. Ruggiero, pp. 259–78 (p. 275).

9. Elizabeth Eisenstein, *The Printing Revolution in Early Modern Europe*, new edn (Cambridge University Press, 2005), p. 337.

10. A parallel suggested in Andrew Hadfield, 'National and International Knowledge: The Limits of Histories of Nations', in *The Renaissance Computer: Knowledge Technology in the First Age of Print*, ed. Neil Rhodes and Jonathan Sawday (London: Routledge, 2000), pp. 106–19 (p. 107).

11. Ann Blair, 'Reading Strategies for Coping with Information Overload ca. 1550–1700', *Journal of the History of Ideas*, 64.1 (2003), 11–28.

12. Brian Ogilvie, *A Science of Describing: Natural History in Renaissance Europe* (University of Chicago Press, 2006).

13. Brian Ogilvie, 'The Many Books of Nature: Renaissance Naturalists and Information Overload', *Journal of the History of Ideas*, 64.1 (2003), 29–40 (p. 38).

14. Ogilvie, 'Books of Nature', p. 39.

15. Daniel Rosenberg, 'Early Modern Information Overload', *Journal of the History of Ideas*, 64.1 (2003), 1–9 (p. 1).

16. Rosenberg, 'Information Overload', p. 2. See also Armand Mattelart, *The Invention of Communication*, trans. S. Emmanuel (Minneapolis: University of Minnesota Press, 1996).

17. Richard Yeo, 'Encyclopaedic Knowledge', in *Books and the Sciences in History*, ed. Marina Frasca-Spada and Nick Jardine (Cambridge University Press, 2000), pp. 207–24 (p. 212).

18. Cited in Alexandra Walsham and Julia Crick, 'Script, Print and History', in *The Uses of Print and Script, 1300–1700*, ed. Alexandra Walsham and Julia Crick (Cambridge University Press, 2004), pp. 1–28 (p. 20).

19. Cited in Ann Blair, 'Annotating and Indexing Natural Philosophy', in *Books and the Sciences*, ed. Frasca-Spada and Jardine, pp. 69–89 (p. 70).

20. E.H. Carr, *What is History?* (New York: Vintage, 1964), p. 30.

21. Geoffrey Elton, *The Practice of History* (New York: Crowell, 1967), p. 148.

22. For an interesting discussion of cultivating historical empathy among students, which draws on the most recent literature, see Stéphane Lévesque, *Thinking Historically: Educating Students for the Twenty-First Century* (University of Toronto Press, 2008), pp. 141–69.

23. See the excellent entry on empathy by Karsten Stueber in the *Stanford Encyclopedia of Philosophy*, accessible at http://plato.stanford.edu/entries/empathy/.

24. *Phaedrus*, 251e–253c.

25. Adam Smith, *The Theory of Moral Sentiments*, ed. D.D. Raphael and A.L. Macfie (Oxford University Press, 1979), I.i.4.6 (p. 21).

26. See Rachel Cohon, 'Hume's Artificial and Natural Virtues', in *The Blackwell Guide to Hume's Treatise*, ed. Saul Traiger (Oxford: Blackwell, 2006), pp. 256–75.

27. The term 'empathy' appears to have been coined by the psychologist Edward Titchener in 1909. See Lauren Wispé, 'History of the Concept of Empathy', in *Empathy and its Development*, ed. Nancy Eisenberg and Janet Strayer (Cambridge University Press, 1987), pp. 17–37 (pp. 20–4).

28. Theodor Lipps, *Ästhetik: Pyschologie des Schönen und der Kunst* (Hamburg: Voss, 1903–6).

29. Ilse Nina Bulhof, *Wilhelm Dilthey: A Hermeneutic Approach to the Study of History and Culture* (The Hague: M. Nijhoff, 1980).

30. Alasdair MacIntyre, *Dependent Rational Animals: Why Human Beings Need the Virtues* (Chicago: Open Court, 1999); Tzvetan Todorov, *Facing the Extreme: Moral Life in the Concentration Camps*, trans. Arthur Denner and Abigail Pollak (New York: Metropolian Books, 1996).

31. Keith Jenkins, *Re-thinking History*, rev. edn (London: Routledge, 2003), esp. pp. 47–57. Jenkins' critique would be more convincing, however, if he demonstrated that valuable historical understanding could be achieved by some other means. His pervasive pessimism on this front and his framing of history as a discursive act largely predetermined by present positionality suggest that he might not find striving for such understanding worth the effort.

32. Bruce Van Sledright, 'From Emphatic Regard to Self-Understanding', in *Historical Empathy and Perspective Taking in the Social Studies*, ed. O.L. Davis, Elizabeth Anne Yeager and Stuart Foster (Lanham, MD: Rowman and Littlefield, 2001), pp. 51–68 (p. 66).

33. John Tosh, *Why History Matters* (Basingstoke: Palgrave Macmillan, 2008), p. 26.

34. Ann Low-Beer, 'Empathy and History', *Teaching History*, 55 (1989), 8–12 (p. 11).

35. V.H. Galbraith, 'Historical Research and the Preservation of the Past', *History*, New Series 22.88 (1938), 303–14 (p. 312).

36. David Lowenthal, *The Past is a Foreign Country* (Cambridge University Press, 1985), pp. 234–5.

37. Denis Shemilt, 'Beauty and the Philosopher: Empathy in History and Classroom', in *Learning History*, ed. A.K. Dickinson, P.J. Lee and P.J. Rogers (London: Heinemann Educational, 1984), pp. 39–84 (p. 44).

38. I use the word 'achieve' here with empathy pursuant to the observations of Peter Lee in his article 'Historical Imagination' in *Learning History*, ed. Dickinson, Lee and Rogers, pp. 85–116.

39. R.G. Collingwood, *The Idea of History* (Oxford: Clarendon Press, 1946).
40. This is a point made by Rosenberg, 'Information Overload', p. 7.
41. John Lewis Gaddis, *The Landscape of History: How Historians Map the Past* (Oxford University Press, 2002), p. 128.
42. http://www.guardian.co.uk/technology/2008/jun/17/surveillance.database.
43. Geoffrey Parker, *The Grand Strategy of Philip II* (New Haven: Yale University Press, 1998).
44. Robert Darnton, 'The Library in the New Age', *New York Review of Books*, 55.10 (12 June 2008). Available online at: http://www.nybooks.com/articles/21514 [accessed 10 September 2010].
45. The many parallels between the transformations of late antiquity and the current age are explored with verve in the absorbing meditation of James O'Donnell, *Avatars of the Word: From Papyrus to Cyberspace* (Cambridge, MA: Harvard University Press, 1998). O'Donnell's perspective is especially valuable and penetrating because he is one of the foremost advocates of the embrace of new information technologies by instructors in the humanities.
46. Adrian Johns, *The Nature of the Book: Print and Knowledge in the Making* (University of Chicago Press, 1998), p. 5.
47. [Editors' note: for further reflection on these connections, see Clarke, this volume, pp. 38–40.]
48. This insight is offered by Leah Marcus in 'The Silence of the Archive and the Noise of Cyberspace', in *The Renaissance Computer*, ed. Rhodes and Sawday, pp. 18–28 (p. 23).
49. O'Donnell points out that the tradition of collective, collaborative and anonymous scholarship is actually quite an old one. He cites the example of the *Glossa Ordinaria*, the medieval Bible commentary of multiple, uncertain and sequential authorship, which was augmented over time. See *Avatars of the Word*, p. 63.
50. Johns, *The Nature of the Book*, p. 36.
51. Mark Edwards, *Printing, Propaganda and Martin Luther* (Berkeley: University of California Press, 1994), p. 5.
52. Johns, *The Nature of the Book*, p. 32.
53. Erasmus, 'Catalogue of His Works', in *The Erasmus Reader*, ed. Erika Rummel, 2nd edn (University of Toronto Press, 2003), p. 45.
54. Robert Scribner, *For the Sake of Common Folk: Popular Propaganda for the German Reformation* (Oxford: Clarendon Press, 1994).
55. See n. 10.
56. A parallel noted by Marcus, 'Silence of the Archive', p. 19.
57. Daniel Headrick, *When Information Came of Age: Technologies of Knowledge in the Age of Reason and Revolution, 1700–1850* (Oxford University Press, 2000), p. 4.
58. Alfred Crosby, *The Measure of Reality: Quantification and Western Society, 1250–1600* (Cambridge University Press, 1997), pp. 61–2.
59. Cited in Daniel Woolf, 'News, History and the Construction of the Present in Early Modern England', in *The Politics of Information in Early Modern Europe*, ed. Brendan Dooley and Sabrina Baron (London: Routledge, 2001), pp. 80–118 (p. 87).

Part 2
The Early Modern and its Others

4
'Other Voices': The Early Modern Past in Provincial America

Jonathan Dewald

Most of my teaching has taken place at second-tier public universities located in provincial American cities, first in southern California, then in upstate New York. That's a distinctive teaching environment, one with few equivalents elsewhere in the world. My students are smart and in many ways astonishingly grown up. But coming as they do from relatively modest social milieux, they arrive at the university with little background knowledge of Europe. Few have travelled outside North America, and even fewer command European languages or anticipate advanced studies in European history. The early modern past is not their history. Its landscapes and monuments – familiar to even the most present-minded young European – are unknown to most, and the standard list of early modern cultural icons is almost as alien.

They will fill some of these gaps during their first years at the university. A substantial minority takes advantage of university programmes that allow a semester or academic year in Europe; and introductory classes in history and literature supply some background familiarity. But the basic fact remains: for most, studying the early modern period is a venture into dimly known territory – and territory that they won't necessarily revisit. Few American universities enforce a cumulative programme of historical studies, in which basic courses on the early modern period might serve as prolegomena to later work. I have to view most of my classes as self-contained intellectual experiences.

In these circumstances, questions about *how* to teach the early modern period start with questions about *why* to teach it: why should students thus situated choose any course on the subject? Especially since there are opportunity costs associated with the choice: their study of early modern Europe will come at the expense of courses on modern South Asia, or on race in American society, or on the numerous other subjects that have more direct implications for their lives now and in the future – to say nothing of the still more practical courses offered elsewhere in the university. My own answers to these questions centre on the ideal of cultural encounter. In some ways my students have an intense awareness of the outside world, the product of contemporary patterns of immigration, technology and politics. Yet in other ways the world is very distant to them, and America's traditional insularity remains as powerful as ever, even as it assumes new forms. Students' concern with global poverty (right now a programme officially titled 'global poverty and practice' is among the most popular at the University of California, Berkeley) and public debate about spreading democracy indicate awareness of the outside world – but these interests also indicate the heavy strain of missionary condescension with which many still view the outside world.

Early modern Europe offers cultural encounter of a different kind. This was clearly an underdeveloped, undereducated society, a society with low life expectancies and a shortage of democracy. But it was also a society that produced a long series of undisputed cultural monuments, whose prestige at least resonates with students. As the world of Shakespeare, Racine, Rembrandt, Newton, Loyola and the rest, it cannot be dismissed as underdeveloped, irrelevant to us moderns save as a counter-example. Despite its poverty, many of its achievements outstrip our own. As such, it is an example for thinking about alterity without superiority or inferiority – a way to bring before students the mix of universality and particularity that characterizes human experience, a way to challenge assumptions about cultural hierarchies.

This fundamental commitment has led to a series of specific pedagogical choices. I use as many visual materials as possible in my courses, to compensate for my students' limited sense of the European landscape and of European art. (In this respect, the new technology is of course an extraordinary resource.) I avoid films, since even the best historical films impose a contemporary sensibility on early modern realities, and thus risk falsifying the cultural encounter I want to achieve. Obviously foreign-language readings are out, given my students' skills, but so also are textbooks and the kinds of knowledge that textbooks best provide; since my courses need to function on their own, as self-contained ventures, I spend relatively little time on the roster of kings, wars, discoveries, great books. Instead, my concern is to place students in direct contact with early modern voices, to see how these men and women dealt with basic human problems. That means a heavy dose of primary sources, usually presented whole rather than in the selective format offered by document collections. My choice of sources has varied widely over the years, of course, partly in keeping with my own whims and changing interests, partly in response to changes in the field and in the world at large. But given the age of my students, most of them in their late teens and early twenties, I have tended to focus on personal documents: autobiographies, accounts of spiritual reflection and struggle, novels.

For a long time I assigned only primary documents in my courses. In the past few years, however, I have given more weight to secondary studies, in response to a further objective I want my courses to address. My students simply do not get much training in thinking about how societies function and fail, and early modern Europe offers a wide array of cases for reflecting on those processes: political upheavals, dramatic instances of economic progress and regress, changing habits and experiences of violence. Hence my reading lists increasingly include books like Jan de Vries' *Economy of Europe in an Age of Crisis*, Joel Mokyr's *Lever of Riches* and Geoffrey Parker's *Military Revolution*. Of course, history classes are not the only forum for this kind of thinking. But history offers an especially valuable introduction to it, because of the discipline's commitment to understanding human complexity and its focus on the interplay between individual and society. Public discourse in twenty-first-century America often favours the simplifying abstractions of the social sciences, especially in assessing human motives. All historical study tends to complicate that discourse; and early modern Europe, with its unsettling combination of the familiar and the strange, offers especially compelling examples with which to do so. As the early moderns themselves would have wanted, my teaching thus retains an ethical orientation. It is a way (powerful though indirect) of developing my own and my students' belief systems, by setting them against another instance of the human condition.

5
Exploring the Limits of the Thinkable

Siep Stuurman

Asked to indicate their favourite periods, high-school pupils usually name contemporary history and antiquity, the familiar and the utterly different. Early modern history is less popular. Many undergraduate history students have only the vaguest inkling of what early modernity is. 'Wasn't it mostly churches and absolute monarchs?' one of them let fall during a coffee break, intimating that these were definitely not topics that would keep her awake for long. As many early modern classes are electives, this state of affairs calls for promotion and seduction skills: one needs to lure students into the subject and, far more importantly, to get them to engage intellectually with it.

As a historian of ideas, a twofold strategy has served me well. One focus is on the significance of content: what people think matters, and what people think about important and controversial subjects matters even more. When students assert that violence, material interests and raw power are historically far more significant than such ephemeral and volatile things as ideas, my return question invariably is: 'so you probably think that your own ideas do not matter much either; and if you really believe that, what are you doing in a humanities department in the first place? If you delete all ideas, what remains of history?' That usually gets me part but not all of the way.

The second tier of my strategy can be summarized in three words: *texts, not textbooks*! Confronted with texts that are attractive but also unfamiliar and 'difficult', I invite students to practise the art of close reading, usually in the format of brief assignments on key texts. One of my favourite texts, and one that unfailingly captivates them, is Diderot's *Supplément au voyage de Bougainville*, accessibly written but less accessibly argued. The *Supplément* is a maze of dialogues and stories, so the first assignment is to make an exhaustive list of all the voices in the text and to explain what they stand for. The 'exhaustive' is vital, for it forces the students to read the text very carefully, lest they inadvertently skip a voice. That prepares them for discussion of issues such as why the nexus of religion and gender is so central to Diderot's argument; what happens to the chaplain in the night-time; how all of that ties in with Diderot's critique of European expansion; and why he opted for this particular literary genre. From here, I can go into questions about what was publishable at the time, and how Diderot performs a balancing act on the shifting boundary of the thinkable in the late eighteenth century. Finally, Diderot's persona of the 'Old Tahitian' is as good an introduction to the Enlightenment as any. A powerful critique of European imperialism is wedded to the inexorable global forward march of European power and culture, in a developmental temporality that is itself part of the Enlightenment discourse of *histoire philosophique* (Dipesh Chakrabarty's 'hyperreality of Europe'[1]). The two contradictory discourses are the centrepieces of the same labyrinthine text. They also happen to be two major vectors of Enlightenment and post-Enlightenment history.

There is, however, a drawback to teaching Enlightenment texts in this framework. Because the Enlightenment is the major turning point on the path to modernity in a cultural – if not material – sense, students easily take for granted that the transition to modernity somehow was on the cards and had to happen sometime in the eighteenth century, as it finally did. In this manner, the Enlightenment may take on the hue of a 'preface to modernity', that is, a mere prologue to contemporary history. This is all the more deplorable because we live in a world darkened by historical amnesia and obsessed with temporalities of futurity.

In such pre-modern readings of Enlightenment texts, a major early modern discourse such as Deism is easily relegated to the questionable status of a historical halfway house, instead of the *Weltanschauung* it undoubtedly represented for numerous Enlightenment thinkers (and not only for them, if we may credit recent sociological reports about the great popularity of 'intelligent design'). To understand the Enlightenment historically one has to relate it not only to what came later, but also to what went before and how incredibly hard, and often counterintuitive, it was to 'invent' the Enlightenment. To discuss seventeenth-century texts, for instance, that show how utterly incomprehensible and frightening the very concept of a cosmic order without God was to the great majority of early modern Europeans, and to make students realize how eminently reasonable and rational the arguments for the necessary existence of a divine 'grand design' were in the intellectual and cognitive framework of post-Renaissance Europe is a significant challenge. To the overwhelming majority of seventeenth-century Europeans, the idea of pitting reason *against* God was tantamount to abolishing the notion of reality and could only end in the death of intelligibility itself.

Over the past couple of years, I have taught an MA seminar on the history of concepts and discourses of equality and cultural difference in world history. Students had to read and do assignments on texts by Homer, Confucius, Herodotus, Tacitus, Sima Qian (Ssu-ma Ch'ien, Grand Historian in the former Han dynasty, c. 100 BC), the Bible, Ibn Khaldun, Montaigne, Descartes, Poulain de la Barre, Diderot, Frederick Douglass, Franz Boas, Martin Luther King and Leila Ahmed. The selection of texts varied somewhat over the years, but the basic template of the seminar remained in place. Teaching the seminar was a worthwhile experience. Of course, the present-day focus of students did not, and could not, vanish overnight. Nonetheless, there somehow emerged among the students an intuitive feeling that the Enlightenment represented a historical innovation, the invention of something novel and unprecedented, a passage to ideas that were previously unthinkable. To them, the first part of the seminar was a close encounter with authors and texts they had – or so they told me – always believed 'too difficult for us beagles' (as Snoopy would put it). That was a revelation: Homer and Herodotus turned out to be not 'difficult' but eminently accessible and frequently thrilling. A further example: Genesis. The first assignment question about Genesis was: how many times in the text is a human being created? Count, count, count, and read the text more carefully than you ever did (as a student from an orthodox Calvinist background, where Bible reading was still a family tradition, confided to me). And so then the class could have a discussion of the possible meanings of creation in Christian discourse. But the students also took home a different lesson: their answers to the question diverged and it proved very difficult to reach agreement on the 'true content' of a biblical text. To have tried themselves to agree on the factual 'truth' of such a canonical text, and failed, taught them an 'existential' lesson about the history of Christianity, and by implication about any other creed or philosophy. Things look so promising: you agree upon the sacred authority of the text. But things turn out not to be so good, for you cannot agree on its meaning.

But that is not all. Reading Diderot is one thing, but reading Diderot after having read Herodotus and Sima Qian is another. The three thinkers have something in common. All of them entice their readers to imagine what the world would look like if you were standing on the other side of the frontier: among the Scythians north of the Black Sea in Herodotus' case, among the Xiongnu (Hsiung-nu) north of the Great Wall in Sima Qian's case, among the Tahitians in Diderot's case. The crucial difference concerns temporality. Diderot's temporal regime presages ruin and Europeanization for the Tahitians: they will be made over in the European mould, unhappy and torn apart, but not of course as powerful as the Europeans. Things are radically different, however, in the two ancient historians. The one thing their ethnographies of the steppe nomads have in common is that there is no global regime of developmental time. The nomads have good reasons to pursue their own way of life, and no good reasons at all to adopt the customs of the sedentary 'civilizations'. Cultural difference was there to stay (for two millennia, the sedentary–nomadic divide was the 'great frontier' of the Eurasian world). Greece, Persia and Han China were real, but they were not hyper-real.[2]

A different perspective on the Enlightenment, focusing on its temporality and its overarching discourse of *histoire philosophique*, permits students to give historical depth to their understanding of the intellectual transformations of the early modern period. Next, students may attempt to figure out how cultural difference fits into the picture, for instance by writing an essay on cultural difference and temporality in Herodotus (or Sima Qian), Montaigne and Diderot. Picturing Montaigne swimming in an ocean of unknown and alarming novelties, keeping himself afloat by holding on to the flotsam and jetsam of his beloved Antiquity, they will perhaps better understand how hard it was to push at the limits of the thinkable, but also what it was that gave the *Essais* their remarkable staying power.

Let me end these brief observations on a note of modesty. When we teach we are not the all-knowing grand masters. We too peer into the early modern maze from the vantage point of the present age. Like all of us who have done research in early modern intellectual history, I know that it is impossible to divest oneself entirely of the cardinal sin of anachronism. I think I came rather close in an article on a proto-feminist woman writer in seventeenth-century Albi, published some ten years ago, but certainty is not to be had in such cases.[3]

Notes

1. See Dipesh Chakrabarty, *Provincializing Europe: Postcolonial Thought and Historical Difference* (Princeton University Press, 2000).
2. See Siep Stuurman, 'Herodotus and Sima Qian: History and the Anthropological Turn in Ancient Greece and Han China', *Journal of World History*, 19.1 (2008), 1–40.
3. Siep Stuurman, 'Literary Feminism in Seventeenth-Century France: The Case of Antoinette de Salvan de Saliez', *Journal of Modern History*, 71 (1999), 1–27.

6
Lobola, Intombi and the Soft-Porn Centaur: Teaching *King Lear* in the Post-Apartheid South African Classroom

Deborah Seddon

This essay centres on my recent experience of teaching Shakespeare's *King Lear* in a final-year undergraduate course on Renaissance Literature at Rhodes University, South Africa. I focus on what I consider to be the most important challenge in teaching the literature of the early modern period: facilitating my students' critical thinking about the connections between culture, politics, gender and representation, not only in relation to one text, but towards their understanding of the global impact of early modern European cultures. One possible approach, I suggest, is to highlight for students how the early modern period, and a text as controversial as *King Lear*, might be assessed in terms of their own complex cultural heritage as young South Africans. My deliberately provocative title, translated from the IsiXhosa, reads 'The Bride Price, the Virgin, and the Soft-Porn Centaur'. As I will demonstrate, my title's mixture of languages and allusions, in its appeal to both the local and the global, seeks to convey something of the heterogeneity of South Africa's socio-cultural environment.

I will describe a teaching strategy that engages directly with elements of contemporary South African experience – from images in cyberspace to evolving forms of indigenous cultural practices – to aid students' assessment of the role of gender and power in the play. This teaching method utilizes my research into the work of South African politician, journalist and novelist Solomon Tshekisho Plaatje, the first translator of Shakespeare into an African language. From 1916 onwards, Plaatje translated five plays into his mother tongue, Setswana. As I will show, Plaatje's conception of the Shakespearean text can provide teachers of the early modern period with a new approach: one that suggests we direct our critical attention to the places where our cultural heritages intersect. Such a strategy may help teachers move beyond the rather limited notions of 'universalism' and 'multiculturalism' and take an active role in cultivating what Christopher L. Miller has termed 'intercultural literacy'.[1]

Global cultures, colonial histories

That my classroom happens to be in South Africa is pertinent to my discussion but so is the contemporary global situation, where 'locality' is not always 'the prime referent of our experience'.[2] The collapse of apartheid coincided with the onset of globalization, and the world South Africa re-entered in 1994 is a place in which 'imagined communities' now extend well beyond national boundaries. As Mike Featherstone argues, 'it is not helpful to regard the global and the local as dichotomies separated in space and time'; instead, in the current phase, 'globalization and localization are inextricably bound'. What we are witnessing is the capacity of individuals 'to shift the frame and move between a varying range of foci' and 'to handle a range of symbolic material out of which various identities can be formed and reformed in different situations'.[3] As a result our students seem now 'more than ever to want to locate themselves as global citizens'.[4] Like undergraduates all over the world, my students use JSTOR, Google, Wikipedia and a range of other web resources to complete assignments, they download music from the Internet, communicate with friends through mobile phones, and participate actively in the popular culture of the international entertainment industry. Likewise, the challenges facing the teaching of early modern literature in South African universities are similar in many respects to those encountered elsewhere. How does one make the text alive in word, sound and image for students? How does one enable the students' willingness and capacity to pay studied attention to the specificities of language, mythological resonance and socio-political context? How does one encourage students to take an active interest in making the text their own?

Teaching strategies, however, also need to remain attentive to the continued impact of history. In South Africa that means not only the recent history of apartheid, but a longer history in which the inauguration of English Literature as a discipline was distinctly tied to its use in the colonial enterprise as what Chris Baldick has called 'a civilizing subject'. As Rajeswari Sunder Rajan points out, it is 'one of the ironies of colonial history that English literary studies should have had their beginnings in India and Africa' in a deliberate attempt at the enculturation of a certain set of socio-political values.[5] We need to resist this approach in our own teaching, particularly when presenting students with the canonical works of the early modern period, perhaps most especially, because of its history in inculcating value, when teaching the works of Shakespeare.

Local specificities

I teach *King Lear* in a final-year course consisting of undergraduates who have chosen the Renaissance Literature course from a choice of three possible first-semester courses. Thus, they might be reading Renaissance Literature alongside a course in Contemporary American Literature, African Literature, New Literatures in English, or the English Novel.[6] The students are taking English Literature as a major along with another subject, sometimes two other subjects, from within the range of disciplines that make up the Humanities Faculty. Rhodes University is situated in a small town in the Eastern Cape but students come from all over the country, and from neighbouring Southern African countries. We also have exchange students from Europe and the United States. So my students speak a variety of languages, have a range of interests and bring different familial, educational and cultural backgrounds to the classroom.[7]

Though much has changed in South Africa and on campus since I was a student in the early 1990s, a great deal is still exactly the same. Rhodes University was founded in 1904, named for the English imperialist, financier and mining magnate Cecil John Rhodes. While the campus is more racially mixed today than ever in its history, South Africa remains a divided country. Despite huge strides towards economic and social redress since 1994, for the majority of the population dire poverty, the lack of electricity, running water, employment, transport and the need for decent housing are still daily realities. Black Economic Empowerment and Employment Equity Policies have meant that the black middle class is expanding rapidly but divisions in income and class remain for the most part racially defined. While people are freer and more empowered in many ways than ever before, the economic and psychological effects of apartheid are still all around us. South Africa often tops the international statistics tables in terms of the gap in the quality of life between the very rich and the very poor, and in the rate per capita for murder, violent crime and sexual violence, the rape of women and children.[8] Many of my students either have themselves been victims of oppression or violence or are close to someone who has been robbed, high-jacked, assaulted, raped, or who was conscripted, imprisoned, exiled or worse under apartheid. Those with families in Zimbabwe remain fearful for their safety as that country has faced years of rigged elections, an economic meltdown, spiralling death-rates and astonishing brutality in the intimidation of opposition supporters.

Thus, there are many elements in *King Lear* which may have a tangible resonance for South Africans and Africans: the tyranny of an aged king against all who dare to contradict him; the irate reaction from those so accustomed to their absolute power towards the individuals they have newly asked to speak; the resentment of those who feel delegitimized or disinherited by the social order; the acts of terrible cruelty possible in quite ordinary people; the need for serious critique to be shaded in madness or jest; the lesson still awaiting those who hold political and financial power when they enter the hovels of the vagrant poor. But, if affinities exist between the text and the world of my students, I would argue that, as a teacher, I should be wary of making too much of them. In more traditional approaches to teaching, the articulation of such affinities was often the means of demonstrating the universal 'relevance' of the canon to modern lives: illustrating the ability of 'the great books' to address all students, situations and times. If there are aspects of *King Lear* that might speak to the young South Africans and Africans in my classroom, there is also much in this play that these students might, quite rightly, refuse. As Amy Gutmann has argued, in teaching the humanities, the reading of 'great books' is 'an indispensable aid' but we need to teach them 'in a spirit of free and open enquiry, in the spirit of both democratic citizenship and individual freedom'.[9] Education fails, she suggests, when we intimidate or seduce our students into blind acceptance of the visions of these books. What Gutmann resists most in those who defend the traditional canon is what she calls 'intellectual idol worship'. She notes that 'it is intellectual idolatry and not philosophical openness and acuity' that supports the claim that the great books 'contain the greatest wisdom now available to us on all significant subjects'.[10]

I chose to teach *King Lear* in the Renaissance course not only because it is considered to be what Gutmann calls a 'great book' but because it is a play that I intensely disliked as an undergraduate. The idea that this frighteningly volatile old man, with his violently misogynist language, should be read as a misguided but magnificent tragic hero, his flaws redeemed by noble suffering, was too much for me. So I rejected *Lear* completely.[11] Although none of my teachers had enabled me to encounter her work back then, I felt a bit like Janet Adelman, who has argued that the realization that 'Shakespeare is complicit in Lear's fantasy', and also requires the sacrifice of Cordelia's autonomy, is 'a very painful recognition for a feminist critic, for anyone who reads as a daughter'.[12] Peter Brook's film adaptation (1971) and Jane Smiley's novel *A Thousand Acres* (1991), both of which discover daughters in the play who are 'not Ugly Sisters but abused children', allowed me the space to reassess my initial reaction.[13] Such engagements, as Kathleen McLuskie puts it, permit a reading beyond 'special pleading on behalf of female characters' by restoring 'the element of dialectic, removing the privilege from the character of Lear and the ideological positions which he dramatises'.[14] My approach to teaching *King Lear* stems directly from the ways in which I found my own route back into this contentious play and from my research into the appropriation, adaptation, rewriting and translation of the Shakespearean text.

Global and local Shakespeares

What, one might ask, is at once more tiresomely familiar and dauntingly strange to any twenty-first-century literature student than the experience of being confronted in class by a Shakespearean text? By the time they get to their third year, my students have been exposed to an international range of poetry, drama and fiction, and hopefully have had their modes of thinking and reading shaken up a little on the way. Yet, in my experience, one of the things that has remained intact since they left school is their sense that 'Shakespeare' is considered 'the real thing': the transcendent centre of the English literary canon.[15] For some, this makes Shakespeare crucially valuable to their education; for others, it renders his work tediously conservative. Both these points of view can be productively challenged by recourse to recent scholarship on Shakespeare's afterlife.

The critical study of Shakespeare's global reception in the past decade has done much to foreground the particularity, specificity and creativity of differently situated responses to Shakespeare, and the function of his works as 'an unusually charged medium of textual exchange'.[16] These projects have assessed Shakespeare's place in history, ideology and culture by highlighting the ways in which both the author-figure and his texts have been 'adapted', 'reinvented', 'reimagined' and 'repositioned' to grant authority and resonance to a multiplicity of subject positions.[17] This critical work has illustrated that, far from distorting an unchanging textual or authorial identity, such reinterpretations, as Jean Howard has suggested, *are* Shakespeare, as Shakespeare 'lives in history, with history itself understood as a field of contestation'.[18]

Teaching strategy: Shakespeare 'lives in history'

One of my first moves then, in introducing the play, is to problematize the two seemingly evident signifiers that appear on the cover of my students' course-handout: 'William Shakespeare' and 'King Lear'. As Ann Thompson argues, because it exists in two versions, *King Lear* is 'the obvious text' to use in introducing students to 'such issues as the transmission and stability of seventeenth-century texts, the ongoing shift from manuscript to print culture' and 'the uncertain status of drama as a popular and ephemeral art form'.[19] Due to its affordability and availability, I set R.A. Foakes' Arden edition of the play as what he calls a 'reading text'. Foakes' edition 'includes, with markers in the form of superscript Q (for Quarto) or F (for Folio)' the words found in one text but not in the other.[20] Foakes also draws attention to the history of editing which has transformed these texts into the modern editions with which my students are familiar and which, as Magreta de Grazia has shown, carry a distinct ideology within their apparatus.[21] I also direct the class to the textual debate in books such as *The Division of the Kingdoms*.[22] For many students, this is the first time they have actively considered how the materiality of the Shakespeare text can affect reader and audience response; some are deeply alarmed by the disparities in characterization and plot between the Folio and Quarto versions. But such discomfort can provide impetus for a closer examination of the history of performance and adaptation. As Thompson suggests, 'the natural extension' of such 'micro-level' textual scrutiny is 'to look at the ways in which *King Lear* has, like any dramatic text, been "unstable" on the stage'.[23] I discuss images from various stage performances, films and artworks while lecturing on different scenes and I provide a range of films for my students to watch.[24] These are not simply visual tools to breathe life into a text for students who might never have seen *King Lear*, or any Shakespeare play, on a stage. The diversity of approaches taken by modern directors such as Peter Brook, Grigori Kozintsev, Jonathan Miller, Michael Elliot and Richard Eyre, and the history of adaptations, from Nahum Tate's 1681 happy ending to Akira Kurosawa's *Ran* (1985), or the 1997 film of Jane Smiley's *A Thousand Acres*, can emphasize how any meaning to be had from the play is not just intrinsic but a matter of national, cultural and sexual politics. In all senses, I tell my students, 'King Lear' is still a work in progress.

I have found my students both astonished and delighted to learn something of the complex history of what has gone into the making of England's national poet. Exposing them to a few of the multiple existences of a 'Shakespeare' who has been constantly in 'production' since the first of his plays was first performed, not only provocatively unsettles their engrained attitudes, it also encourages students to attend to, and thus value more highly, their individual interpretations. This empowerment of their own perspectives prompts keener attention to the details of the text than a teaching method focused ostensibly on 'close reading' alone. For there is no place outside ideology or history from which the plays may be approached and a successful teaching strategy should enable my students to recognize their own part in the 'production' of Shakespeare. By this I do not mean performing the play, but in the sense of developing a performative understanding. In designing my course, I have been influenced by John Biggs' simple but important assertion that 'it is what the students do to achieve understanding that is important not what the teachers do'. As Biggs argues, 'the acquisition of information in itself does not bring about such a change, but the way we structure that information and think with it does'. He notes that 'students *act differently* when they really understand' and 'the very highest levels of understanding are thus performative'.[25] This teaching goal requires that the course facilitates my students' capacity to critique the history of representation, and the function of literature in various societies.

But if Shakespeare 'lives in history' then how might the play live, here and now, for my students, in South Africa? There is no simple answer to this question. With 11 official languages and a mixture of peoples of African, Asian and European descent, South African identities are themselves a work in progress.[26] Since the brutal inception of the nation with the Act of Union in 1910:

> to be 'South African' has historically meant no longer fully to be something else, no longer to be plainly something one might style as uncomplicatedly as 'Dutch,' 'Xhosa,' 'English,' 'Tswana,' or any of the other language and cultural formations making up the country's brimming residual fund of identities.[27]

As David Attwell has argued, Fernando Otiz's notion of 'transculturation' is an apt description of conditions in South Africa where the impact of cultures on one another 'has had the effect of disallowing everyone from remaining unchanged, and therefore has kept histories, traditions and identities radically in flux'. Where I find Attwell's argument most valuable is in his acknowledgement that colonial violence is often a condition of transculturation, which 'not only suggests multiple processes, a dialogue in both directions', but also 'processes of cultural destruction followed by reconstruction on entirely new terms'.[28] The global reach of early modern European economies is part of the story of that violent transculturation. In 1602, a few years before *King Lear* was first performed in London, the Dutch East India Company (VOC) was created to ensure Dutch monopoly over the spice trade in the face of competition from the British and Portuguese. The VOC was the first company in history to issue stocks in order to build their business. This created a means of access to millions of guilders, and provided a blueprint for the development of stock markets all over Europe.[29] The decision of the VOC in 1652 to use the Cape of Good Hope as a refreshment station en route to India was the beginning of the colonial encounter in South Africa, and was followed shortly by the importation of slaves from Dutch East Asia and violence against the indigenous peoples of the Cape.[30] For South Africans, the country's long history of racialized conflict has irrevocably marked and altered us in response to each other but it has also kept cultures apart. The self-reflective awareness of what Leon de Kock has called our 'radical heterogeneity' as a nation tends to co-exist with our daily habits of division into more discrete ethnic identities.[31] At one end of the spectrum in my classroom, I have bi- or multilingual students who participate simultaneously in a variety of cultural ways of being, and at the other, monolingual students enclosed within a still-dominant white middle-class worldview. How is it best to engage all these young men and women? My decision has been to read the play through the lens of differently located responses and to present specific examples of South African engagements with Shakespeare that are, in themselves, a profound deliberation on the transculturation of identity.

Solomon Plaatje

A key focus of my own research has been the engagement with Shakespeare's texts by one of South Africa's most important political and cultural figures – Solomon Tshekisho Plaatje (1876–1932). Plaatje was a member of the Barolong clan of the Tswana but because of his fluency in Setswana, Sesotho, IsiXhosa, IsiZulu, English, Dutch and German and his groundbreaking work as a novelist and journalist, and as a founding member of the African National Congress, Plaatje was committed at a number of levels to addressing the vexed question of South African identity.[32] The first African translator of Shakespeare, Plaatje translated five of the plays into Setswana (*Julius Caesar, The Comedy of Errors, The Merchant of Venice, Othello* and *Much Ado About Nothing*) but political and financial restraints meant that only one translation was published in his lifetime.³³ Plaatje's work has been central to the questions I have asked myself about how best to teach the plays in a South African context. His sense of the equivalence of function between Shakespeare's plays and South African orature is crucial to understanding Plaatje's translations.³⁴

Orature refers to the class of oral verbal art forms in all cultures which may be understood to function in a manner akin to 'texts' because, to use Karin Barber's description, they have been 'constituted *as* texts' by those cultures.³⁵ That is to say that these oral forms have achieved a certain 'object-like' solidity, detached from everyday utterances, and thus durability in time. Detaching the utterance in this way invites comment, analysis and interpretative participation from a community of users. In performance there is often scope for improvisation, reinterpretation and adaptation, but this does not call the status of an oral text as a durable formulation into question.³⁶ The various genres of South African orature may be roughly designated as poetry, proverbs, riddles, songs and folktales but, because the textuality and the performativity of these different oral forms are often culturally specific, these English-language descriptors are not always an exact parallel.³⁷

Plaatje was one of a host of South African writers in the late nineteenth and early twentieth centuries who combined the literacy skills they had developed through mission education with a thoroughgoing knowledge of vernacular history and orature. These poets and writers developed a flexible, dynamic relationship with the printed word, which potentially could reach a far wider audience than an oral performance and could also be used to record and transmit oral texts in the face of devastating socio-political change.³⁸ As I will show, Plaatje's conception of the continuities between oral texts and Shakespeare's plays stemmed from his own work as a cross-cultural writer grounded in Setswana orature. I will suggest how Plaatje's understanding of Shakespeare can aid students in examining the oral resource-base of a play like *King Lear* and how this might contribute to the development of intercultural literacy.

In Plaatje's initial writing on Shakespeare, an essay included in the publication that marked the tercentenary of Shakespeare's death, *A Book of Homage to Shakespeare* (published by the British Academy and edited by Israel Gollancz), he first raises the possibility of translating the plays. He links the idea to his already nuanced understanding of the commensurability between Shakespeare's culture and his own: 'that this could be done is suggested by the probability that some of the stories on which his dramas are based find equivalents in African folk-lore'.[39] As I have argued elsewhere, Plaatje's essay provides an important index of how Shakespeare's works were in circulation amongst urbanized black South Africans in the early years of the twentieth century. In response to the ways in which the educated black petty bourgeois were oralizing and incorporating Shakespeare's texts into their own cultural practices, in the form of both folktales and proverbs, Plaatje recognized that he might use printed translations of the plays to disseminate threatened Setswana orature, particularly the Setswana proverbs that, as the first indigenous ethnographer of the Tswana, he had spent much of his energy collecting into print. Plaatje's free translation of the Shakespearean text had far-reaching implications – the most important being his deploy-ment, where appropriate, of Setswana proverbs to replace Shakespeare's imagery and metaphors. Replete with these indigenous idiomatic forms, his translations aimed to both preserve and perform the orature of his culture. A primary aim of Plaatje's translations was to provide school books in the vernacular to a new generation of Setswana speakers who were growing up in a radically changed cultural environment, where oral cultural practices and the ethical and social systems encoded by proverbs were being distorted or forgotten, and where there was little to read in the vernacular except religious texts provided by Christian missionary presses. His engagement with Shakespeare provides a sin-gular instance of the use of the playwright's work to affirm, safeguard and, most importantly, locally disseminate an African oral culture in print form.

Plaatje's translations were thus a reactivation of the oral elements of Shakespeare, a registering of Shakespeare's relationship with an oral tradition that was long absent from English assessments of the play-texts in the early twentieth century. As Adam Fox has demonstrated, the situation in early modern England is particularly important 'as a case study for examining the relationship between oral and written forms':

> On one hand oral exchange remained the primary mode of receiving and transmitting cultural capital for most people. On the other hand this was the period in which significant advances were made in popular literacy and the new technology of print first made a real impact on society.[40]

Fox notes that 'any crude binary between "oral" and "literate" culture fails to accommodate the reciprocity' that had been achieved between speech, script and print by the Elizabethan period. His detailed examination of the different media in which ballads, proverbs and folklore existed in early modern England demonstrates that 'print did not destroy circulation by word of mouth. Sometimes it enshrined material picked up from the oral realm: certainly it fed back into it' and that 'far from undermining oral circulation', print 'reinvigorated and refreshed something which was in danger of disappearing'.[41]

Plaatje's translation project indicates precisely this recognition of the reciprocities between oral and print media and what he viewed as the productive resemblances between Shakespeare's cultural environment and his own residually oral South African context. His conception of Shakespeare's orality was the source of, and remained at the heart of, Plaatje's relationship with the playwright. Plaatje is not alone in his consideration of the plays' relationship to orature nor is he the only South African writer to engage in a deliberate appropriation of Shakespeare in support of an emergent South African identity.[42] The most famous South African stage adaptation is Welcome Msomi's *Umabatha* (1969), *Macbeth* in IsiZulu, which toured America and Europe, most recently with two seasons at the Shakespeare's Globe Theatre in London (1997 and 2001). Msomi's adaptation utilizes Zulu proverbs and poetic styles derived from Zulu panegyric verse (*izibongo*) to tell the story of Shaka's murder by Dingane.[43]

The importance of orature

Taking my lead from Plaatje, a now consistent focus of my preparation for teaching Shakespeare is an examination of a play-text's rootedness in the residually oral culture of early modern England. Of course, attention to sources (both written and oral) has long been a focus of Shakespearean scholarship. But studied attention to the oral sources of a Shakespearean play can achieve a number of important goals in teaching. One of these is to ground the work more firmly in its own specific socio-historical context. As Mary Ellen Lamb has shown, the encounter with the fairies in *A Midsummer Night's Dream* takes on new, sometimes sinister, meanings when read in terms of the metaphorical function of fairy practices in the oral culture of early modern England.[44] A consideration of oral sources can thus allow students to develop a better sense of the response to the play by Shakespeare's early modern audience.

In terms of *King Lear*, Alan R. Young has argued that Shakespeare's play deliberately distorts 'the folk-pattern on which the story [...] is based' and awareness of its oral sources is vital to assessing the impact of the catastrophic ending.[45] Young draws attention to two groups of folktales 'which represent an oral tradition related to the original source of Geoffrey of Monmouth's tale of King Leir from which derive the various written transmissions leading up to Shakespeare's play'. The first group of tales, classified by folklorists as Types 510A and 510B, are 'Cinderella' stories: 'tales not only among the oldest known' but also the most 'widely disseminated'. Folktales of this type exist in European, Arabic, Indian and Chinese versions. The second group, classified as Types 923, can be termed 'love like salt' stories which exist 'all over western Europe, in Scandinavia, Malta, the Balkans, South Africa, Turkey and India'. In England, the tales closest in pattern to the King Leir story are known under the general title of 'Cap O' Rushes'.[46]

Young notes that both sets of tales possess a common pattern. All begin with a love test: a father's demand that his adult children put a value on their love for him. The youngest child (often a son in Indian versions) refuses to flatter the father and gives a cryptic response. This is misinterpreted by the father, who then expels the child from his house. The child survives by disguise, finds his/her own way to good fortune and eventually meets with the father to reconcile. In a version of the Cap O' Rushes story from Suffolk, the youngest daughter is banished after her reply: 'Why, I love you as fresh meat loves salt.' She hides her rich apparel under a humble garment of reeds, and finds work in the house of a prince who later discovers who she is and marries her. At the wedding feast, to which her father is invited, the daughter orders that only unsalted food be served. On eating the tasteless meal the father realizes his error, his daughter reveals her true identity and they are reconciled.[47] In his consideration of these folktales Young argues that the tragic ending of Shakespeare's play completely thwarts the expectation of a comic conclusion that has been 'evoked in the minds of his audience by their familiarity with both literary and oral sources'. This explains the immense impact of the ending: Lear's defeat, the father and daughter's imprisonment, and the death of Cordelia are thus 'as unexpected to the audience as [they are] to Lear'.[48]

I have found that attention to the oral sources of the Lear story can go even further than this – a comparison with pre-existing folktale traditions is also helpful in considering a question often crucial to feminist readings of the play: that of Lear's incestuous desire for Cordelia.[49] As Christine Goldberg's discussion of the 510B folktale cycle indicates, not all these stories begin with a misunderstanding: in some versions, the father wishes to marry his daughter and this is what prompts her escape from his household. In some of the more gruesome versions, from both Africa and Europe, her disguise is fashioned from human skin, so that the banished child literally becomes another person in order to survive.[50]

For my first seminar on *King Lear*, I set Young and Goldberg as preparatory reading and ask my students to Google the 'Cap O' Rushes' or 'love like salt' stories. In discussion we compare notes; a few students are completely new to these tales but many have encountered similar stories in childhood, either from older relatives, or from books. In the classroom, this encourages attention to the nuances of the text as students begin to understand the differences between source and play in terms of plot, characterization, genre and so forth. What is intriguing to note here is the way in which Shakespeare's play splits the folktale material into two by doubling the role of the father: while Cordelia is banished by Lear, Edgar takes the part of the child humbly disguised.

Orature is at the root of all cultures, but in advocating the importance of oral sources in teaching Shakespeare I would like to clarify that I am not suggesting anything as simple, or as patronizing, as a search for origins: the idea that all of us, from whatever culture, have such folktales in our heritage and this might allow my disparate students to find some common ground. Instead, I would suggest the opposite: that the consideration of orature in relation to Shakespeare actually complicates the notion of origins. I wish my students to see Shakespeare's play as itself an innovative retelling, recombination and complex appropriation of much older oral materials. Coupled with the students' knowledge of Plaatje's Setswana translations and Msomi's IsiZulu adaptation, attention to Shakespeare's deliberate rewriting and deviation from oral sources can help extend the notion of adaptation as usually applied to Shakespeare's afterlife in the opposite direction. For South African literature students, an encounter with Shakespeare's relationship to orature (a form of cultural expression long denigrated in colonial assessments of non-Western societies) provides a valuable realignment of a sensibility that still tends to view Western civilization as the major producer and exporter of literature via colonialism. Here is a Shakespeare rooted in an oral tradition, and, like so many South African writers, actively involved in reworking that tradition by producing new forms of cultural expression.

Intercultural literacy

I am also concerned to develop in my students what Christopher L. Miller has termed 'intercultural literacy', which he describes as an ambitious and worthy goal of undergraduate and graduate education. He defines it as:

> a mode of inquiry that respects the accumulation of shared symbols (thus the term 'literacy') but also invites research into the processes by which cultures are formed and particularly encourages analysis of how cultures constitute themselves by reference to each other.[51]

Such an understanding is crucial to the reconstruction and development of culture in South Africa. Miller sets his approach against E.D. Hirsch's advocacy of a national 'cultural literacy' which, he argues, runs 'the risk of confining oneself to the study of "one's own" culture' so that 'theory and reading will operate in a closed circuit, smoothly confirming each other and leaving the appearance of universal validity'.[52] But Miller is also critical of the way in which multiculturalism 'is too often conceived as the mere multiplication of discrete cultural or national units' – thus, in 'expanding the number of cultures about which a student should be "literate" [...] multiculturalism is plural nationalism'. Will this, he asks, 'advance the understanding of culture as a process or will it simply reinforce boundaries and further balkanize the curriculum?'[53]

For Miller, 'multiculturalism is an inadequate formula, an expedient, incapable of handling the challenge of international and intercultural reality'. As he points out, 'the histories of Africa, Asia and Europe have been intertwined for millennia', and in Africa, any question of 'one's own' national culture is extraordinarily complex, as 'the incongruity between nations, languages and culture' is 'the most basic fact of intellectual and political life'.[54] African writers tend to use the languages of former colonial powers in their work, yet that work is also frequently marked by the influence and strategic deployment of indigenous oral traditions. Thus it is impossible to consider literature in any broad sense 'without taking orality into account'. As Miller suggests, attention to these intersections of orality and literacy can help shift students' most basic assumptions about the discipline of 'literature' itself.[55] I would argue that such questions are particularly important when teaching early modern play-texts produced within a residually oral English culture.

My course on *King Lear* is designed to involve my students in an active investigation of 'culture as a process' by facilitating their understanding of the ways in which different cultures have interacted and transformed in response to each other. As Edward Said has asserted, in the post-imperial world all 'cultures are involved in one another; none is single and pure, all are hybrid, heterogeneous, extraordinarily differentiated and unmonolithic'.[56] In the final section of this essay, I will describe briefly how a teaching strategy directed towards intercultural literacy can enable students' critical responses to the most contentious aspect of *King Lear*: the depiction of women. I will look at two examples, one 'global' and one 'local' but inextricably linked.

Whose misogyny is it anyway?

LEAR   Down from the waist they are
centaurs, though women all above. But to the girdle do
the gods inherit, beneath is all the fiend's: there's hell,
there's darkness, there is the sulphurous pit, burning,
scalding, stench, consumption! Fie, fie, fie! Pah, pah! (IV.6.121–5)

Here, in Lear's identification with Ixion 'bound upon a wheel of fire' (IV.7.46–7), he sees himself as father to the centaurs. But his image of his offspring, and by extension all women, as half human, half beast is a particularly disturbing one: the mutation of a mythological idea within the realm of private fantasy. The vision is linked to his notion of the vagina as hell itself, and is the clearest example of Lear's revulsion of women.

Exploring this passage with a class is not easy, especially given the information needed to decode the imagery. Who is Ixion? What is a centaur? Why does Lear think he is father to such mythological creatures? But the passage is crucial to assessing the representation of women in the play and a useful means of illustrating how careful attention to the mythological elements is required to grasp characterization. As Peter L. Rudnytsky has suggested, Lear's diatribe splits the female body in two: 'the line of demarcation is the loins, with the human or divine region above and the bestial or demonic below'. He argues that the passage repeats the polarization of women into angels or demons, virgins or whores, pervasive in patriarchal culture, and conspicuous in Cordelia's idealization and her sisters' demonization.[57] In preparing to discuss this passage, I made a chance discovery of my own, which became a valuable teaching tool. Looking for a suitable visual example of a centaur to use in my lecture overheads, I typed the word 'centaur' into the Google Images search engine and I couldn't believe my eyes. There, at the click of a mouse, entire pages of 'photo-shopped' images of erotic female centaurs appeared. I decided to show my class the most unforgettable image of the lot: a photograph of a sleekly airbrushed naked blond woman with the body of a four-legged pony. She appears on a site devoted to myths and monsters called Monstrous.com.[58] Verging on soft-core pornography, the image variously stunned, amused and disgusted my class but it achieved its intended aim – to revivify the passage and explain the importance of the mythological reference. It also helped demonstrate something else for my students: Lear's vision of the woman as centaur is not just the obscure concoction of a madman drawn from mythological references too tedious for them to bother with – it is the powerful articulation of a shared male sexual fantasy which is alive and well in twenty-first-century cyberspace.

The explosion of information in print was one of the fundamental technological revolutions of the early modern period. Today it is mirrored in the global dissemination of ideas through the resources of the Internet. If grasping the cultural journey that takes us from Lear's 'monstrous' daughters (I.1.218) to the image on www.monstrous.com is a lesson in intercultural literacy then it is one that works in a number of ways. Lear's reference to the centaur is important for my students to understand because it will help them to grasp not only his speech, but also something of the history of representation and the relationships between culture, gender and power. The redeployment of classical mythology is seen as one of the greatest achievements of English Renaissance literature and is a prime example of how different cultures constitute themselves in relation to one another. The Internet image of the female centaur illustrates vividly the implications of Lear's use of mythology, and the continued perpetuation of that fantasy today. The Internet image works, then, as a potent corrective to criticism of the play that condones and repeats Lear's misogynistic assessment of his daughters.[59] It demonstrates the need, as Rudnytsky puts it, 'to emancipate ourselves from the gender arrangements of patriarchy, even as we continue to reread the literary masterpieces in which its fantasies are most powerfully inscribed'.[60]

In the South African context, the exploration of patriarchal attitudes in the play can also be illuminated by reading Lear's behaviour in the first scene in terms of the contemporary debate over *lobola*, or the bride price. The ritual of negotiating and paying *lobola* is a custom amongst many indigenous cultures in Southern Africa. The word stems from the transitive verb *ukulobola* (in IsiXhosa), and traditionally meant the payment of cattle for a wife in compensation to her father. The practice, which continues in some rural areas and is incorporated in mediated form into the lives of many Christian or urban couples, is well known but by no means uncontroversial. Defenders of the tradition argue that *lobola* works to strengthen kinship ties and offers the protection of the extended family to married women and their children.[61] Detractors argue that the fact that a man or his family has parted with resources – either cattle or money – in order to acquire a wife affects women's rights and male perceptions of the marriage relationship.[62] Recent research has shown that many men consider the ritual a purchase and women therefore as 'property to them'.[63] A number of solutions have been proposed, including formalizing contractual arrangements in line with Western prenuptial agreements.[64]

Whatever their individual cultural backgrounds, my students are much more familiar with the practice of *lobola* than with the similar Western tradition of the dowry paid by the bride's father on the marriage of his daughter. Thus the debate over *lobola* is constructive to developing students' understandings of Lear's revocation of Cordelia's dowry and his utterance, 'But now her price is fallen' (I.1.198). A comparative discussion of the practices can thus be fruitful. For example, in response to the essay question, 'What is your assessment of the portrayal of women and sexuality in *King Lear*?' one of my students chose to produce a close reading of the first scene centred on a comparison of the patriarchy in the play and in her own Xhosa heritage. As she observed: 'Many of the perceptions of women in this play are still perpetuated today, and I will show how this is true of the Xhosa culture in South Africa.' While recognizing the clear distinctions between a dowry and *lobola*, she argued that Lear's description of Cordelia's 'price', and his retraction of her dowry, delegitimizes his daughter. In Xhosa terms, she observed, Lear's words attempt to rob Cordelia of any worth by denying her position as *intombi*, the IsiXhosa word for both 'a daughter' and 'a virgin'. His scheme is only foiled by France's generosity in choosing to wed Cordelia without her father's blessing or dowry. In their earlier forms, she suggested, both English and Xhosa cultures shared a system of patriarchal relationships in which masculine kinship ties were formed and maintained through the exchange of wealth for daughters and in which, without her father's or another man's kinship, a daughter's identity is reduced to nothing. Here, I would argue, is Miller's notion of intercultural literacy in action. This student has produced a reading of an early modern play that is also a performative understanding – a feminist critique of her complex South African heritage.

Conclusion (or, here and there, then and now)

In their evaluations of my course this year, in response to the question, 'What is the most interesting thing you have learnt during this course about *King Lear* or Shakespeare?' half my class (exactly 50 per cent) highlighted their learning about the links to and deviations from the oral sources of the play. Of the other half, 23 per cent pointed to the fact that *King Lear*, as one student put it, 'has been read and performed from *so many* points of view'. For those in the former category, a few students were disappointed but most were intrigued to learn that Shakespeare was not the primary inventor of the story told by the play. As one student noted: 'learning about the history it has in folklore was interesting because Shakespeare has always seemed an entirely English thing to me, but the story is actually older than that'.

With stories derived from a variety of folkloric, historical and mythological sources and set in a variety of time periods and locations, Shakespeare's theatre was never, even on the early modern stage, 'an entirely English thing'. But, as Michael Dobson has demonstrated, in the century between the Restoration and the Stratford Jubilee, the twin processes of adaptation and canonization transformed Shakespeare into a respected Enlightenment author-figure and a symbol of English national identity. Granted this status, Shakespeare was exported all over the world by means of the British Empire. Ironically, once relocated on these terms, Shakespeare was no longer 'the exclusive possession of any one social group or cultural formation' and became 'an enabling and empowering resource' deployed and appropriated in a variety of contexts in the service of an extraordinary range of political, national and cultural needs.[65]

This essay has focused on the teaching approach to one play but I would like to conclude by suggesting that the teacher's deliberate location of any Shakespearean play in terms of its oral and written sources, its materiality, and its varied history in performance, criticism and culture, is part of establishing the play-text for students within a much older story – a story in which, for centuries, cultures have continued to co-exist, coalesce, react, conflict and thus compose themselves in response to one another. This story can alter students' fixed ideas about Shakespeare, literature, the early modern period and about themselves. To teach early modern literature in contemporary South Africa is to teach the literature of a time and a place from which we are profoundly estranged. Paradoxically, however, due to the history of imperialism, it is also a time and a place which, for better or for worse, will always form a part of who we were, are and might become. For like Shakespeare, our own identities as South Africans are and always have been in 'production'. As Stuart Hall suggests, identity is not 'an already accomplished fact', but a 'production', which is 'never complete, always in process, and always constituted within, not outside, representation'.[66] Intercultural literacy as a goal of educational practice can, I would suggest, increase my students' recognition of their own place and, more importantly, their own agency within a transnational cultural history where identities, and what they might mean, are being constantly articulated, relocated and contested. This approach to teaching English literature of the early modern period cannot and should not collapse the very real differences between here and there, then and now, but it might allow us to better map what we bring together in one South African classroom.

Notes

1. Christopher L. Miller, 'Literary Studies and African Literature: The Challenge of Intercultural Literacy', in *Africa and the Disciplines*, ed. Robert H. Bates, V.Y. Mudimbe and Jean O'Barr (University of Chicago Press), pp. 213–31 (p. 217).
2. Mike Featherstone, 'Localism, Globalism and Cultural Identity', in *Identities: Race, Class, Gender, and Nationality*, ed. Linda Martín Alcoff and Eduardo Mendieta (Oxford: Blackwell, 2003), pp. 342–59 (p. 351).
3. *Ibid.*, pp. 342 and 347.
4. David Attwell, *Rewriting Modernity: Studies in Black South African Literary History* (Scotsville: University of KwaZulu-Natal Press, 2005), p. 6.
5. Chris Baldick, *The Social Mission of English Criticism, 1848–1932* (Oxford: Clarendon Press, 1983); Rajeswari Sunder Rajan, 'After "Orientalism": Colonialism and English Literary Studies in India', *Social Scientist*, 4.7 (1986), 23–35 (pp. 24–5).
6. The undergraduate degree at Rhodes is three years. The course on *King Lear* is part of a semester-length course on Renaissance Literature, and consists of a total of seven (45-minute) meetings: five lectures and two seminars over two and half weeks.
7. Tuition at Rhodes University is in English. IsiXhosa is the predominant language in the Eastern Cape.
8. For a range of statistics on South Africa see 'Information by Country: South Africa', *UNICEF* website, http://www.unicef.org/infobycountry/southafrica_statistics.html [accessed 4 September 2009].
9. Amy Gutmann, 'Introduction', in *Multiculturalism: Examining the Politics of Recognition*, ed. Amy Gutmann (Princeton University Press, 1994), pp. 3–24 (pp. 12–15).
10. *Ibid.*, pp. 15–16.
11. My teachers' approach to Lear also appeared in the introduction to my set work, the Arden edition (Second Series) in which Kenneth Muir argues that Lear has, by the end of the play, freed 'his heart from the bondage of selfhood. He unlearns hatred and learns love and humility' (London: Routledge, 1989, p. l). This reading of the Shakespearean tragic hero draws on A.C. Bradley's *Shakespearean Tragedy*, published in 1904, and played out in the criticism of Maynard Mack, Kenneth Muir, Richard Levin and others. For Bradley, 'there is nothing more noble and beautiful in nature than

Shakespeare's exposition of the effect of suffering in reviving the greatness and eliciting the sweetness of Lear's nature'. He suggests that we would be 'near to the truth if we called this poem *The Redemption of Lear*' (*Shakespearean Tragedy* (London: Macmillan, 1963), pp. 234–5). Maynard Mack argues that Shakespeare provides a 'tragic vision of the creature whose fate it is to learn to love only to lose (soon or late) the loved one, and to reach a ripeness through suffering and struggle, only to die' (see Mack, '*King Lear*' *in Our Time* (Berkeley: University of California Press, 1965), p. 79). In 1988, Richard Levin took issue with the 'denigration of the tragic hero' in feminist criticism of Shakespeare which he asserted, in diminishing his stature and thus negating 'the tragic effect', amounts to a misunderstanding of the genre of tragedy (see 'Feminist Thematics and Shakespearean Tragedy', *PMLA*, 103 (1988), 125–38). Compare G. Wilson Knight's perceptive examination of the way in which the tragic effect of *King Lear* is in fact *enhanced* by moments of grotesque humour at Lear's expense, where the audience is tempted to laugh at his absurdly comic words and actions. See *The Wheel of Fire* (Oxford University Press, 1930). Madeleon Sprengnether observes that when we look at Shakespeare's plays from a perspective different to the implicit identification with the tragic hero, 'a dislocation occurs so profound as to alter our very understanding of tragedy'. Such an approach, she argues, historicizes tragedy and reveals the interrelation of genre and gender. See 'Introduction', in *Shakespearean Tragedy and Gender*, ed. Shirley Nelson Garner and Madelon Sprengnether (Bloomington: Indiana University Press, 1996), pp. 1–27 (p. 9).

12. Janet Adelman, *Suffocating Mothers: Fantasies of Maternal Origin in Shakespeare's Plays, Hamlet to The Tempest* (New York: Routledge, 1992), p. 125.
13. For a view of what is achieved by Peter Brook's RSC production (1962) and film version (1971) in comparison with more conservative recent productions see Carol Rutter, 'Eel Pie and Ugly Sisters in *King Lear*', in *Lear from Study to Stage: Essays in Criticism*, ed. James Ogden and Arthur H. Scouten (Madison: Fairleigh Dickinson University Press, 1997), pp. 172–225 (p. 174); Jane Smiley, *A Thousand Acres* (London: Flamingo, 1992); and Iska Alter, '*King Lear* and *A Thousand Acres*: Gender, Genre, and the Revisionary Impulse', in *Transforming Shakespeare: Contemporary Women's Revisions in Literature and Performance*, ed. Marianne Novy (New York: St. Martin's Press, 1999). Jane Smiley discusses her novel on the BBC website, *BBC World Service*, 'World Book Club', originally broadcast March 2008, http://www.bbc.co.uk/worldservice/specials/133_wbc_archive_new/page5.shtml [accessed 4 September 2009].
14. Kathleen McLuskie, 'The Patriarchal Bard: Feminist Criticism and Shakespeare', in *Political Shakespeare: New Essays in Cultural Materialism*, ed. Jonathan Dollimore and Alan Sinfield (Manchester University Press, 1985), pp. 88–108 (p. 106).
15. For criticism of this approach to Shakespeare, see Alfred Harbage, 'Shakespeare and the Myth of Perfection', *Shakespeare Quarterly*, 15.2 (1964), 1–10, and Marjorie Garber, 'Shakespeare as Fetish', *Shakespeare Quarterly*, 41.2 (1990), 242–50.
16. Thomas Cartelli, *Repositioning Shakespeare: National Formations, Postcolonial Appropriations* (London: Routledge, 1999), p. 23.

17. See, for example, Michael Dobson, *The Making of the National Poet: Shakespeare, Adaptation and Authorship, 1660–1769* (Oxford: Clarendon Press, 1992); Gary Taylor, *Reinventing Shakespeare: A Cultural History from the Restoration to the Present* (London: Hogarth Press, 1990); Jean Marsden, *The Re-Imagined Text: Shakespearean Adaptation and Eighteenth Century Literary Theory* (Lexington: Kentucky University Press, 1995); and Cartelli, *Repositioning Shakespeare.*

18. Jean E. Howard and Marion O'Connor, 'Introduction', in *Shakespeare Reproduced: The Text in History and Ideology* (London: Methuen, 1987), p. 4.

19. Ann Thompson, '"King Lear" and the Politics of Teaching Shakespeare', *Shakespeare Quarterly*, 41.2 (1990), 139–46 (p. 145).

20. William Shakespeare, *The Arden Shakespeare: King Lear*, ed. R.A. Foakes (London: Cengage Learning, 1997), pp. 127 and 4.

21. Margreta de Grazia, *Shakespeare Verbatim: The Reproduction of Authenticity and the 1790 Apparatus* (Oxford: Clarendon Press, 1991) and 'The Question of the One and the Many: The Globe Shakespeare, *The Complete King Lear*, and The New Folger Library Shakespeare', *Shakespeare Quarterly*, 46.2 (1995), 245–51.

22. Gary Taylor and Michael Warren, *The Division of the Kingdoms: Shakespeare's Two Versions of King Lear* (Oxford: Clarendon Press, 1983).

23. Thompson, 'King Lear', p. 145.

24. The Royal Shakespeare Company online archive is a useful source of images from their productions, including photographs, costumes, paintings, prints and prompt books, http://www.rsc.org.uk/searcharchives/home/index.jsp [accessed 4 September 2009].

25. John Biggs, 'What the Student Does: Teaching for Enhanced Learning', *Higher Education Research and Development*, 18.1 (1999), 57–75 (pp. 60–6).

26. The 11 official languages in South Africa are, in descending order of mother tongue speakers, IsiZulu, IsiXhosa, Afrikaans, Sepedi, English, Setswana, Sesotho, IsiNdebele, Tshivenda, SiSwati and Xitsonga.

27. Leon de Kock, 'Does South African Literature Still Exist? Or: South African Literature is Dead, Long Live Literature in South Africa', *English in Africa*, 32.2 (2005), 69–83 (p. 72).

28. Attwell, *Rewriting Modernity*, pp. 17–18.

29. See Clem Chambers, 'Who Needs Stock Exchanges', *Mondo Visione Worldwide Exchange Intelligence*, http://www.exchange-handbook.co.uk [accessed 4 September 2009].

30. 'The Dutch East India Company', *SA History Online*, http://www.sahistory.org.za [accessed 4 September 2009].

31. De Kock, 'Does South African Literature Still Exist?', p. 74.

32. For details of Plaatje's career see Brian Willan, *Sol Plaatje: South African Nationalist* (London: Heinemann, 1984).

33. Sol T. Plaatje, *Mabolelo a ga Tsikinya-Chaka: Diphosho-phosho* (*The Sayings of Shakespeare: The Comedy of Errors*) (Morija Press, 1930). Plaatje's translation of *Julius Caesar* was published, after his death, by Witwatersrand University Press in 1937. Of the other translations, only fragments of the manuscripts, or Plaatje's mention of these works in his letters and other publications, remain.

34. See Deborah Seddon, 'Shakespeare's Orality: Solomon Plaatje's Setswana Translations', *English Studies in Africa*, 47 (2004), 77–95; and 'The Colonial Encounter and *The Comedy of Errors*: Solomon Plaatje's *Diphosho-phosho*',

The Shakespearean International Yearbook, 9: Special Section, South African Shakespeare in the Twentieth Century (2009), 66–86.

35. Karin Barber, 'Quotation in the Constitution of Yorùbá Oral Texts', *Research in African Literatures*', 30 (1999), 17–41 (p. 18). There is considerable debate among scholars of orature as to what constitutes the essence of the oral verbal art form: the text or the performance. Barber's essay demonstrates that this dichotomy is a false one by drawing on a more inclusive notion of 'text' as that which refers to any configuration of signs coherently intelligible to a group of users (p. 17).

36. Barber, 'Quotation', pp. 18–19.

37. For instance the English term 'praise poem' is an inadequate means of describing the cultural practice of South African panegyric verse such as Setswana *maboko* or IsiXhosa *izibongo* as these forms of poetry also operate as a crucial means of socio-political critique.

38. See Deborah Seddon, 'Written Out, Writing In: Orature in the South African Literary Canon', *English in Africa*, 35.1 (2008), 133–50.

39. Sol Plaatje, 'A South African's Homage', in *A Book of Homage to Shakespeare*, ed. Israel Gollancz (Oxford University Press, 1916), pp. 336–9, and reprinted in Plaatje, *Selected Writings*, ed. Brian Willan (Johannesburg: Witwatersrand University Press, 1996), pp. 210–12 (p. 212).

40. Adam Fox, *Oral and Literate Culture in England, 1500–1700* (Oxford University Press, 2000), p. 12.

41. *Ibid.*, pp. 3–11.

42. For details of the South African Shakespeare created by the writers of *Drum* magazine see Natasha Distiller, *South Africa, Shakespeare, and Post-Colonial Culture* (Lampeter: Edwin Mellor Press, 2005).

43. Welcome Msomi, *Umabatha: An Adaptation of Shakespeare's Macbeth*, trans. by the author (Pretoria: Via Afrika, 1996).

44. Mary Ellen Lamb, 'Taken by the Fairies: Fairy Practices and the Production of Popular Culture in *A Midsummer Night's Dream*', *Shakespeare Quarterly*, 51.3 (2000), 277–312.

45. Alan R. Young, 'The Written and Oral Sources of *King Lear* and the Problem of Justice in the Play', *Studies in English Literature, 1500–1900*, 15.2 (1975), 309–19 (p. 318).

46. *Ibid.*, pp. 310–11.

47. *Ibid.*, pp. 311–13.

48. *Ibid.*, p. 317.

49. See, for instance, Adelman, *Suffocating Mothers*, pp. 116–29; Lynda E. Boose, 'The Father and the Bride in Shakespeare', *PMLA*, 97.3 (1982), 325–47 (pp. 332–5); and Stanley Cavell, *Disowning Knowledge in Seven Plays of Shakespeare* (Cambridge University Press, 2003), p. 70.

50. Christine Goldberg, 'The Donkey Skin Folktale Cycle (AT 510B)', *The Journal of American Folklore*, 110.435 (1997), 28–46.

51. Miller, 'Literary Studies and African Literature', p. 217.

52. *Ibid.*, p. 226.

53. *Ibid.*, p. 216.

54. *Ibid.*, pp. 216 and 225.

55. *Ibid.*, pp. 221–6.

56. Edward Said, *Culture and Imperialism* (London: Vintage 1994), p. xxix.

57. Peter L. Rudnytsky, '"The Darke and Vicious Place": The Dread of the Vagina in "King Lear"', *Modern Philology*, 96.3 (1999), 291–311 (p. 301).

58. 'Female Centaur', *Monstrous.com*, http://monsters.monstrous.com/female_centaur.htm [accessed 4 September 2009].

59. For Bradley (*Shakespearean Tragedy*), Goneril is 'the most hideous human being (if she is one) that Shakespeare ever drew' (p. 249), whereas Cordelia is a thing 'enskyed and sainted' (p. 264). Bradley sees the play as concerned with 'the tragic effects of ingratitude' and, although sympathetic to Cordelia, he includes her as well as her sisters in this charge. In the introduction to the Second Series of the Arden edition (London: Routledge, 1989) – reprinted into the 1990s – Kenneth Muir also ventriloquizes Lear, stating that in the play: 'the selfishness and ingratitude of children, no longer trammelled by the restraints of morality or modified by filial affection, are projected onto the monstrous figures of Goneril and Regan' (p. xlvii), who 'become centaurs, their rational minds instruments of the animal body' (p. li).

60. Rudnytsky, 'The Darke and Vicious Place', p. 311.

61. See Peter Mtuze, *Introduction to Xhosa Culture* (Lovedale Press, 2004), pp. 28–33.

62. See Sarah C. Mvududu, *Lobola: Its Implications for Women's Reproductive Rights in Botswana, Lesotho, Malawi, Mozambique, Swaziland, Zambia and Zimbabwe* (Harare: Women and Law in Southern Africa Research Trust, 2002); Danai S. Mupotsa 'Lobola for my Love', *Mail and Guardian*, 23 July 2008, http://www.mg.co.za/article/2008-07-18-lobola-for-my-love [accessed 4 September 2009].

63. 'Lobola – A Price for a Bride', *Research and Educational Trust for Women and Law in Southern Africa*, http://www.wlsa.org.zm/zambia/pages/26apr01p1.htm [accessed 10 January 2009] (§ 16 of 17).

64. 'Lobola for a New South Africa', *South African Info*, http://www.southafrica.info [accessed 4 September 2009].

65. Kate Chedgzoy, *Shakespeare's Queer Children: Sexual Politics and Contemporary Culture* (Manchester University Press, 1995), p. 2.

66. Stuart Hall, 'Cultural Identity and Diaspora', in *Identity: Community, Culture, Difference*, ed. Jonathan Rutherford (London: Lawrence and Wishart, 1990), pp. 222–37 (p. 222).

7
Windows of Gold

Ruth Whelan

There is a folktale that captures something of my evolving experience of researching and teaching early modern French literature and culture, and, indeed, of teaching and learning in general. Here is my version of it by way of a prologue to this brief reflection on those changes:

> Once upon a time there was a girl who lived on a hillside overlooking a valley, which was covered with a carpet of trees as far as the eye could see. On sunny mornings (which were not all that frequent where she lived) she would gaze across the valley only to be dazzled by the windows of a house that stood on the opposite hill.
>
> — 'They have windows made of gold, but ours are only made of glass. How come?' she wondered. But no-one in her family could provide an answer that satisfied her.
>
> Her curiosity grew and grew until she was determined to find an answer to her question; so one afternoon she set out down the hillside along a path not much frequented, judging by the look of it. Her sense of direction was a bit unreliable and she was glad to meet another person journeying in the same direction, who seemed to know the way, and a lot of other things besides. She was a bit afraid of getting lost in the hundreds of trees that stood all around them because she thought they all looked alike, but her companion could actually detect patterns. As they talked, she too began to perceive the different varieties and how they were grouped into discrete woods threaded with paths.
>
> Towards sunset they arrived at the house with the golden windows but to her astonishment the girl saw that its windows were in fact made of glass.

— 'We must have taken a wrong path in the woods', she said to her companion.

— 'Let's knock and ask directions to the house you are looking for', her companion replied.

The person who answered the door listened to the girl's question, smiled, and said:

— 'Yes, I know the house. You have come quite the wrong way, but probably because the golden windows can only be seen at a particular time, around sunset in fact. See, if you turn around and look across the valley, you will see the house you are looking for; see, over there, on the opposite hill.'

The girl turned, gazed, and gasped in recognition. There, across the valley, was a house whose windows were made of gold; it rose in the distance ... on the site of her own home. It *was* her own home! Laughing in delight, she turned to her companion, who laughed back, although apparently not at all surprised by her discovery. Shortly afterwards she took her leave.

As she walked away, she heard a voice behind her saying:

— 'The gold that you were seeking is now in you. Take care of it! Farewell!'

With a start she realized that her companion was right. She stood absolutely still for a moment and contemplated the powerful radiance that was emanating now from within her own self. Then with one last wave she set off down the path, eager to share her new awareness with anyone who would listen.

Over a whole lifetime of learning and teaching, with everything shifting and changing (including, I hope, myself), I have had a beacon, consistent yet not static, glinting, guiding: flashes of gold – a bee. I was 18 when I spotted it, in a book and not a garden, a book significantly entitled *Essais*, which its author understood to mean essaying, trying out, flexing, exploring, developing what he calls the 'natural faculties', as my tiny undergraduate marginalia remind me now. In his celebrated essay on the education of children, Montaigne weaves together the bee and the child to express the learning outcomes he desires: 'Les abeilles pillotent deçà delà les fleurs, mais elles en font apres le miel, qui est tout leur; ce n'est plus thin ny marjolaine: ainsi les pieces empruntées d'autruy, il les transformera et confondera, pour en faire un ouvrage tout sien: à sçavoir son jugement.'[1] Although it was written in 1580, that one sentence still encapsulates for me the richness of the humanist paradigm which shaped my university education and early career – but it also implicitly expresses its shortcomings.

In contrast to the Sophists of Montaigne's time and perhaps our own, for whom education is acquisition and consumerism, skills and display, the bee reminds us that learning and teaching are processes whose objective is metamorphosis, or at least facilitating the possibility of it. And, as my folktale suggests, I see this process as both journey and quest, which lead away from the parental home, or the comfort of a more limited vision, towards the wider world beyond, or the broader understanding that is creative selfhood. Obviously, this process is dialogic in as much as it involves the teacher and the taught, both of whom are transformed (ideally) by the process.

Less immediately obvious is the cultural dialogue that is also at work here: Montaigne borrows the concept of the bee from Plato's *Ion* but transplants it into an educational context, thereby transforming it, making it his own; he is in fact modelling the metamorphosis he seeks from learning.[2] All education is dialogic in this way, but researching, teaching and learning early modern French is especially so. For we are engaging with a language and a culture that (if we are Anglophone) is not our own and with a past which is a foreign country for a generation marked by the historical amnesia symptomatic of the post-modern condition.[3] The flashes of gold that we enable our students to glimpse, here and there during their undergraduate studies, are an attempt to place them in creative dialogue with a past that has shaped our present in a multiplicity of ways and to encourage them to incorporate it into their awareness of the world.

However, while the humanist paradigm of education as creative dialogue with the 'great minds' of the past is heady in its implications, like all human artefacts it is also deeply flawed. It usually comes packaged in the myth of disinterested and dispassionate enquiry and often results in presentations – whether in the classroom or at academic conferences – that claim to be impersonal and objective. I am amazed in retrospect that I was taught French and French literature almost as if it were Latin and classical antiquity, and that I was required in my essay-writing to speak in the first-person plural and refer to the reader or critic with what was assumed to be a 'universalizing' pronoun – in reality male – and to the human subject as Man, as if the capital letter somehow made the word inclusive. Naturally, my teaching and writing in early career operated within this model of knowing and also reproduced it. I presented lectures that were models of 'objective' in-depth textual analysis of the great names and the great books of France's golden age, and in tutorials I urged and prodded students in the same direction.

There was and is a value in this. We are creatures of the word; consequently, learning to be attentive to the diction, syntax and grammar, the subtleties, images and nuances of language – in sum, to its headiness and possibilities – fosters insight and empowerment. All the more so when the language in question is not our own, and we learn to listen and hear, read and speak in a tongue foreign to our experience. Such learning is a journey that promotes *dépaysement* – meaning literally a change of country, relationships, habits and perspective, which may be uncomfortable, at least at first, but ultimately enables us to return to ourselves different, or at least more aware. But was the humanist model sufficiently open-ended to promote those ends? Or were its ideological limitations inhibiting both me, and the students I taught, from learning to speak in a voice that was our very own? Answering those questions triggered certain shifts in my approach to early modern French literature and culture.

The first was a shift of perspective. Gender as a conceptual tool is one of the most significant critical innovations in literary and cultural studies of the last decades of the twentieth century. My own reading of feminist theory and literary criticism prompted me to offer an experimental course on women writers and attitudes to women in seventeenth-century French literature and culture. The change of perspective seemed as energizing for the students who signed up for the course as it was for me; we studied authors not traditionally included in the canon of 'the greats'; deconstructed Molière and laughed just as much; considered Sabine as attentively as Horace, Camille as Curiace; pondered the paradoxes of power and women in Racine, Lafayette and Villedieu, and did the rounds of early modern misogyny and feminism.

Was I being anachronistic? Was I politicizing my classroom? The questions were not so much asked as flung at me by colleagues, but not by students; but I found and continue to find them unexamined and naïve. For they confuse myth and reality, misconstrue the nature of objectivity, and assume that the humanist paradigm is apolitical. However, as Montaigne's essay and his weave of bee and boy-child reveal, the humanist educational model was anything but disinterested; on the contrary, it served the social and political ends of a (white) male elite. So (ahem!), the humanist classroom being already politicized, why not place it in a dialectical interaction with another paradigm, a feminist one, and see what emerges? Would rewriting Montaigne's model in the feminine singular be lacking in objectivity somehow? Is it lacking in objectivity to be aware that all human knowledge is a discursive construct and that everyone – woman, man, child – operates within certain assumptions? Surely objectivity refers to the intellectual integrity with which we conduct enquiry (which includes an awareness of our own focalization) and the respect we show for the results?

My version of the folktale, with its girl-protagonist, learning as an associative quest, heuristic methods and open ending that is non-acquisitive, is designed to suggest alternatives to the myth of the enquirer as an autonomous rational subject, historically male (women enquirers usually having been occluded by the humanist paradigm), and whose quest has often proven to be a *self-interested* appropriation of knowledge for reasons of power or even domination.[4] In my experience, using gender as a conceptual tool in the classroom can be liberating for both teacher and taught – whether they be men or women – because it helps us to realize that we do not perceive the world independently of discursive, textual, narrative, cultural or ideological contexts. As a result we become free to deconstruct and reconstruct knowledge, and by means of that process our findings become incorporated into our very self. In this way we come to understand that knowledge is gaze; and the wider, the more informed the gaze, the better the knowledge.

The second shift was more progressive, and involved making space for feelings in the classroom – an approach also criticized by purveyors of 'objectivity'. In some ways, it is hardly surprising that Nicolas Sarkozy has been so dismissive of *La Princesse de Clèves*, given the way the novel is often taught: as a historical artefact, a stage in the development of the novel form. Of course it is; and these historical and formal aspects are important and must be communicated to students. But, I believe that it is important not to stop there. It is also a novel about a woman's emotional, psychological, sexual and social development, and the conflict which she experiences between, on the one hand, her love for her husband and her loyalty to him, and, on the other, her attraction to Nemours and her desire for him.[5] Somehow, by divers means, we must teach the formal aspects in such a way as to make it possible for students to catch the sound, or even a distant echo, of the heart beating in the novel, or the play, or the letters, or the autobiography, or the poetry, or whatever it is we teach. Because, as Elaine Showalter remarks, 'at some level [...] all of us who teach literature believe that it is important not only in education but in life'.[6] Making the connection between literature and life is not always easy where seventeenth-century literature and culture is concerned. But helping students not only to understand what they are reading but also to feel it is, I believe, an important step on the way.

Language, as Julia Kristeva remarks, is translation;[7] and so is teaching (and learning), in my opinion. If early modern studies are to avoid being a merely antiquarian interest that we pass on to our students, we need to engage constantly in acts of translation in the classroom. Otherwise, as Kristeva also observes: 'si je ne suis plus capable de traduire ou de méta-phoriser, je me tais et je meurs'.[8] How is this to be achieved? By making connections for students between language, thought, feeling and life, and by guiding them to make such connections for themselves. I am not suggesting that we encourage autobiographical or confessional ramblings based loosely on the course material, but rather that we find ways to make what we teach come alive. Dramatic readings, whether in the form of commercial recordings, or spontaneous performance by teacher or student, give life to flat words on a page. Turning language into clues ('find all the words referring to love in this passage'; 'count the verbs in this paragraph, now look at the tenses'; 'spot the epithets and adjectives used by the protagonist'; 'identify the rhythms in these alexandrines that express feelings') and getting students to argue out together the significance of what they see, are ways of engaging them in the art of translation that is vital not only in education but in life. Sometimes, I use modern protest songs as a way into Huguenot polemical writings, or clips from films set in seventeenth-century France to convey aspects of early modern political symbols. Am I being anachronistic? Perhaps. But are we not always gazing at the past through the lenses of the present? Is it not that very dialogue which makes the past interesting to us?

The third shift in my teaching was spatial. My research on Huguenot refugees in the period 1680 to 1720 had long made me aware of the multiple effects of place, and of changing places, on human thinking, feeling and creativity. I was able to explore such matters with students in graduate teaching, but there was rarely much room for them on the undergraduate curriculum. However, the sense almost of betrayal I carry from my own undergraduate experience of learning French literature as if the country and society were incidental to the experience, means that I have consistently tried to weave all of these things together in my teaching, so that the study of the society is not reduced to dry insti-tutional matters, and the literature does not seem to have drifted into the classroom on a cloud.

In my modern teaching, these concerns have evolved into courses with titles such as 'Poetics and politics of space' (which started out as

'Paris and the regions'); and I strive to find authors that lend themselves to reflecting on social or political issues, or representations of interior and exterior space, among other things. My early modern teaching is similarly inflected: the *huis clos* of court society and its poetics and politics recur when teaching La Fayette, La Fontaine or La Bruyère. But I also like to explore the imaginary spaces hinted at, the social issues raised, the patterns of behaviour represented, or even the outrageous misconducts denounced in and by early modern writing.

Of course, over the years, I have regretfully had to discard courses when the texts became too linguistically or conceptually difficult for students to read in the time they are prepared to devote to their studies, or when the subject matter no longer appeared to be in dialogue with our own time. So time and again I set off down the hill in search of the windows of gold, hoping to bring back a fresh perspective, a new awareness, or different course materials that might capture the attention of students. However, sometimes I wonder how long I will be able to go on teaching early modern French literature and culture to the successive generations of students who pass through my classroom.

The electronic age, in which we work, fosters an expectation of immediacy where knowledge is concerned and an impatience with anything that may not be instantly consumed. Yet this context of flat-screen learning (with its implicit narcissism) makes it even more important, I believe, to retain and develop the early modern elements of our teaching programmes. Obviously, the poetry, plays, novels and prose of France's golden age, its court system and political conflicts, its music, architecture and painting continue to inflect its culture in the present. And it is vital that students be made aware of those cultural associations and references if they are to learn how to appreciate France and its people, and to interact and communicate with them. But there are also other compelling reasons why the early modern matters.

Enquiry into cultures distant from our own introduces an important element of heterochronicity into the immediacy of our post-modern culture. That is to say, studying early modern France makes us embark on symbolic transmigrations to and from different timeframes, to and from discursive, social and political spaces different from our own.[9] We derive from this an awareness of the layers of time that inhabit us and shape our present, and a sense of cultural perspective and depth. Moreover, the linguistic, conceptual and cultural differences (and difficulties) of early modern French literature and society mean that, as an object of study, they are resistant to easy consumption. Such resistance is good because it has the potential to make us work at understanding what is different from ourselves and to come to respect it on its own terms. In the process, we may recognize the relativity of our own cultural assumptions and perspectives, and learn to question them where necessary. In other words, learning about early modern France is an invitation to embark on a journey that displaces, that contests the closure of ignorance, and challenges the arrogance of post-modern amnesia.

But the last word must be given to Michelle, who took my course this year on the politics and poetics of court society. She emailed me to say that when she was revising La Fontaine's *Fables* for the examination, one of them in particular had made her laugh out loud. 'Humour', as Freud wrote, 'is not resigned; it is rebellious. It signifies not only the triumph of the ego but also of the pleasure principle.'[10] This is perhaps the most important point of all: learning about early modern France and its rich culture opens up a world of pleasure unsuspected until we begin to discover it. The sound of Michelle laughing with La Fontaine in the library lingers like music – an accompaniment to the days spent seeking the windows of gold.

Notes

1. Michel de Montaigne, *Essais*, ed. Pierre Villey, 3 vols (Paris: Quadrige/Presses Universitaires de France, 1988), I.26: 'De l'institution des enfants' (p. 152): 'Bees browse the flowers here and there, but afterwards they produce honey which is peculiarly their own and no longer thyme or marjoram. So the fragments he borrows from others he will transform and blend to make out of them a work altogether his own, that is to say his judgement.'
2. Plato, *Ion*, 534b, as pointed out by the editors of M. de Montaigne, *Essais*, ed. Denis Bjaï, Bénédicte Boudou, Jean Céard and Isabelle Pantin (Paris: Librairie Générale Française, 2001), p. 233, n. 3.
3. See Fredric Jameson, 'Post-modernism and Consumer Society', in *Postmodern Culture*, ed. Hal Foster (London and Sydney: Pluto Press, 1983), p. 125.
4. On this see Craig Owens, 'The Discourse of Others: Feminists and Postmodernism', in *The Post-modern Reader*, ed. Charles Jencks (London: Academy Editions and New York: St Martin's Press, 1992), pp. 334, 339; Susan R. Bordo, *The Flight to Objectivity: Essays on Cartesianism and Culture* (New York: State University Press, 1987); Genevieve Lloyd, *The Man of Reason: 'Male' and 'Female' in Western Philosophy*, 2nd edn (London: Routledge, 1993 [1984]).
5. Traditionally, the novel is interpreted as portraying a conflict between duty (to the husband) and love (for the object of desire); in my opinion, the language of love used by the protagonists suggests that the conflict is between two kinds of love: *amour-estime* and *amour-inclination*.
6. Elaine Showalter, *Teaching Literature*, 2nd edn (Oxford: Blackwell Publishing, 2007 [2003]), p. 24.
7. Julia Kristeva, *Soleil noir: dépression et mélancolie* (Paris: Gallimard, 1987), p. 53.

8. *Ibid.*: 'if I am no longer able to translate or to metaphorise, I become silent and I die' (p. 54).
9. I borrow this understanding of 'hétérochronie' from Thomas Pavel, *L'Art de l'éloignement: essai sur l'imagination classique* (Paris: Gallimard, 1996), pp. 23–4.
10. Sigmund Freud, 'Humour' (1927), quoted by Marina Warner, *From the Beast to the Blonde: On Fairy Tales and their Tellers*, 2nd edn (London: Vintage, 1995 [1994]), p. 151.

8
A Renaissance Woman Adrift in the World

Merry E. Wiesner-Hanks

For a variety of reasons, the breadth of courses that many early modernists teach is much greater than they anticipated, particularly for those who finished graduate school a number of decades ago. As department sizes shrink and full-time faculty are replaced by much cheaper part-time or non-tenure track instructors, many people are asked to teach courses for which they have no graduate training, not simply in a closely related field (Milton along with Shakespeare, the Middle Ages along with the Renaissance and Reformation) but in completely different cultural traditions or time periods. As more and more colleges and universities, particularly in the United States and Canada, add world history or world literature to courses in Western Civilization or American and English Literature, historians and literary scholars are increasingly required to become comparativists, or to teach about cultures in which they have little background. This drive to expand geographically has also come from inside as well as outside for many of us, as we increasingly have found teaching courses that focus only on Europe unsatisfying.

As teachers (and often also as scholars) we have thus entered new intellectual territories, but as we cross geographical boundaries, we often perceive of ourselves as frauds or interlopers, floating around in a huge ocean of material without a compass. We ask ourselves: how do we begin? What do we seek to gain? Knowing that whatever materials we choose for our courses will become representative of a culture, how do we choose? How can we ask the right kinds of questions, so that we are not simply dabbling in an unfamiliar area? To what extent can we escape our own cultural perspective, especially one reinforced by graduate training? How do we measure the credibility of a newly informed perspective? How do we balance difference and familiarity,

113

both for ourselves and for our students, to avoid orientalizing and exoticizing and yet not to erase otherness? What are the problems particular to teaching about the pre-modern world, when using written sources privileges certain cultures? Should our teaching be affected by the increasing numbers of students with non-European backgrounds in our classrooms, or is this generalized stereotyping and false identity politics akin to the overgeneralizations about 'women's role' and 'women's experience' we have all learned to avoid? How should, and can, our teaching and writing about areas beyond Europe shape our approach to European topics? Are there any borders that cannot or should not be crossed?

These are not questions to which I have a ready answer, and they are ones I continue to ask myself as I 'globalize' every one of my courses. That process has become less daunting, however, once I realized that I was following a course that was surprisingly familiar: just as gender is an appropriate category when looking at every historical development and every text (a point I have been making throughout my entire career), so is global context.

For just one example, take the decidedly canonical figure of European intellectual history, Jean Bodin. In *The Six Books of the Republic* (1576), Bodin argues that the state is like a household:

> So we will leave moral discourse to the philosophers and theologians, and we will take up what is relevant to political life, and speak of the husband's power over the wife, which is the source and origin of every human society.[1]

That husbandly authority came from God, for Bodin, and royal power was an extension of this. Resisting either would lead to anarchy, which was worse than the worst tyranny. Bodin's ideas about royal power are a standard element in the story of the development of political theory, but unless the focus is on the debate about female rule, his ideas about the power of husbands are rarely discussed. But not only are they part of the same work, they are part of the same sentence! Thus ignoring gender leads to a skewed reading.

But what about global context? Here we might have to take a step backwards to broaden our view somewhat, but only a small one. Bodin's opponents were French Protestants, the originators of what has come to be called 'resistance theory', a body of ideas that is increasingly seen as central to the eighteenth-century revolutions on both sides of the Atlantic – American, French and Haitian. But did his opponents, and their intellectual heirs, also disagree about the power of husbands? Here's the radical Parliamentarian Henry Parker:

> The wife is inferior in nature, and was created for the assistance of man, and servants are hired for their Lord's mere attendance; but it is otherwise in the State between man and man, for that civill difference [...] is for [...] the good of all, not that servility and drudgery may be imposed upon all of the pompe of one.[2]

And here is a slightly better known resistance theorist:

> Were our state a pure democracy [...] there would still be excluded from our deliberations [...] women, who to prevent deprivation of morals and ambiguity of issue, should not mix promiscuously in the public meetings of men.[3]

Those are the words of Thomas Jefferson, who, as the genetic research on the descendants of Sally Hemings has made clear, knew very intimately about 'ambiguity of issue'.

To follow another line of Bodin's thought to the New World: along with writing the *Six Books of the Commonwealth*, Bodin wrote several books about witchcraft, in which his horror at wives' revolts against their husbands or subjects' revolts against earthly monarchs is matched by his horror at the witches' supposed rebellion against God and the divinely ordained order:

> Those too who let the witches escape, or who do not punish them with the utmost rigor, may rest assured that they will be abandoned by God to the mercy of the witches. And the country which shall tolerate this will be scourged with pestilences, famines, and wars; and those which shall take vengeance on the witches will be blessed by him and will make his anger to cease.[4]

Such enemies of God were not only to be found in Europe, but also in the Americas, where native women practised the same kind of witchcraft as the women at home. Bodin makes this comparison several times in his work, and Jean de Léry, a French Calvinist explorer, adds a description of the witches' sabbath, taken directly from Bodin, to the third edition of his travelogue about the Tupinambá of Brazil. Lery comments:

> I have concluded that they have the same master; that is, the Brazilian women and the witches over here were guided by the same spirit of

Satan; neither the distance between the places nor the long passage over the sea keeps the father of lies from working both here and there on those who are handed over to him by the just judgment of God.[5]

Pierre de Lancre, a French magistrate appointed in 1609 by King Henry IV to investigate the activities of witches in the Basque region of France, noted that the reason there were so many more witches in his day than earlier was the coming of European missionaries to the New World, which had forced more of Satan's demons to return to Europe. The demons travelled, in de Lancre's opinion, with Basque fishing ships, remaining with 'impudent and undisciplined' Basque women when their husbands left again in search of cod. These women's only market-able agricultural commodity was apples, and they 'ate with abandon this fruit of transgression, which caused the trespass against God's com-mandment, and they ignored the prohibition made to our first father'.[6] De Lancre's statement reminds us that the *Malleus Maleficarum*, the guide to demonology and the interrogation of witches that shaped the witch-trials in much of continental Europe, was published only six years before Columbus' first voyage. Early modern people saw connections between these, and so should we.

Going global does the same thing that first noticing that women's experience differed from men's did: it allows us to sail (or drift) into new areas, and return home with exciting new goods that force us to see familiar things in new ways. I certainly do not teach the Renaissance or the Reformation in the same way that I did when I thought of them as European events, or, even more narrowly, as Italian or German events. I certainly do not think about my beloved German working women without thinking about where the linen cloth they were weaving was going, what the guns they helped to make were doing and where the diseases they were treating might have come from.[7] This does not mean that I no longer have doubts, or am no longer struck by the hubris of the enterprise – who can pretend to know the history or the literature of the whole world? – but I cannot imagine being stuck on the shore.

Notes

1. Jean Bodin, *Six Books of the Republic,* quoted in Christine Fauré, *Democracy Without Women: Feminism and the Rise of Liberal Individualism in France,* trans. Claudia Gorbman and John Berks (Bloomington: Indiana University Press, 1991), p. 40.
2. [Henry Parker], *Observations upon some of his Majesties Late Answers and Expresses* [1642], p. 14.

3. Thomas Jefferson, 'Letter to Samuel Kerchival' (1816), in *The Works of Thomas Jefferson*, ed. Paul Leicester Ford, 12 vols (New York: G.P. Putnam's Sons, 1904), X, p. 46.

4. These include *De la démonomanie des sorciers* (1580) and *Vom aussgelasnen wuetigen Teuffelsheer*, trans. Johann Fischart (1591) (Graz: Akademische Verlagsanstalt, 1973). The quotation is from the second, p. 256. My thanks to Gerhild Scholz Williams for alerting me to this work and providing the translation.

5. Jean de Léry, *History of a Voyage to the Land of Brazil, Otherwise Called America* (1585), ed. and trans. Janet Whatley (Berkeley: University of California Press, 1990) p. 248, n. 14.

6. Pierre de Lancre, *Tableav de l'inconstance des mavvais anges et demons, ov il est amplement traicté des sorciers et de la sorcelerie* (Paris: J. Berjon, 1612), translated and quoted in Gerhild Scholz Williams, *Defining Dominion: The Discourses of Magic and Witchcraft in Early Modern France and Germany* (Ann Arbor: University of Michigan Press, 1995), p. 111.

7. My first book was *Working Women in Renaissance Germany* (New Brunswick, NJ: Rutgers University Press, 1986).

9
Worlds Apart, Worlds Away: Integrating the Early Modern in the Antipodes

Susan Broomhall

Teaching the early modern period in Australia has its own particular challenges in addition to others borne of contemporary student communities and institutional pressures that are perhaps shared the world over.

There is, for example, a constant need to argue the relevance of the early modern period to contemporary lives, one that may not be immediately present and obvious to students here. Although many are well travelled, we cannot assume that they are aware of the early modern heritage that is discernible in the built culture of modern Europe and North America. And Australia too is shaped by encounters with early modern Europeans in powerful ways which study of this period provides an opportunity to articulate to students, through seventeenth-century Dutch and later shipwrecks that litter the west coast, city placement and nomenclature resulting from rivalries between French and British naval empires, the relationship of eighteenth-century colonization of 'New Holland' to the lines of the 1494 Treaty of Tordesillas, as well as early modern European assumptions about indigenous peoples whom they encountered here.

While Australia does itself have an early modern European physical and material presence to analyse, it also has significant cultural connections to those societies that colonized it in the late eighteenth century. Even in today's multicultural Australia, it is possible to find strong resonances of concepts derived from Western Europe which underpin contemporary institutional structures, gender assumptions and religious ideologies, to name a few. To examine them is not to prioritize these in Australia's rich and diverse past and present cultures, but simply to recognize what impact early modern Europe has had, and to enable students to contextualize it in relation to other influences on contemporary Australia.

Social, gender and cultural history approaches are especially strong in early modern teaching in Australia, where advocates such as Patricia Crawford, Charles Zika and Judith Richards among others have been both influential researchers of the gender relations of early modern Britain and Europe as well as supervisors of the current generation of Australia's early modern history teaching staff.[1] Gender analysis is embedded through examination of gender ideologies central to most courses, specific courses exploring women's experiences and, lately, emerging thematic topics such as masculinities. Indeed it would be rare for any course in this area not to take gender into consideration, along with class, ethnicity and religious persuasion, as standard elements for identity construction, political formations and social experiences.

Many historical courses are formulated along the lines of particular themes, rather than discrete chronological periods. Some are teaching programmes developed strategically to align with collaborative research projects, and are highly flexible. Other courses offering early modern historical content are designed to introduce students from diverse areas to relevant historical contexts. In recent years I have taught for example on a course entitled 'Quills to Mice: A History of Communication', designed as a contribution to a Communication Studies major, and another entitled 'Plagues, Pox and Pandemics: The History of Death and Disease', offered to a combined cohort of Medical, Population Health and Arts students. Australia's humanities staffing is often not as deep in these areas as may be found in Europe or North America, so some teaching structures combine medieval and early modern teaching. The specificity is thus not 'early modern' as opposed to 'medieval', but rather encompasses more broadly the period in between the classical and the modern worlds.

In addition, teaching early modern at some universities, including mine, has been conducted not just under disciplinary demarcations such as History or English, but also as a studies area known as Medieval and Early Modern Studies (MEMS) ranging from approximately 500 to 1800. These same conceptualizations are also applied to the nation's small but dynamic community of teachers and researchers, represented by the Australian and New Zealand Association for Medieval and Early Modern Studies (ANZAMEMS) and the recent 2004–9 Australian Research Council Network for Early European Research.[2] Indeed, as MEMS, a discrete studies area recognized as having area-specific skill sets and content, the field has become increasingly popular among students in recent years. Among younger students, the period is often perceived as something 'exotic' compared with areas of more vocationally oriented content, although there are also some who see MEMS as a way into future work opportunities in Europe. An increasing number of mature students, many high-level professionals from a diverse range of occupations, are now also returning for Masters-level tuition and seek to specialize in MEMS to stimulate them intellectually and explore research topics as a matter of personal enquiry.

Multidisciplinary approaches in team-taught courses encompass sources and analytical approaches stemming from English, History, Fine Arts, European Literature and occasionally Music incorporated in rich programming. These have introduced students to questions of how distinct sources are approached through analyses taught by specific disciplinary practitioners. Students are offered strong foundational teaching on distinct sets of theories, approaches, source types and skills necessary for research such as palaeography, iconography, medieval literary theory and historiography. Interdisciplinarity, on the other hand, is a deeper challenge we explore at the advanced level of the MEMS major. Students at this level are expected to acknowledge and critically analyse the theoretical positions underpinning scholarship in the field, and interdisciplinarity is an explicit point of examination through the curriculum.

Early modern teaching in Australia, perhaps because of its distance from original sources, tries to make as much use of them as possible. Contemporary documents are made part of the tutorial readings and are used in lectures throughout the curriculum, and it is generally expected that research arguments even for first-year essays develop from primary sources. Modernized editions are rarely used, requiring students to become familiar with period English formulations, if not always its palaeography. Perhaps 20 years ago historians would have relied more heavily on their own cache of materials transcribed from archives; now the range of online archival and printed sources, museum displays and walkthroughs of heritage buildings have opened up access to a huge range of new documents, material objects, and historical and archaeological sites. Searchable documentation, however, reduces sources to bite-size chunks, meaning students often have less appreciation for their broader documentary context.

The Internet has also enabled some expansion beyond a fairly dominant English-language source tradition, particularly increasing availability to early modern art, objects, historical and archaeological sites. Australia has not generally prioritized language training in high school and this has limited students' access to original written sources.[3] Translations therefore have served a critical role, and look set to continue to do so. Foreign-language material must be approached in translation: so, while students are encouraged to explore the challenges of their use, they are still widely employed in conjunction with period English sources.

Information technology has been influential in other ways too, changing the way the early modern is taught. Most students may still be full-time but few have no part-time job as well. Podcasting has changed the lecture-room dynamic as students are able to access lectures off-campus and use them for revision at the end of the semester. New online presentations of history have made for some lively assessments. Having students write model Wikipedia entries provides an opportunity to consider how history is being written by and for online communities. Another university has created a virtual Georgian London in Second Life.[4] Other techniques that are deemed to operate under the rhetoric of 'teaching smarter' include web-based teaching, allowing for discussion areas, bulletin boards and collaborative workspaces. As supplements to the tutorial and seminar, these have been important whilst not as yet being proposed as replacements for them. An important purpose they can serve is to allow students a forum for semi-anonymous exploration of ideas, dialogue and contact in an increasingly physically distant environment.

Role-plays are another increasingly popular student-centred approach to the early modern past, one that encourages students' intellectual, emotional and physical engagement in a range of tasks that also develop generic social skills such as debating, negotiation and brainstorming.[5] These are not designed to have students 're-enact' the past or learn to understand historical events by 'being closer to them'. Instead, role-plays can be designed not only to convey the strangeness of the past but also to explore the quality of empathy for the decisions taken and choices exercised by people in this period. Students have responded well to a Tulipomania game that explored some of the dynamics of the emerging market and consumer society in seventeenth-century Netherlands. In another, students recreated the 1649 Putney Debates within the parliamentary army. A sequence exploring religion and the ordering of space involves a case study in which each group took on sequentially a different identity (Catholic, Protestant or Absolutist Ruler) and designed a town plan for rebuilding a destroyed city. Another role-play had students apply as paupers for relief from a board of Poor Law Governors in the early seventeenth century and another asked students to pose for a family group portrait, using their understanding of iconography as well as familial, gender and status relationships to position themselves according to the assigned characters and roles. Such whole-class role-plays can work well to support student understanding of historical process, the role of imagination and empathy in historians' practice, as well as in developing knowledge of historical social and cultural dynamics. My experiences with these delivery formats suggest that the impact of content learnt in simulated, student-centred formats is powerful in terms of student memory and recall, particularly in sessions that require students to be personally responsible for performing roles or tasks within a broader team context.

Finally it is worth noting that there are further, lateral opportunities for scholarly teaching and exposure of the early modern beyond the academy.[6] An increasing number of Australians have time and income to spend on their leisure pursuits and both the academy and tourism are potential beneficiaries. A greater proportion of the travelling public is made up of participants who are seeking an educational experience as they travel. Generating knowledge capital is critical to the ongoing success of tour operators responding to a sophisticated consumer market. Europe remains a pivotal destination for travellers worldwide and its early modern past offers a point of entry for tertiary teachers to speak to new audiences. Australian educational tourism companies, for example, are now turning to academic scholars to provide intellectually rigorous material for tour programming in addition to roles as tour presenters and site specialists.

In 2010, a national Centre of Excellence that focused on the period 1100 to 1800 won $24.5 million from the Australian Research Council, the largest amount of funding ever provided to the arts, humanities and social sciences in Australia. This is indicative of a vibrant and dynamic research community that is underpinned by strong teaching programmes across the country. Australian early modern teaching offers a diverse range of practices and delivery styles, packaged in different ways to meet institutional demands, but which also respond to student interest in new areas of curriculum, and which continually expand the range of students who are exposed to the period in universities and beyond.

Notes

1. See Stephanie Tarbin, '*Limina* Interview: Interview with Professor Trish Crawford, May 1995', *Limina: A Journal of Historical and Cultural Studies*, 1 (1995), 77–84; Andrew Broertjes, Nicole Crawford, Natalie Lloyd, Alicia Marchant, Lesley O'Brien and Kate Riley, 'Interview with Patricia Crawford', *Limina: A Journal of Historical and Cultural Studies*, 10 (2004), 6–15; Susan Broomhall, 'Recent Australian Research on Early Modern Studies of Gender,

and Science and Technology', *Renaissance Studies Bulletin*, 22.2 (2005), 19–25, and the edited collection in Crawford's honour, *Women, Identities and Communities in Early Modern Europe*, ed. Stephanie Tarbin and Susan Broomhall (Aldershot: Ashgate, 2008). On earlier and other approaches, see Roslyn Pesman Cooper, 'Bruce Mansfield and Early Modern European History in Sydney', *Journal of Religious History*, 15.4 (1989), 384–7.
2. See Anne M. Scott, 'The Network for Early European Research', *Renaissance Studies Bulletin*, 22.2 (2005), 1–2.
3. On the paucity of language skills of Australian students and its impact on German history research (as well as the place of early modern German history teaching in Australia), see Stephen Welch and Charles Zika, 'German History in Australian Universities: An Overview', *Zeitenblicke*, 2 (2003), http://www.zeitenblicke.de/2003/02/zika.htm
4. Katherine Ellison and Carol Matthews, 'Virtual History: A Socially Networked Pedagogy of Enlightenment', *Educational Research Journal*, 52.3 (2010), 297–307.
5. See papers developed as a result of a University of Western Australia Teaching Fellowship: Cedric Beidatsch and Susan Broomhall, 'Teaching Smarter? The Place of Workshops in the Curricula for Undergraduate History Teaching', in *Educating for Sustainability: Proceedings of the 19th Annual Teaching Learning Forum, 28–29 January 2010* (Perth: Edith Cowan University, http://otl.curtin.edu.au/tlf/tlf2010/refereed/beidatsch.html [accessed 10 September 2010]). See also Cedric Beidatsch and Susan Broomhall, 'Is This the Past? The Place of Role-Play Exercises in Undergraduate History Teaching', *Journal of University Learning and Teaching Practice*, 7.1 (2010), 1–20.
6. See our publication, Susan Broomhall, Tim Pitman and Joanne McEwan, *A Classroom Like No Other: Learning and Teaching in Australian Educational Tourism* (Perth: Uniprint, 2011), developed as a result of an Australian Learning and Teaching Council grant that ran from 2007 to 2009.

10
Paradise Regained? Teaching the Multicultural Renaissance

Jane Grogan

The field of English Renaissance literary studies today is a good deal wider than it used to be. While it has been left largely to the historians to argue over denominations – Atlanticist or archipelagic? national or globalized? – in English departments from Aberdeen to Seattle and beyond the Anglophone world, there is a broad critical consensus about the wide and diverse purview of English literary studies of the period, social, geographical and generic. Writings from Ireland, Scotland, Wales and the early settlers in America and the Caribbean have attained an almost over-determined literary respectability – post-theory, post-new historicism, post-colonialism, post-New British history, post-revisionism and more. Position papers and polemical pamphlets, instructions for travellers, women's diaries and manuscript spiritual autobiographies, histories and pseudo-histories, prophecies and sermons, even legal textbooks and depositions enlarge the corpus of Renaissance literary writing studied within the scholarly domain. Literature in English was written not just in metropolitan London but in rural Ireland, Ottoman Aleppo and at the court of the great Moghul; it was printed not only in London and the English university towns, but also in places like Antwerp, Dublin and Geneva; manuscript, of course, flourished every-where, and women writers from Virginia to Kilkenny tested its limits across a range of genres. Yet in the universities of Ireland and the UK, this geographical and generic range is rarely reflected in the workhorse, lecture-centred, undergraduate survey courses. Despite the drive towards research-led teaching, an unhealthy, unspoken divide between the two exists, and in particularly acute form in periodized undergraduate survey courses: those overviews of 'Renaissance' or 'Early Modern' Literature that, Shakespeare aside, constitute most undergraduates' only exposure to writ-ing of the sixteenth and seventeenth centuries. Instead, non-canonical or sensitive texts are trusted only to postgraduates (or, occasionally, final-year undergraduates) in specialized research seminars, while the vast majority of their undergraduate colleagues are left to the company of Tillyard's old Platonizing favourites.[1] Within the traditional protocol of the lecture-hall – distant, formal, *en masse*, and with the weight of tradition and students' sometimes exalted expectations behind it – the canon and platitudes surrounding the 'Renaissance' are disseminated more easily than the more complex picture of diffuse and diverse literary production in manuscript and print visible in scholarly research of the period, it seems.[2]

More worryingly still, this high canon now flourishes in the name of a progressive, multicultural pedagogy for a progressive, multicultural society.[3] Folded into this outdated but all too accessible canon of Renaissance literature is a more troubling anachronism still: a tendency to homogenize the student body, at least across the UK and Ireland, as an undifferentiated mass, not now of royal or imperial subjects but of peaceful, multicultural consumers, more globalized than localized in their concerns, more wedded to Shakespeare than to his less famous contemporaries, citizens of a tolerant, multicultural society without history – or, indeed, reality. This prevailing conception of the student body across the UK and Ireland as a deracinated, passively multicultural mass is not just socially and ideologically naïve, it is also pedagogically suspect. At the very least, it is a missed opportunity to confront the real challenges of living in a multicultural society. Tenuous and troubled though the concept of multiculturalism may be in its various social, political, economic and ethical aspects in the present moment, the 'circumstances of multiculturalism' are here to stay – and have been since at least the sixteenth century.[4] I would like to suggest in this essay that whatever our political persuasions, as teachers in an uneasily multicultural world, we should use the influential survey courses of Renaissance literature to trace the troubling origins of those 'circumstances' and to pursue with our students the forgotten quarrels and awkward moments of early modern multiculturalism. Moreover, we should consider doing so in terms that are both more consonant with our research and more open and alert to our students' experiences of contemporary multiculturalism.

Renewed, reframed, even sidelined though it may be by Renaissance scholars in their critical work, the canon remains *the* force to be reckoned with in the teaching of Renaissance literature. We can apportion some of the blame for the relative uniformity and durability of an outdated myth of 'English Renaissance literature' to students' prior familiarity with Shakespeare and 'the Renaissance' in the collective cultural present, and the subsequent ease with which a certain appealing story of Renaissance literature and its kings, queens and crises can be transmitted to ready ears. The difficulty lies not just in the texts populating the canon, but in the conceptual vocabulary and cultural politics suggested by the canon, more stubborn formations still, reupholstered though they may be in a more contemporary critical idiom. But we might also detect an element of complacency with a dehistoricized model of multiculturalism, even a naïve, unilateral politics of difference in the dissemination to all students across the UK and Ireland of that same, easily packaged 'Renaissance' myth of tradition and innovation, public and private, queen and country, theatre and court, Shakespeare and Marlowe, selfhood and otherness, metropolitan London and unremarkable elsewheres. The Tillyardian canon is the vehicle for these familiar, fossilized ideas, and its endurance in undergraduate survey courses (as I will show later) testifies to a troubling, generalizing attitude towards the student body read as a tranquil multicultural mass. This is a multiculturalism that can look strangely monocultural in its blindness to the social and historical legacy that Renaissance texts hold for first-, second- and third-generation immigrants from former British colonies, for descendants of Ulster planters and Munster tenant-farmers, for British and Irish students whose mixed racial inheritance may not even be known to them. The pedagogical challenge posed by the canon is not simply a question of repudiating false claims to universalism; it is one of recognizing individual subjectivities in the classroom or lecture-hall, and their ethnic, historical and social connections with the texts we teach. But such a student-centred approach is very rarely evident in the descriptions of survey courses that I have reviewed.

Thus, in acquiescing for teaching purposes with the entertaining and accessible version of 'Renaissance' already inchoate in popular culture and other social and cultural norms (the 'Renaissance' embedded in the curricula of the secondary educational systems of both countries but thoroughly discredited in scholarship of the field), we do both our students and our research a disservice, and disregard the real challenges of living in a multicultural society: living with the histories of oppression – political *and* literary – that have created it, and facing the imperative to remember, respect, take responsibility and forgive. By simply repackaging the familiar, essentially Burckhardtian view of 'Renaissance' that students expect, we take away from them the possibility of a more difficult and challenging engagement with a body of texts that speak powerfully – and even formatively – to their own struggles to live their pasts, presents and futures in a multicultural society.[5] What I suggest in this essay is a more sensitive and optimistic bridging of the gap between research and teaching in ways that seek to awaken and acknowledge students' social, historical, political, geographical or other connections with the texts. The challenges – and flaws – of multiculturalism are many, and all the more visible and pressing after 9/11 and the 7/7 attacks on London's transport system.[6] The full range of Renaissance texts, written at what we might arguably locate as the origins of multiculturalism, its colonial provenance at least, offers a powerful opportunity to confront and reflect on the past and present formations of multiculturalism.

This essay draws on my experience of teaching Renaissance literature at two universities in the UK, and two in the Irish Republic over approximately nine years from the fateful 2001, and is necessarily impressionistic, wilfully polemical and conspicuously crude in its terms of reference: for example, the broad distinctions between 'UK' and 'Irish' students without regard to socio-economic and ethnic distinctions among or within the various universities, or indeed, to other relevant factors such as issues of access to higher education and the internationalism of lecturers in Renaissance studies in both countries. For hard evidence, I take the set texts of undergraduate survey courses of Renaissance literature together with brief module descriptors (as accessed on department websites in September 2009) as voluble indicators of pedagogical approach. Thus, I am assuming – not without support from the particular selection of texts on the Renaissance Literature survey courses I studied, as we will see – a syllabus-based model of curriculum theory, the province of the so-called liberal educationalists. The limitations of my approach are obvious. But if genuine pedagogic concerns can be observed, painted in these broad and exaggerated brushstrokes, we might be encouraged to steel ourselves to trust our students with a more troubled and troubling narrative of 'the Renaissance' than heretofore.

Syllabi and teaching materials

All seven universities in the Irish Republic, two in the north of Ireland and a representative selection from England, Scotland and Wales populate my case study.[7] The vast majority have a second- or third-year core lecture module on Renaissance Literature (including Shakespeare) and more flexible offerings in specialized second- or third-year seminar (small-group) modules, although where staff numbers are lower, Renaissance material is occasionally incorporated into more wide-ranging genre-based or thematic first- and second-year courses. The long eighteenth century looks to be alive and well in UK universities (more so than in Irish universities), with some universities at the top end of the research ratings in a position to divide their core module offerings in Renaissance Literature into separate Elizabethan/Jacobean and long eighteenth-century components. Of these courses, the old favourites dominate: Shakespeare, Marlowe, Spenser, Donne, Marvell, Milton. Turning to women writers, Aphra Behn is a popular choice in the later period, and survey courses that begin with the Civil War or Restoration increasingly accommodate women poets such as Margaret Cavendish and Katherine Philips. Only Mary Wroth troubles the Elizabethan/Jacobean courses, and then only occasionally. One interesting pattern to be seen in the UK universities is that the traditional canon flourishes most strongly at universities at the higher levels of the RAE table – in other words, at universities with the strongest research strengths in Renaissance studies and, often, larger staff numbers and, correspondingly (we must assume), greater diversity of interests. Here, where research is nominally (or quantifiably) at its strongest, the gulf between research and teaching is also at its greatest, following my assumptions about a syllabus-based model of curriculum theory. On the other hand, in the middle and bottom half of the table, a greater interest in 'lesser studied writers' (University of the West of England, Bristol) or 'the diverse texts and contexts of early modern culture' (Northumbria) is evinced.[8] Turning to Ireland, we find that the work of women writers is explicitly treated in undergraduate English Renaissance survey courses of just three Irish universities (University College Cork, National University of Ireland Maynooth and University College Dublin), and with one exception for prose romance (UCD) all courses treat only major Renaissance poetic and dramatic genres. Dramatic texts are repre-sented by Shakespeare, Marlowe, Jonson and Middleton, while poetry admits of just a little more range. None of the survey courses feature Irish-based poets besides Spenser, nor do they focus on any material specifically related to early modern Ireland. The same is true of UK universities; even in Scottish universities, contemporary Scottish material is largely sequestered in modules on Scottish literature rather than on survey courses of 'Renaissance' literature. Only King's College, London, makes overt and specific use of its geo-historical location to explore connections with Renaissance literature.[9] Rather, the canon and its values are often explicitly and exclusively promoted in course descriptions. The result, then, is a strikingly uniform set of texts, contexts and values taught across the universities of the UK and Ireland, at least in 2009.

The case is exacerbated by the teaching materials available. Primarily divided between drama and poetry (although the Norton anthology combines the two and the Blackwell anthology includes prose with its selection of poetry), only one anthology considers a wide and diverse range of authors, forms and cultures. Popular anthologies (the Norton, Blackwell, Routledge and Penguin anthologies) cleave largely to the old-fashioned canon of male, London-centred writers of tragedy, comedy, epic, satire and sonnets.[10] Women writers are usually relegated to their own anthologies which can be prescribed for seminar courses but are unlikely to form the primary anthology for survey courses taught by lecture (and did not appear on any of the courses I viewed); survey courses tend to stick to the few women writers who appear in the established anthologies. *The Penguin Book of Renaissance Verse* is a notable exception, mixing female and male writers, and even including a poem in Irish (Gaelic). But even there, the representation of non-metropolitan authors and genres is sparse, and the systematization of its diversity under themes ('The Public World'; 'Images of Love', etc.) actually serves to obscure, in some instances, the literary acumen and political complexity of less canonical authors. Certainly, the cost of books is a factor on these survey courses, but the popularity of fairly conservative anthologies of Renaissance literature, and the minimal exploration of authors in less privileged genres and forms in the Renaissance survey courses studied here, implies that the demand for a more up-to-date and diverse canon of Renaissance texts must be small indeed.

Unmaking and remaking 'Renaissance'

In teaching Renaissance literature and especially Shakespeare at university level, a certain amount of undoing of the knowledge that students bring to the subject is usually necessary. But so entrenched and cherished are wider cultural ideas about Shakespeare's 'genius', about 'Renaissance man' and the sudden, quasi-miraculous appearance of 'individuality' and 'science', that the breaking is often undertaken gently and in strikingly corollary terms. What is apparent from the syllabi of UK and Irish universities and my own experiences at some of those universities is that students are disabused of the Elizabethan World Picture only to be mollified with something approximating the Liberal World Picture instead, often mediated through the very same texts: Shakespeare's *Richard II*, Marlowe's *Dr Faustus*, Jonson's *Epicoene*, Spenser's *The Faerie Queene*. Thus we teach not the sceptred isle but the troubled monarchy, not the rise of the individual but the death of God, not high scholarly classicism but gender-bending city comedy, not the virgin queen but the critical poet. The new orthodoxy proves no less ordered, centrifugal and Anglocentric than the old, and students are kept far away from texts that might challenge that new self-regulating, liberal order: awkward texts such as Marlowe's anti-Semitic (and anti-Christian) *The Jew of Malta*; a host of anti-Islamic 'Turk' plays and polemical pamphlets; the fervid spiritual autobiographies of Lucy Hutchinson and Anne Bradstreet; the psalm translations of Mary Sidney; the embittered treatises and crowd-pleasing romances of Barnaby Riche and so on. The case of early modern literary treatments of Islam in particular merits more sustained attention given the present climate of suspicion and fear, one partly formed by a long orientalist textual tradition but also simultaneously challenged in much of the literature of the period of our study. The capacity for Renaissance texts to be *both* complicit and critical of Islamic belief, practices and peoples, and (as frequently seems to happen) to come unstuck in their more vituperative moments, strongly recommends relevant pamphlets, histories, poetry and plays to the attention of our undergraduate students. But thus far, these texts remain notable for their absence from such undergraduate survey courses.

Recent critical theory also does students a potential disservice. From the conservative neo-Victorians such as A.C. Bradley and Tillyard and G. Wilson Knight who consecrated its high culture, through the slash-and-burn deconstructionist years (as its enemies would have it) and the entertaining historical appeasements of the new historicists, the same Renaissance canon has anchored university teaching. But the recent dominance of historicism new and old in the research culture of Renaissance studies in the UK and Ireland has actually disempowered the student reader even further, I would suggest. On the one hand, historicist research has not generally been imported into university teaching to introduce students to new and relevant texts. On the other hand (and perhaps underlying that refusal to join research values with pedagogical practices), in critical practice, historicism has sidelined interrogative, open-ended close reading in favour of context and winsome example, the infamous anecdotes of new historicism now expanded into powerful critical narratives, or the dustier arcana of old historicism heaped one upon the other into indubitable touchstones. But in the pedagogical sphere, this historicist disavowal of direct engagement with the text has more serious consequences: a pure and rigorous historicism can alienate and diminish the student reader by devaluing close reading and promulgating the resolution of all critical problems at the level of context – wide fields of knowledge with which students are, almost by definition, unfamiliar and ill-equipped. It is left to the typically charismatic Renaissance context – or the vicariously charismatic lecturer – to produce the clever device that will unlock the text or problem and rescue it from its less palatable themes (and, indeed, from its insufficiently historicist student readers). No wonder, then, that we do not trust undergraduate students to engage with texts such as *A Christian Turned Turk*, *A View of the Present State of Ireland*, or Ben Jonson's *Gypsies Metamorphosed*, texts that express anger or discomfort about their own multicultural moment. Academics' complaints about depoliticized or apathetic students are a self-fulfilling prophecy in the UK and Ireland, where students are not given the texts or tools with which to examine them directly, but are instead made subservient to the overweening authority of the lecturer, the prevenient authority of historical context and the comforting authority of the canon as confirmation of what they already vaguely knew about good Queen Bess, great Shakespeare and greater London. (I exaggerate the case, of course, but not by much.) Ironically, the school of criticism that has done so much to expand the literary canon of English Renaissance writing to include some of the most important explorations of early modern multiculturalism has also fostered pedagogical techniques that have effectively excluded and alienated students from them.

Relinquishing 'Renaissance'

If the substance and methodologies of research and teaching under the sign of historicism are either divorced from each other or inimical to each other, as I have described, how then should we go about teaching Renaissance literature? The answer lies, I think, in relinquishing a certain amount of pedagogic authority and releasing the texts to our students who bring their own particular interests and needs to bear on them, unevenly historicized though those engagements may be. In fact, those interests and needs are often rooted in the troubled multicultural situations to be found in the texts and history of this earlier, formative multicultural moment: the early modern is a formative period in the history of colonialism, slavery, racism, sectarianism, the oppression of women and so on. In teaching Renaissance literature, we have a wonderful opportunity to expose those links, to test the texts of the time for their engagement with those issues and to show their contribution in the formation of relevant attitudes and institutions. Moreover, we can do so with students for whom these are still live issues. What I suggest is that we should pay closer attention to our students' social, ethnic, religious and historical differences, and the particular problems of multiculturalism that they face as individuals and as communities: the failure of integration, the homogenization of Otherness, the chimera of multicultural 'community', the reification of victimhood, the perpetuation of synchronic and diachronic inequality, the obliteration of class awareness or awareness of privilege, as well as the very real and immediate politics of everyday living as part of an ethnic minority or diaspora. Our students have cultural and historical connections to these texts, and a truly heuristic historicist pedagogy should be able to accommodate and even take advantage of these connections – as, indeed, Deborah Seddon does by attending deliberately and openly to her students' 'complex cultural heritage as young South Africans' as part of her teaching practice, described in her essay in this volume.[11]

To trust students with the full range of Renaissance texts, palatable or not, and a conceptual and critical vocabulary equal to them means that we need first to refuse to fulfil their expectations of the Renaissance myth, and instead to draw them closer to debates and theories from the world of research. This means confronting the idea not just of 'nation' but of political imaginaries; not just individuals but identity politics; not just a sudden discovery of the classics but the rise of textual authority; not just the age of print but the healthy co-existence of manuscript culture; not just the plain facts of Reformation and schism but the fundamental changes in everyday life and eschatological hopes that ensued; not just 'voyages of discovery' but state-sponsored piracy and oppression; not just trade but imperial designs; not just Protestant isolation but a deep and attractive interest in Islam too; not just superlative English male writers from the new grammar schools and universities but home-educated female poets and diarists, translators and biographers; not just English-language literary culture in England but in Ireland, Scotland and Wales too; not just the Globe but the touring companies ... the list could go on. All of it is familiar to scholars in the area – but not, thus far, to students of those survey courses of Renaissance literature.

In practice, this means prescribing a wider range of texts, genres and authors, and drawing attention to the pressure points where national, racial and ethnic identity are in formation, are unstable or conflicting, in order to give students direct points of access into the text and grounds to engage with it in its own terms and theirs. Making more of the Moor is only half of the challenge: making the students reflect more on the embedded values of Shakespeare's multicultural Venice is a more pressing challenge still.[12] The history of multiculturalism itself must become an issue for discussion, and its ambitious virtues – tolerance, community, celebration of difference – explored as the difficult, willed and not always even-handed things they really are. For the lecturer, this means not so much drawing parallels between Renaissance England and twentieth-century Ireland, say, as tracing lines of descent, showing the formation of modes of being and of social and political imaginaries in a wide range of literary works, and helping students to uncover the specific problems and terms (not all of them political) of such literary works. We are fortunate that Renaissance literature is particularly hospitable to such approaches, and its obsessive re-enactment of competing authorities and its many moments of indecision, of contingency, of doubt are prime points of entry for student readers – as they were for their first readers.

Prescribing a wider range of texts is the first step; the next is to resist the temptation to prescribe interpretations of them and instead to turn those texts over to student readers. The aim is not a new formalist exercise in close reading, but an interrogation of the text's encoding and configuration of its society's intellectual culture in ways that may have designs – and certainly have effects – on the reader, past and present. One strategy for countering students' embedded sense of 'Renaissance' and its canon is to reintroduce them to the sense of contingency, of belatedness, of apology, of uncertainty that prevailed among writers in the sixteenth and seventeenth centuries and which critical, popular and especially pedagogic dogma of the centuries that followed – as well as the aggressive self-representations of the embattled poets themselves – has deliberately whitewashed.[13] Encouraging close reading, with minimal historical context but these few text-destabilizing cues, helps to incorporate and engage students in the text and its moment, to reanimate the choices writers made, the decisions they struggled with and the roads they did not finally take as well as those they did. In providing contextual guidance for a particular text, we can take our cues from its readerly qualities and the students' own experience of the text, keeping sight of the social and political realities of the particular students in the classroom, something that can make a big pedagogic difference, but without sacrificing historicist integrity. And we can encourage students to pay attention to the success (or not) of the formal and technical qualities of the text in its exploration of themes of multiculturalism. Other techniques might include communal close readings of pressure-points in different kinds of texts, examining Renaissance translations, or asking students to compare a range of roughly contemporary poems in a particular genre, including (importantly) bad poetry. Where possible, it can be very productive to give students the opportunity to recommend new texts for the next year. As a teaching strategy for encouraging commitment and enthusiasm, this has obvious benefits, but the subsidiary effect of destabilizing the idea of the canon or curriculum is invaluable. And making space for the idea of a student-prescribed syllabus also works to equalize the relations and socially ratified differentials of power between teacher and student in still deeper ways.

A productive exercise that I have used for a seminar accompanying a lecture is a variation on a familiar strategy (one already in use at UK and Irish universities) that does attempt to bridge the gap between research culture and pedagogy. This involves brainstorming students' sense of what they understand by the term 'Renaissance' and trying to inculcate in them a sense of critical self-reflectiveness about their assumptions and expectations of texts of the period. What associations has the term 'Renaissance'? What kinds of concepts and theories does it sustain or foster? How might they apply it, and what other kinds of terms and ideas does it generate? What does the term 'Renaissance' value that 'early modern' does not? Having gathered and displayed these, I then hand out extracts from *The Civilization of the Renaissance in Italy* and ask students to identify key ideas, to describe the language and to elucidate the underlying ideas and ideologies. Students tend to be quick to work through Burckhardt's writing and to uncover his values and prejudices. Next, I ask students to discuss the connections (of which there are usually many) between their own ideas of 'Renaissance' and those of Burckhardt, and the durability of Burckhardt's terms and concepts, their permeation in popular culture. (It is always easy to find supporting materials from newspapers and websites designating a sports hero or musician as a 'Renaissance man', and I usually bring along an example.) Finally, I ask them to consider the implications of their discussion for their imminent study of specific authors and texts – Shakespeare among them. We conclude by returning to the concepts and theories that they had first outlined and reinterrogate them, choosing a few to carry with us for testing as the semester proceeds.

The gains of unsettling students in this way at the beginning of a course on Renaissance literature more than justify spending a precious class without any primary texts. The aim is not to demonize or make a scapegoat of Burckhardt for distasteful trends in intellectual history but rather to examine his influential theories at source and to help students to recognize and work through their unexpected thraldom *already* to a particular notion of literature, culture, race, nationhood, moral, political and aesthetic value, their exposure to hegemonic forms of history and culture, all wrapped up in their understanding of the term 'Renaissance'. With the help of this exercise, women writers, Irish writers, ventriloquized or derided voices all return to the fray; further-more, the precedent of tackling an influential secondary source for ideological motivation can help students to exercise critical alertness and even a measure of suspicion in their choice of both secondary and primary reading thereafter. The exercise also quietly allows for redress of the national bias of 'English Renaissance literature'. That the spirit of Burckhardt's theories would likely disregard and exclude Irish people and culture is not lost on my Irish students. Here, interestingly, in direct confrontation with Burckhardt (rather than mediated diffusely in Anglophone culture), the long-established colonial sense of ethnic difference – the ethnic inferiority imputed to the Irish under British rule – returns to trouble the earlier easy acceptance of English-language literature from England, and especially Shakespeare, as a universal cultural gold standard. The exercise allows Irish students to test a challenging and often distasteful series of subject positions, and to begin to take cognizance of their situatedness as post-colonial readers of these texts, as well as their historical exclusion from the cultural consensus that did the canonizing. The exercise is one that I build on later in the semester in order to address difficult issues such as racism and sexism contained in some of texts of the period. Although I am fortunate in being able to accompany a lecture with a seminar, many of these approaches have potential for the lecture-only format too.

Navigating the Irish Sea: personal experiences

I suspect that much of the discussion above will be old news, at least for those who teach Renaissance literature in Ireland and who are therefore already especially aware of the peculiar challenges and pitfalls of that task. (I suspect, too, that it might strike a chord with other non-English teachers of the subject in England.) That in itself is revealing: we have long since been informed by cultural theorists and globalization gurus of the obsolescence of the nation state, but even working with some version of Leopold Bloom's broad theory of nationhood, the texts of the sixteenth and seventeenth centuries force the issue quite stridently for Irish students at least. Once again, the celebratory politics of difference that operates in high multicultural theory underplays the social and historical difficulties in practices of nationality, accent, race and, tellingly, the 'imagined sense' of multiculturalism in Ireland proves insufficient to inoculate against this prickly nationalizing instinct.

Teaching Renaissance literature from an Irish perspective brings the problems with the established taught canon to the fore, and the lessons of this experience will be my focus for the remainder of this essay.

As an Irish woman teaching Renaissance literature in England, my experience was largely positive but sometimes unexpectedly challenging. At times, students exhibited signs of discomfort at being taught what they considered some of the most sacrosanct (male) authors of English literary culture by a woman, and a woman from the west of Ireland at that. When I expressed my sense of this discomfort, a mentor once remarked delicately (as he thought) that perhaps the students did not understand my accent. But the issue ran deeper than that and his overcompensating elision of it may have been yet another symptom of a wider unease with the Irish in Britain in the years not too long after the IRA's sustained bombing campaign in London and the UK – or, perhaps, simply a conservative unease with the idea of UK students being taught 'their' national literature, this fixed canon of stellar Renaissance authors, by a 'non-national'. My experience as an Irish woman teaching Shakespeare to English students was not, perhaps, as alienating or shocking as that reported by Elizabeth Butler Cullingford, called a 'British imperialist bitch', not by her students but by an Irish male academic! And if, in 2001, swaddled in the vaunted tolerance of the research environment, 'a feminist critique of nationalism risks being interpreted as support for British troops on the streets of Belfast', it may not be so bizarre that in 2001 an Irish woman teaching *Henry V* in England raised some hackles.[14]

Teaching English Renaissance literature in Ireland brings a different set of challenges, further compounded by whether one is Irish, English or another nationality or ethnicity. Spenser's *The Faerie Queene* necessarily means something different to a student from Cork than it does to a student from Cardiff or a student from Cambridge, whatever narrative of nationality or ethnicity is invoked. But so too do the writings of Queen Elizabeth, the four captains in *Henry V*, the Protestant poetry of Mary and Philip Sidney, Marvell's 'An Horatian Ode Upon Cromwell's Return from Ireland', Milton's *Samson Agonistes*, the Jacobean and Caroline court masques and the many and varied engagements with civil war politics and Protestant schism from both sides of the Atlantic – a fact that the exclusionary logic of the existing canon also disavows. If teaching the traditional canon of English Renaissance literature in England can prove a somewhat hostile environment for an Irish woman, however, it can be deeply discomfiting to teach the same texts to a lecture-hall full of Irish students. While Irish students are quick to locate and feel disenchanted by overt expressions of anti-Irish sentiments in Renaissance texts, and prove sensitive readers of Burckhardt when left to deal directly with his writings, they are, conversely, markedly comfortable with the idea of being taught an English 'national' literature and, in my experience, seem even more bewitched by the glorious givens of a high English Renaissance than UK students.[15] This might not surprise a post-colonialist, but despite Irish students' exposure to post-colonial theory (primarily mediated through Irish studies), they remain reluctant to bring those ideas to bear on the cherished high 'Renaissance' of Shakespeare and Donne.

Self-reflectiveness is vital, and here the teacher or lecturer can show the way. Acknowledging one's own social identity and investment in the texts being taught – whether historical or ideological – becomes a relevant pedagogical strategy in these situations. Where teaching is imagined not as the transmission of a fixed canon by an expert to an ignorant mass but as process, formation through dialogue, it becomes absolutely necessary. But it can also invite suspicion, particularly if the reader (whether teacher or student) holds strong religious or political views or belongs to a minority group. Here, again, our subject area brings opportunity: it would not have been such a strange idea to Renaissance authors to whom *ethos* – real or faked – was just another essential part of the rhetorical apparatus with which they framed their formal writings and expression. That so many of the writings produced in the period (and not just the sonnet) engage directly with this problem of *ethos* means that just such a focus on persona, voice and the teacher or student's own stake in the text can help to uncover the political and ideological mechanisms of the text, and make students more engaged and self-aware about their own relationship with Renaissance literature and its shaping of particular kinds of subjectivities through their reading experience.

The dynamic of uneasiness and suspicion can therefore be curiously productive in the teaching situation. Attentiveness and a degree of self-reflection, and not just hostility, come into play, and students become more aware of what might be at stake in texts, in the idea of culture and especially in the idea of a national culture. Again, this involves challenging the residual force of the canon, but it also sparks a more readerly and 'presentist' understanding of context. The historical and geopolitical particularities of teachers and students are allowed to come into play in a way that is seldom recognized in pedagogical theory or practice in the UK and Ireland but that has long been recognized in the USA.[16] This operates even when the student's experience of the text is a negative one. An example: Sheila T. Cavanagh recounts her experience of teaching Book V of *The Faerie Queene* to American undergraduate students, and her habit of supplying them with a reading-pack of sixteenth-century writings about Ireland and twentieth-century analyses of colonial and racial discourse *not* for their integral scholarly interest and historical connections with the text, but for more immediate pedagogical reasons: the purpose of this customized reading-pack is to stave off her students' loss of 'patience and interest' with Artegall and Talus by making explicit connections to their own politicized interests and experiences.[17] Given their educational backgrounds and the clear Irish resonances of Book V, Irish students are unlikely to suffer this type of impatience and disinterest – but English students might, for quite different reasons to their American counterparts: the forgetting of empire is all too easily achieved by the Tillyardian canon and Burckhardtian 'Renaissance'. Cavanagh's method is exemplary for facing up to the readerly challenges *as much as* the difficult and topical issues of Spenser's text, and for trusting students to confront these difficult issues in terms that they recognize and relate to. But it might be even more instructive were she to confront students with the fact of their own disinterest as well as her redress for it.

If discourses of race are Cavanagh's way into the English Renaissance for her American students, class can be an effective way into a more complex conception of Renaissance literature for UK students. Raymond Williams long ago showed the bloodied claws of a particular kind of English Renaissance pastoral poetry, and his writings, at least, have bridged the gap between research and teaching. But this opportunity is more true of UK students than of Irish students, the latter being traditionally less attuned to either racial or class issues because of the relative monoculturalism of Irish society and the persistence of the early state's 'apparently unifying but essentially archaic and coercive social norms' until quite recently.[18] Unlike UK students, however, Irish students do have the benefit of the contribution of Irish studies to the field, a contribution that has been well intentioned if not particularly successfully carried through. One tentative Atlanticist attempt at redress in critical scholarship of the English Renaissance has been to point out the co-existence and equivalence of cultures living alongside each other, though (as Yeats saw it) painfully and tragically divided from one another.[19] Where, for Yeats, this division was irrecuperable (for him conveniently so), recent scholars have attempted to connect Irish and British literary cultures synchronically and politically – albeit, like Yeats, nostalgically or even in valedictory benediction. The recent two-volume

Cambridge History of Irish Literature tries to right what it perceives as a historical wrong by devoting significant space to Irish writers in earlier centuries but finally connects them not to their British counterparts in the period but instead to the stars of the 'Irish Literary Renaissance' of c. 1890–1925.

Some scholars have paused a little longer, looked a little farther east than the Dublin of the early twentieth and sixteenth and seventeenth centuries. Declan Kiberd declares of Edmund Spenser and of the Irish historian Seathrún Céitinn that '[b]oth men, after all, were courtiers without a court'.[20] But this rich scholarly insight has not led to the inclusion of Céitinn in translation on undergraduate English syllabi, nor has it influenced Renaissance teaching at Irish universities. Renaissance studies has not done much better with efforts from Irish studies. The inclusion of an extract in Irish (Gaelic) from the Maguire bard Eochaidh O hEóghusa's poem on his patron's alliance with the rebel Hugh O'Neill in the *Penguin Book of Renaissance Verse* ostensibly matches the catholic outlook of its Introduction to acknowledge the existence of other literary cultures within the dominions of Queen Elizabeth I. As the sole example, however, ultimately the poem stands as an inconvenient intruder – or, better, a remote and isolated hermit – outnumbered by the shiny phalanx of the more familiar, primarily Anglocentric poems surrounding it. Despite such false horizons and missed opportunities in the teaching materials available, one of my guiding beliefs in this essay has been that the Irish classroom may yet offer a better opportunity for confronting literary histories and texts across Britain and Ireland than literary journals or publications, simply because teaching, even more than research, needs to work with and towards its particular, immediate audience.

The gains of a pedagogy more closely attuned to the specific historical, ethnic and religious identities of one's students, even where all of these factors contribute to a suspicion of Renaissance literature, are made beautifully clear in Ramona Wray's important 1997 essay on teaching Shakespeare in post-ceasefire (but pre-Good Friday Agreement) Belfast.[21] She begins by noting that Northern Irish students are often actively uninterested in Shakespeare having encountered him in the classroom, and that this antipathy usually emerges from a conviction that Shakespeare stands for the 'cultural hegemony' that has disenfranchised them – a conviction closely and urgently related to the highly politicized experiences of her students.[22] She shows how sectarian bias and these politicized experiences can be channelled in the classroom in order to shift Shakespeare away from prevailing England-centred interpretative paradigms and closer to home. Her interest in allowing (and encouraging) students to read from their own subject positions, to explore political topics and themes of immediate relevance and concern to them through the 'safety of metaphorical positions', forces a dialogue between past and present in which present needs ultimately, necessarily, predominate.[23] However, the texts are not simply mined for relevant content, but are instead approached in a more open and searching way, their doubts and decisions confronted and scrutinized as costly decisions, not inevitabilities.

The situation was different among Wray's student counterparts in the Irish Republic then, as Wray notes, and arguably even more so in recent years among the consumer-cultured Celtic Tiger cubs of the Irish Republic, who were eventually turned out into a corrupted and failing Irish economy by their duly tigerish mother.[24] But the kind of genuine emotional and politically sensitive engagement with the texts that Wray describes remains rare at universities north, south and east. Wray's courage in addressing the live issues and personal vulnerabilities of the students in her teaching, as well as the superficial and embedded flashpoints of the texts themselves, allowed these issues space to be faced – or faced by proxy, if necessary, and with no less value – in the university classroom. Her example demonstrates the receptiveness of Renaissance texts to being taught productively in ways that confront difficult issues of sectarianism and political and religious conflict, albeit when those are experienced far more intensely in Belfast than in the Irish Republic or in England. The spectrum of political and religious conflict in a multicultural society is wide, and the Belfast example is perhaps at one extreme. However, Wray's success testifies to the conviviality of Renaissance texts to less metropolitan, Anglocentric, 'high' literary approaches, and to the sensitivity of these texts of an earlier multicultural moment to the many kinds of conflict and tension found in multicultural society and still experienced by our students.

In light of Wray's pre-1997 experience in Queen's University, Belfast, perhaps it is not so odd that, after the Good Friday Agreement (1998), it should be a Northern Irish poet and former teacher who gives the most thoughtful direction on how we might take on the challenge of teaching early modern literature, in all its difficult diversity, in ways that engage and interrogate the realities of our students' lives in an unequal multicultural society, and that help students to consider the roots, routes and contingent histories of contemporary multicultural society in a range of early modern texts. Seamus Heaney's recent series of comments on the subject of how to read and live with Elizabethan poets whose colonizing endeavours were as wholehearted as their poetry is attractive concludes *Stepping Stones*, his 2008 book of interviews with Dennis O'Driscoll. Heaney suggests how we might (and should, I think) in our multicultural society teach not even Shakespeare, but a more ideologically compromised poet still, Edmund Spenser. He espouses a humane and searching engagement with poets and texts whose values and histories are troubling and even egregious – but without ever countenancing any kind of forgetting of the wrongs that they stood for or sought. 'So it would be an instructive, self-educational thing at this minute to read Edmund Spenser in relation to Iraq, for example,' he notes. 'You shouldn't have to accuse Spenser of writing bad poetry, but you'd have to understand him historically, in the full and present realization that civilized people can do wrong things ....'[25] Heaney suggests that as readers we *should* read these texts and acknowledge their literary and political legacy – but in so doing, we should 'change the plane of regard [...] in other words, not [...] respect the imperial drive, [but] come forward and say expropriation and brutality and force are evil'.[26] To shelter students from such a challenge does them no favours; to teach the more accessible, palatable Renaissance canon underestimates students' interest, skills and needs. We – and they – have everything to gain from a more diverse, open and difficult engagement with the forgotten history of early modern multiculturalism, a history that can and should be addressed in the most relevant and urgent terms with respect to the particular student body that we teach.

A caveat

For the purposes of this essay, I have capitulated, as I mentioned at the outset, to a crude division between UK and Irish students, one based on two broad categories of my own experience of university teaching. It is a tenuous and unreliable distinction: quite apart from the ethnographic and social diversity of the various student bodies of different universities, and indeed the varied ideals and origins of the university systems in both countries, globalization and the Americanization of youth culture have served to both draw together and divide students on a whole set of different bases. Irish students have BBC television and are just as avid viewers of (and participants in) reality television, imported American cult shows from HBO, and globalized Internet and electronic fora. Whatever the different stripes or configurations of the various and complicated identities of British and Irish students, the implied homogeneity under which they currently suffer under an assumption of passive, benign multiculturalism does nobody any favours. In effective pedagogy, even more so than in research, the audience needs to be identified, their stake in the material recognized and the texts turned over to them for direct consideration – a task that is not necessarily facilitated by the established structures and conventions of university teaching.[27] The fallacy that texts and cultures mean the same thing across time and space is one that has long since been dispatched, and the rise of multiculturalism is no reason to revive it. We would do better to live and teach multiculturalism within a full and searching analysis of its history, of the texts and ideas and movements that shaped it, of the cultural frameworks that it fosters (and that foster it, in turn) as well as those it disavows. In teaching Renaissance literature, we have a wonderful opportunity to do just that.

Notes

1. Thus *Paradise Lost, The Faerie Queene* and the poetry of Donne feature heavily alongside major chunks of Shakespeare, as do Wyatt, Jonson and Sidney. My intention is not to join in the exhausted tradition of criticizing Tillyard, but rather to point out the very familiarity and durability of the high canon of Renaissance texts.
2. Another significant factor is, arguably, the concentration of performance indicators in the domain of research at the expense of teaching in the UK by the RAE system for allocating public funding to universities from 1986 to 2008 (soon to be replaced by the Research Excellence Framework), and in Ireland, with the ever-increasing sway of the Higher Education Authority (HEA) in funding and policy issues, and the establishment of the Irish Research Council for the Humanities and Social Sciences (IRCHSS) in 2000.
3. As Dominic McGlinchey notes in a recent essay, the term 'multiculturalism' is a slippery one. He cites the ten forms of multiculturalism classified by Gerard Delanty in *Community* (London: Routledge, 2003), pp. 92–110, noting dryly (but aptly for our purposes) that 'many social and political communities [...] have an imagined sense that they are multicultural'. See 'Multiculturalism and Its Discontents', *Human Rights Law Review*, 5.1 (2005), 27–56 (p. 28).
4. From Paul Joseph Kelly's introduction to *Multiculturalism Reconsidered* (Cambridge: Polity Press, 2002), p. 1, cited by McGlinchey, 'Multiculturalism', p. 34.
5. This is an enterprise that has been far more effectively achieved in US universities, by and large, although the dominance of identity politics with only secondary historical interests has, arguably, not treated Renaissance texts with the sensitivity that they merit.
6. Anne Phillips offers a useful overview of the 'retreat' of multicultural ideals in the UK and the Netherlands since 2005, as well as a compelling argument about the subversion of feminist principles in the multiculturalism debate, both academic and political, in her recent book, *Multiculturalism Without Culture* (Princeton University Press, 2007), esp. pp. 4–8.

7. In order to use a representative sample, I worked from the 2008 RAE rankings of English departments in the UK (the most recent set of results available), choosing every fifth university from 1 (York) to 85 (Bolton). As this method of sampling happened not to touch on any Scottish, Welsh or Northern Irish universities, I then chose the top two and bottom two from each, using the same table of rankings. I used course details available online for core modules on Renaissance Literature that would ordinarily be taken by a BA student of English, whether single- or joint-honours. Although the RAE listing initially offered only a convenient framework for my sample, its evaluation of universities in terms of their research outputs turned out some surprising and valuable evidence of my theory about the gulf between teaching and research. All details are derived from the websites of the relevant universities, accessed 10 September 2009.

8. Listed under 'Second and Third Year Module Provision 2009', http://www.uwe.ac.uk/hlss/english/undergra.shtml [accessed July 2010].

9. See http://www.northumbria.ac.uk/?view=CourseDetail&page=module&code=UUFENL1&mod=EL0527 [accessed July 2010].

10. The *Norton Anthology of English Literature*, ed. Stephen Greenblatt et al. (London and New York: Norton, 2006), vol. I: *Renaissance Literature: An Anthology of Poetry and Prose*, ed. John C. Hunter (Chichester: Wiley Blackwell, 2010); the *Routledge Anthology of Renaissance Drama*, ed. Simon Barker and Hilary Hinds (London: Routledge, 2002); the *Penguin Book of Renaissance Verse, 1509–1659*, ed. David Norbrook (Harmondsworth: Penguin, 2005). The Routledge anthology of sources and documents for the period (edited by Kate Aughterson) is generally considered too expensive to ask students to buy as a supplement to their primary texts, given the wide variety of texts generally prescribed on Renaissance survey courses. The *Penguin Book of Renaissance Verse* and the *Norton Anthology of English Literature* (volume I) seem to be the market leaders, but even these do not dominate where multiple editions of the familiar primary texts exist, and where the curricula tend not to deviate too far beyond the established canon. Until this year (2010), the University of Sheffield used the Broadview anthology (volume II), which is committed to representing the work of lesser-known writers alongside their more familiar contemporaries, supplemented with a course handbook (see http://www.shef.ac.uk/english/ugmodules/lit234.html [accessed 12 July 2010], and we find other cases of dissatisfaction with the anthologies currently on the market: the University of Leeds, for example, has produced its own anthology of Renaissance poetry (see http://www.leeds.ac.uk/english/undergrad/modules/L23Cores201011.pdf [accessed 12 July 2010). But Andrew Carpenter's excellent recent anthology, *Verse in English from Tudor and Stuart Ireland* (Cork University Press, 2003) is nowhere prescribed on the Renaissance survey courses examined here.

11. See above, Seddon, p. 81.

12. The reference to Emily C. Bartels' important article ('Making More of the Moor: Aaron, Othello, and Renaissance Re-fashionings of Race', *Shakespeare Quarterly*, 41.4 (1990), 433–54) reminds me that an obvious omission in this essay is a consideration of the place of criticism in teaching, in terms of both the reading-lists of secondary sources supplementing the set texts and the influence of critical debates on the teaching of canonical texts.

But my contention is partly that this connection between research and teaching is made only in secondary or belated ways: if critical scholarship had truly come into confluence with teaching, the set texts would be more diverse and challenging.

13. The debate about the labels 'Renaissance' and 'early modern' has worn on for years now. Both have reasons to recommend them. Despite the accretion of unhelpful values and concepts around it, I favour 'Renaissance' for its insistence on the importance of history and versions of the past in the culture of the sixteenth and seventeenth centuries, something that 'early modern' can lose sight of – but I still find it helpful to use it interchangeably with 'early modern' to give it more flexibility and to highlight its status as an intellectual and ideological category rather than a self-conscious historical formation.

14. Elizabeth Butler Cullingford, *Ireland's Others: Ethnicity and Gender in Irish Literature and Popular Culture*, Field Day Monograph Series (Cork University Press, 2001), p. 5.

15. I suspect that, consciously or not, the appropriation of a more up-to-date idea of 'Renaissance' to describe 'the Irish Literary Renaissance' (or 'Revival') of Yeats, Joyce and so on, has left the 'English Renaissance' firmly stuck with the most conservative and unreconstructed form of the idea. Certainly, the term has cachet, but of a dubious kind, and even proponents of the Irish Literary Renaissance have expressed unease with upholding the term.

16. The prominence of studies of gender, race, sexuality and ethnicity in the United States has in many cases enabled a more open and interrogative classroom experience, although it too has its critics: the radical educationalist Peter McLaren, for example, suggests that in the USA, 'modernism has unified coercively the heterogeneous culture of the Other through the values of patriarchy, self-perfection, and individual autonomy'. See 'Critical Literacy and Postcolonial Praxis: A Freirian Perspective', *College Literature*, 20 (1992–93), 7–22 (p. 9).

17. Sheila T. Cavanagh, '"That Savage Land": Ireland in Spenser's Legend of Justice', in *Approaches to Teaching Spenser's 'Faerie Queene'*, ed. David Lee Miller and Alexander Dunlop (New York: MLA, 1994), pp. 143–52 (p. 143).

18. The relatively recent arrival of economic and political immigrants to Celtic Tiger Ireland is one factor that continues to generate lively debate about Irish cultural identity and social consciousness. For a sample of these debates, see *Nationalism and Multiculturalism: Irish Identity, Citizenship and the Peace Process*, ed. Andrew Finlay (Muenster: Lit Verlag, 2004), especially the essay by Piaras Mac Éinri (pp. 85–109), from which this quotation is taken (p. 94).

19. Yeats' essay on Spenser is the classic example: 'When Spenser wrote of Ireland he wrote as an official, and out of thoughts and emotions that had been organized by the State. [...] Could he have gone there as a poet merely, he might have found among its poets more wonderful imaginations than even those islands of Phaedria and Acrasia.' Instead, '[l]ike an hysterical patient he drew a complicated web of inhuman logic out of the bowels of an insufficient premise – there was no right, no law, but that of Elizabeth, and all that opposed her opposed themselves to God, to civilisation, and to all inherited wisdom and courtesy, and should be put to death.' *The Poems*

of Spenser, edited and with an introduction by W.B. Yeats (London: Caxton Publishing, 1906), pp. xxxiii and xix.

20. Declan Kiberd, 'Literature and Politics', in *The Cambridge History of Irish Literature*, ed. Margaret Kelleher and Philip O'Leary, 2 vols (Cambridge University Press, 2006), II, pp. 9–49 (p. 13).

21. Ramona Wray, 'Shakespeare and the Sectarian Divide: Politics and Pedagogy in (post) Post-ceasefire Belfast', in *Shakespeare and Ireland: History, Politics, Culture*, ed. Mark Thornton Burnett and Ramona Wray (Basingstoke: Macmillan, 1997), pp. 235–55.

22. *Ibid.*, p. 237.

23. *Ibid.*, p. 251. It should be noted that this was not, however, a lecture course but a small-group seminar that Wray taught, and it seems clear that within seminar courses much more of the ground of contemporary research is covered with undergraduate students in both Ireland and the UK than in their lecture courses.

24. Wray is careful to distinguish between the Irish and the Northern Irish students on the basis of the intensity with which political issues are felt (*ibid.*, p. 237).

25. Dennis O'Driscoll, *Stepping Stones: Interviews with Seamus Heaney* (London: Faber & Faber, 2008), p. 455.

26. *Ibid.*

27. McLaren notes that both teachers and students have already been 'inserted into language' and notes the consequent 'unavailability of subject positions in which students are permitted to practice forms of radical critique' ('Critical Literacy and Postcolonial Praxis', p. 16). Although pursued from an entirely different set of bases, his argument parallels mine in its concern about the kinds of agency allowed to students in current educational models.

11
Shakespeare and the Problem of the Early Modern Curriculum

Andrew Hadfield

Teachers of early modern English literature are both blessed and cursed by the gargantuan figure of Shakespeare. Blessed, because Shakespeare's presence means that the study of the period will always be in demand and we will never have to face the bleak prospect that often assails our colleagues teaching the eighteenth century which lacks an equivalent figure unless the new queen of English literature, Jane Austen, is co-opted for that role. Cursed, because Shakespeare can blot out the culture from which he has emerged, especially now that so few advanced school students study Chaucer. Shakespeare serves as an intellectual and emotional focus on his own, so that many students will *only* want to study him. In a worst-case scenario, universities, with more than one eye on their popularity ratings, will allow students to study a course on 'Shakespeare on Film' *instead* of a course of real early modern literature (there is no problem, of course, if students take both).

The problem of university teachers being forced to promote a version of the English Renaissance that is all but obscured by Shakespeare is exacerbated by the availability of texts, their particular status and the ways in which they have been edited. Students will find Shakespeare texts cheap and easy to acquire: if Arden, Oxford and Cambridge editions prove too expensive, there are always Wordsworth editions, which, if not prime examples of their craft, are at least readable. More importantly, Shakespearean texts are modernized and standardized, unless they come in specialist editions for the true scholar (I am thinking in particular of the Cambridge first quartos series). Other plays and poems are not, so that they seem to new readers as though they come from a different age, whereas Shakespeare is always presented as our contemporary. Some years ago it was fashionable to insist that students study texts in their original old-spelling editions. This has not, I think, been a success. Instead of enabling teachers to introduce students to a new and exciting world of original texts as they were first read, the effect was to make what seemed obscure more obscure and actually restrict the teaching canon to what could be easily understood. Perhaps the impact has been most detrimental to women's writing, which started to become available in editions in the 1980s and 1990s, but which often appeared in scholarly old-style editions, making it look more Spenserian (old, dull, archaic and arcane) and less Shakespearean (modern, exciting, racy, easily understood).

What, then, can be done? The first trick is to meet the students where they are and to convince them that you can teach them something they need to know. How the teacher does this will depend on the higher education institution at which they teach. The process is easy at old, established universities which require high entry grades and which will attract students who will be easily susceptible to intellectual pressure and snobbery and who will have already read (or at least heard of) other early modern texts and authors. But it has always seemed to me axiomatic that no degree qualification can be called 'English Literature' if students do not spend at least a quarter of their time studying literature written before 1650, which would disqualify a lot of programmes in the British Isles, including that at my own institution (students can at present complete the degree having studied only eight to ten pre-1650 works). Early modern literature courses only ever really study drama and poetry: prose has virtually disappeared from the undergraduate curriculum, unless a bold soul sneaks in *The Unfortunate Traveller*.

In these days of student surveys, the pendulum has swung too far in favour of giving students exactly what they think they want and university authorities are eager to shun any possible confrontation. Many students avoid early modern courses because they are frightened of studying older texts, because the language is unfamiliar and they feel out of their depth, and because they have not studied enough relevant or challenging material at school. Even very gifted students avoid early modern literature because they are not equipped to study it and will opt for the Shakespeare course with nice, edited familiar texts. What we need is a powerful subject group that stipulates what a student needs to study in order to qualify as an English graduate. This suggestion will horrify many university teachers who saw the idea of the canon as the enemy in the 1980s, but abandoning the requirement to study core texts has done us untold damage both inside and outside the academy. Nevertheless, other subjects insist on stipulating what needs to be done and it is the basis of all primary and secondary school education in

England on the model of the National Curriculum. Of course, what needs to be studied has to be set out in the hard sciences. In the QAA (Quality Assurance Agency) benchmarking statement, chemists are told what they need to know in order to be awarded a degree in the subject. Under the section 'Subject Knowledge and Understanding', teachers of bachelor's degrees are told that they must ensure that their students 'are fully conversant with major aspects of chemical terminology', 'demonstrate systematic understanding of fundamental physicochemical principles' and 'gain knowledge of a range of inorganic and organic materials'.[1] The benchmarking statement for psychology sets out a similar list of core disciplines that students need to learn, which are 'research methods, biological psychology, cognitive psychology, personality and individual differences, developmental psychology and social psychology'. The benchmarking statement for English is, I would suggest, extraordinarily vague, and establishes a series of concerns and principles, not a prescriptive list of areas of knowledge, stating only that students need to acquire 'knowledge of literature and language, which in the case of literature should include a substantial number of authors and texts from different periods of literary history. For single honours literature students this should include knowledge of writing from periods before 1800.' Students studying English with another subject at undergraduate level can clearly skip anything older than Jane Austen if they – or their institution – wish. Otherwise the statement is a description of how texts should be taught and thought about, not what should be taught. Students need to acquire: 'knowledge and understanding of the distinctive character of texts written in the principal literary genres, fiction, poetry and drama, and of other kinds of writing and communication [...] appreciation of the power of imagination in literary creation; awareness of the role of critical traditions in shaping literary history; knowledge of linguistic, literary, cultural and socio-historical contexts in which literature is written and read'. Few teachers of English would object to these principles – but that surely is a weakness as well as a strength. If institutions wish to get rid of much of their early period teaching, the benchmarking statement gives them a green light to do so.

Familiar complaints about falling standards would be offset if we, as university teachers, went on the offensive and stated exactly what our subject is, a process that is supposed to be happening anyway through benchmarking and the application of universally agreed standards to our research outputs through the RAE (Research Assessment Exercise) and the new REF (Research Excellence Framework) in the UK, as well as indices provided by European and Australian research councils which are seeking to rank scholarly journals in order of merit and importance. The process may be irresistible and it is better to use it as we see fit and not to wait for things to be imposed: if we sit back and let the authorities act it may be too late for us to seize any sort of initiative. And, of course, in order to teach the early modern period effectively, we need cheap, well-edited, modernized texts of non-Shakespearean works so that students can range a bit more widely. Many, of course, do exist, and there are a number of anthologies – Broadview, Longman, Norton – that make texts available in consultation with higher education teachers. It would be of great benefit for teachers to co-operate in order to ensure that certain texts are made available and are used. Through the development of an e-mailing list, a number of conferences and other events, and some judiciously edited anthologies and essay collections, the once invisible subject of 'Tudor literature' now has a presence within the academy, and is now taught at some institutions. Early modern prose is another subject that could easily be revived in the next few years.[2]

What then might we actually teach? A common complaint is that what teachers now find tiresome, students find exciting, so that there is a time lag between research and teaching. Many of us struggle to avoid teaching classes in which the right answer to the question is 'metrosexual cross-dressing in *Twelfth Night*'. Perhaps this is right and the process of getting there has become as stale as the answer; perhaps we should be pleased that students are so excited by what once excited many of us. But it is hard to state exactly what we should teach when there are equally good cases for making students read romance, varieties of narrative poetry, satire, medical literature, travel literature and so on. One way forward is for us to teach long cross-period courses, that range from the Middle Ages to the present day, on such subjects as 'Islam and Literature', 'Colonial and Post-Colonial Writing', 'Life Writing', or some of the categories outlined in the previous sentence. Early modern literature does not then become cut off from later periods and some of the artificial divides that we habitually establish seem less concrete and easier to challenge or circumvent. Furthermore, it has the healthy result of forcing teachers to become a bit less obsessed with being experts who can only teach small, specialized periods, a process exacerbated by the ways in which we have to define ourselves as researchers, but which students tend to resist. Research should always feed into teaching, but should not circumscribe or define what is read and discussed in the classroom, and academics should always be prepared to range beyond their immediate knowledge-base, seizing the initiative in designing courses in order to meet students where they are and transporting them in directions we think they should want to go, bringing our ideas to them and so moving them forward. And, if we accept that they have things to teach us, and that we are not sages who know all the answers, we will learn ourselves and know slightly better where we might want to go in the future. Establishing a symbiotic relationship between teaching and research, a desirable goal in my view, does not mean simply teaching our research.

Notes

1. All references are to the QAA benchmarking statement available online at: http://www.qaa.ac.uk/academicinfrastructure/benchmark/honours/english. asp#4 [accessed 8 September 2010].
2. [Editors' note: in this regard, readers may find interesting the recent publication of *Teaching Early Modern English Prose*, ed. Susannah Brietz Monta and Margaret W. Ferguson (New York: MLA, 2010).]

Part 3

The Early Modern in the Contemporary Classroom: Course Design and Classroom Practice

12
An Early Modern Challenge: Finding the Student In-road

Patrick Cheney

For the early modern courses I teach at Penn State, the primary challenge remains relatively unchanged over 30 years: for any given work, how can I find a student in-road?

By 'student in-road', I mean a way into a work or text. For me, a student in-road needs to be intellectually challenging, something that catches the eye; it also needs to be emotionally engaging, making the heart beat. It is always grounded in the text – a word, a phrase, a line, a short passage, maybe a scene. But it can't be just any part of the text; it has to be one that takes us to the heart of the work as a literary form, to the centre of the author's literary career, and thus outward to the period concept; so that finally we can situate the text, the work and the author along the road from antiquity to modernity.

In my graduate seminars, I concentrate on the areas of my research, so the link between research and teaching remains intimate. In my undergraduate courses, however, I let authors and works dictate the direction. Nonetheless, in both sets of courses, I look for the student in-road, even if it often leads outside my area of expertise, to something I find fascinating yet cannot fathom. That feeling, I think, helps animate the course.

Here is an example, from the opening scene of Shakespeare's *Tragedy of Antony and Cleopatra*. It is a mere four lines long, as we catch up with the lovers for the first time, in the middle of a dispute:

> *Cleopatra*. If it be love indeed, tell me how much.
> *Antony*. There's beggary in the love that can be reckon'd.
> *Cleopatra*. I'll set a bourn how far to be belov'd.
> *Antony*. Then must thou needs find out new heaven, new earth.[1]

First, I ask students what the source of the dispute is; they quickly see the comical paradox: it is about who has authority to *reckon love, count desire*. Antony derides the idea, but Cleopatra retorts by claiming that it is her role to determine the bounds 'set' for her 'to be belov'd'. Exasperated, Antony concludes by marking off the impossibility of her claim: 'Then must thou needs find out new heaven, new earth.' It is in this last phrase that I find a student in-road.

New heaven, new earth. I ask the class if they have heard the phrase before, and typically at least one student has, or gets us close. I then read the Book of Revelation, chapter 21, verse 1, when St John of Patmos says, 'And I sawe a new heaven, & a new earth'.[2] Students are shocked to discover a pre-Christian Roman, Mark Antony, of military and erotic fame, voicing the divine comedy of Revelation. I encourage them to see the vastness of what Shakespeare stages: he encourages the audience to view the most important world event before the Incarnation, the defeat of Antony and Cleopatra at Actium in 31 BC by Octavian, through the future lens of the Christian Apocalypse.

How can that be? How can a late first-century BC Roman general speak the language that a Christian prophet will not voice till the first century AD?

I start my teaching of *Antony and Cleopatra* with this temporal conundrum. To show students that the tragedy's scriptural stitching is not idle, I jump to the play's conclusion, when the Eastern Star tells Charmian, 'I'll give thee leave / To play till doomsday' (V.2.231–2). As he does in both *Lear* and *Macbeth* – to a certain extent *Hamlet* – Shakespeare invites the audience to view his tragedy through the lens of the Last Judgement. Yet, unlike major authors from Dante and Petrarch to Spenser and Milton, Shakespeare limns a defining blackout about what happens at 'the promis'd end [...] / Or image of that horror' (*King Lear*, V.2.264–5). Alone in Western literature, the Shakespearean cosmos graphically includes the Christian endpoint but hauntingly leaves the promise of eternal bliss vacant.

This lens helps explain the performance that controls the conclusion to the play: Cleopatra and her attendants do not simply commit suicide 'after the high Roman fashion' (IV.15.87), or even present themselves regally to the living; they carefully prepare themselves for resurrection in the afterlife. As the Clown quips of the asp he brings, 'his biting / is immortal [...] / I wish you joy o' th' worm' (V.2.216–17, 279). Subsequently, Cleopatra says, 'Give me my robe, [...] I have / Immortal longings in me. [...] / I hear Antony call; / [...] / Husband, I come' (280–7). When Iris goes first, however, the queen becomes furtive: 'If she first meet the curled Antony, / He'll [...] spend that kiss / Which is my heaven to have' (301–3). And after the queen and her attendants lie dead, the First Guard tells Caesar of Charmian, 'I found her trimming up the diadem / On her dead mistress' (342–3). As Harold Goddard helps me see, when Caesar then looks at the corpse of the dead queen, and observes, in one of Shakespeare's supreme moments of *poesis*, 'she looks like sleep / As she would catch another Antony / In her strong toil of grace' (346–8), Shakespeare uses the word 'grace' to provide the most mysterious evidence in his canon for the substance of things hoped for, the evidence of things not seen.[3]

The epiphanic moment has an intriguing gender dynamic to it: a man looks at a woman he perceives to be beautiful and witnesses a transcendent act immanent in her face. Like Antony at the outset, a male intimates messianic significance in the body of a female. Miraculously, Caesar beholds a dead woman who, in perception, appears alive, at once quietly asleep yet toiling in her loving work.

What, then, I finally ask my students, are historical figures living on the cusp of the Incarnation doing in an early seventeenth-century tragedy speaking the language of Scripture? Here, I need not say, but instead recall W.H. Auden, who voices one of the most profound ideas I know made of this author: 'the vision of Eros', which Auden distinguishes from our ordinary desire for a gendered individual, allows Will of the *Sonnets* to perceive the beloved as a 'single person [...] of infinite sacred importance'.[4] In the Gospel of Luke, Christ says, 'for beholde the kingdome of God is within you' (17.21). He does not mean that the kingdom of God is *only* within you, but his message is epochal for directing the godly person to look within for the divine light without. Following Auden, we might say that in the epoch of Shakespeare *the kingdom of God is within the other*. Shakespeare's genius is to perceive the other as a special person of eternal value. He does not so much 'invent the human'[5] as *value the human*, right when the Church was contending with Calvin, for whom the human is 'depraved', the 'mind' a 'sink', the 'body' a 'rotting tabernacle'.[6]

By encouraging students to see in what sense Cleopatra 'find[s] out new heaven, new earth', I try to help discover a historical frame for the play at large, for Shakespearean tragedy as a literary form, for Shakespeare's significance as an early modern author, for his centralizing representation of gender perception and finally for the early modern period itself as a cultural epoch. What Stanley Cavell finds in this period, 'the advent of skepticism', with men and women struggling 'to live [...] in a groundless world', and confronting 'the problem of the other as the replacement of the problem of God', is not accurate.[7] For Shakespeare, the universe is neither Cavell's secular nor Spenser's Christian one, but a literary space in which the two meet. Like Cleopatra's Charmian, the 'human' in Shakespeare's works has leave to play till doomsday, yet does not know what lies beyond. Consequently, Shakespeare does not 'replace' 'God' with 'the other' but instead finds a god animating the other. As the Eastern Star puts it of her dream of Antony: 'His face was as the heav'ns' (V.2.79).

The student in-road proves valuable because it allows students to read the text closely, to understand gender perception as central to genre-formation, to widen out understanding to an author with a literary career using poems and plays for epoch-making 'cultural work', to come to terms with the period concept and finally to situate the early modern period between antiquity and modernity.

Notes

1. *Antony and Cleopatra*, I.1.14–17, *Riverside Shakespeare*, ed. G. Blakemore Evans et al. (Boston: Houghton, 1997).
2. Revelation 21.1, in *The Geneva Bible*, ed. Lloyd E. Berry (Madison: University of Wisconsin Press, 1969).
3. Harold Goddard, *The Meaning of Shakespeare*, 2 vols (University of Chicago Press, 1951), II, pp. 204–7.
4. W.H. Auden, 'Introduction', *Sonnets and Narrative Poems* (New York: Signet, 1964), p. xxx.
5. Harold Bloom, *Shakespeare: The Invention of the Human* (New York: Riverhead-Penguin Putnam, 1998).
6. John Calvin, *Institutes of the Christian Religion*, ed. John T. McNeill, trans. Ford Lewis Battles, 2 vols (Philadelphia: Westminster Press, 1960), II, pp. 498, 604.
7. Stanley Cavell, *Disowning Knowledge* (Cambridge University Press, 1987), pp. 3, 11.

13
Teaching Shakespeare Historically

Mark Thornton Burnett

As a critic of the early modern period interested in the relations between texts and histories, I use my final-year undergraduate seminars as a means of introducing students to the joys and perils of interdisciplinary approaches. Because, for me, knowing how to read a play is inseparable from knowing how to deploy historical evidence and to mobilize a theoretical frame, I continually flag up in class three principles of critical engagement – textual, historical, theoretical. Most recently, such an approach has been facilitated by the arrival of EEBO, the online resource that makes available the wealth of early modern literature and culture, and this fundamental change proffers infinite possibilities for contextualization and scholarship in our teaching. In short, changes in resources have precipitated a transformation in attitudes towards, and the methodologies that surround, the teaching of the period, not least at the level of advanced courses on Shakespeare. At Queen's University, Belfast, I teach a final-year research-led module on 'Reading Shakespeare Historically'. As subsidiary aims, the course is directed towards a de-canonization of Shakespeare: firstly, 'Shakespeare' and 'History' are equally prioritized and, secondly, the range of texts studied goes against expectations created by survey modules in earlier phases of the curriculum. Hence, we bypass the tragedies, concentrating instead on the histories, comedies and problem plays.

Given these aims, orientation is essential. The opening session accordingly is proactive from the tutor's point of view. 'What is history, and where can we find it?' are some of the questions posed as I discuss and distribute the relevant course materials. The context pack – which comprises extracts, illustrations, citations, lists of further reading and so on – is a first port of call, but there is always the proviso that this represents a starting point only. I also direct attention to pertinent areas of the library, to collections of facsimiles, to early printed book holdings and, most importantly, to Early English Books on Line (EEBO), with group exercises being organized in relation to their applications. Vital, too, is how we might learn from, and put to work, our two core texts, the Norton edition of Shakespeare and Russ McDonald's frequently reprinted Palgrave collection, *The Bedford Companion to Shakespeare*. Throughout, I spend part of each seminar focusing attention on particular passages or on suggestions for reading in these texts, the idea being that the information provided is a springboard for subsequent analysis. In this way, a question that frequently occurs – that is, how, exactly, do we historicize at the level of an argument? – is confronted via practical examples of the application of the relevant methodology.

Orientation is inseparable from the assumption of certain kinds of student responsibility. In years one and two, the general teaching structure is organized around tutorials with the addition of lectures, an arrangement that makes for a two-prong 'go' at a particular text. By year three, however, students are allowed to take a free-standing seminar, with the result that time needs to be spent on easing the way into a new – and more individually oriented – teaching situation. The seminar presentation (a module requirement) is designed to encourage students to take responsibility for what they learn. The presentation takes the form of two to four pages of questions/comment that are distributed, in advance, to the rest of the class. At least two examples of early modern historical contexts are to be provided (that is, a copy of a title-page or a one-paragraph quotation from the historical document) in order to illuminate the Shakespearean example; the principle is not to reward the verbal rendition but to register the importance of the material itself. The significance of the provision of material to the other members of the class is explained as follows: each presentation represents a potential body of evidence to be taken up in later endeavours. If each student completes his/her presentation, the class will possess, by the end of the semester, a file of references and positions that can be marshalled in the assessed essay. The individual value of discrete pieces feeds into this final compilation; each member of the class can shape, and have an effect on, the writing process. Students, I try to show, are working for themselves and for each other. A 10 per cent mark for participation and attendance also helps: student-led seminars, it is recognized, are all the better for maximum input.

Where is theory in all of this? Implicitly and explicitly, the dislodgement of a canonical Shakespeare – he is always already implicated in other discourses, practices and frameworks – invites theoretical readings and facilitates the identification of names and movements. Most obviously, the need to read according to theoretical templates is impressed upon students in the session devoted to writing skills. Rather than seeing students individually, I offer a group discussion, having assembled a generalized list (from a reading of the non-assessed essays) of the positive and less positive aspects of the work submitted. This has the advantage of de-individuating students (everything is anonymous) while, at the same time, speaking to particular constituencies (there is invariably private recognition). Once again, this is a group exercise; students are asked to comment on a particular construction, phrase or formulation, and they are free to ask other members of the class for clarification and comment. Dialogue and a sense of a significantly shared enterprise are generated as a result. Questions of expression enter the conversation but so, too, do issues relating to construction: in reflecting upon how we describe 'character', and the ways in which we might wish to foreground 'history' as a fixed point of comparison, we achieve a self-consciousness about essentialist and materialist tendencies in the execution of our thought. 'Hal is constructed as fundamentally determined by the anxieties of his time' and 'Hal is worried about his family and inheritance' are put on the board as examples for students to adjudicate between. Of course, most favour the former statement as a critical formulation, but the fact that debate has been initiated helps to alert students to the need for due reflection as the writing process begins.

No less important to the acquisition of theory is the sample model essay. (To use history is not enough, I suggest, since we also need to reflect theoretically upon how such a critical manoeuvre is conducted.) The sample essay is also anonymous: either the essay circulated belongs to one of the students or it is the work of a critic. We discuss the essay as a group, pointing out its flaws and merits. Conceptually, at stake is an exercise in authority: students are more ready to value their own contribution if they see its features reproduced elsewhere. A process of decentring is encouraged at the same time: if part of the module is the de-canonizing of Shakespeare, another is the uncrowning of particular attitudes towards criticism. Critics, I suggest, are the prompts to further insights rather than the embodiment of an opinion that cannot be contested. They stimulate interpretation: they do not substitute for it.

More generally in the module, I offer regular instruction on how 'history' and 'literature' interact. I canvass opinion among the class as to the most appropriate terms we can invoke to describe this relationship. Invariably, discussion concentrates – in highly useful ways – on the differences between terms such as 'reflect' and 'intervene'. 'Reflect', we conclude, may connote a mimetic and straightforward connection; by contrast, 'intervene' points to textual agency, to the possibility of friction and discontinuity. Once again, our new familiarity with resources assists in the generation of dialogue. An informed engagement with terminology would not be possible without the availability of EEBO, which has opened students to a world beyond Shakespeare, to the plural environments in which early modern drama participates. If there has been a sea-change in teaching the period, it has been in the expansion of the resources, a development that has made us more pressingly aware of the need to adjust our generic horizons and to take advantage of the multiple interactions that technology affords.

14
The Importance of Being Endogenous

Alain Viala

In the course of my academic career, from the Sorbonne to Oxford, I have had two different experiences of teaching and research in the field known here in the UK as early modern France, and in France as the *ancien régime* or *l'époque moderne*. I think it a useful exercise to share here certain lessons I have learned from this experience, as they currently stand. I shall do so primarily in the form of a narrative, and – since we are all well aware that theory exists only as the result of practice – I shall start by speaking of practices.

I would like to take, briefly, as my starting point, a seemingly trivial but significant detail, namely the difference in terminology employed in France and in the English-speaking world. In French usage, *ancien régime* emphasizes a (political and social) contrast, while *époque moderne* renders the very notion of modernity problematic (this concept cannot be exclusively associated with the most recent period of history since many intellectuals of the earlier period explicitly claim it). By contrast, in the English-speaking world, 'early modern' allows some sort of connotation of continuity or progression to emerge, allowing at least a greater sense of a link rather than a break. These fluctuations between similarity and difference, and the possible tensions they suggest, invite us to ponder on a dialectic which seems to me to be worthy of some attention. I shall speak of it in the light of my most recent experience to date.

This consists of teaching the history of *ancien régime* France to students of French at Oxford. I do not think it is necessary to go into how I came to be giving such a class: the need for historical references is clear to us all, with regard as much to the state of the language as to the contextualization of works studied, a grasp of literary and artistic history, and an understanding of key concepts of the period. This need exists in

France but, frequently, when faced with the gaps in students' knowledge, the reaction of university teachers of literature there is to shift the responsibility onto colleagues in other subjects – not only history, but also philosophy, the visual arts, music – and onto previous teachers: the core curriculum shared by students at each stage of their education makes such a transfer of problems to one's associates easy. In Britain and Ireland, and within the context of the study of a foreign language and culture, no such means of avoiding the issue is available. The solution is, then, a history class for the benefit of students of French as a language, as literature and as culture.

For such students, priority is perforce given to cultural history. Hence – given that the number of teaching hours is necessarily limited – political, economic and social history are allocated little space. The cultural history provided – which is itself brief – is divided, in accordance with the needs of the students, into three sections: knowledge, beliefs and practices. Of course, given that ideas do not circulate in some Empyrean Heaven, they cannot be separated from the ways in which they are put into practice. Accordingly, the history of ideas delivered under the heading of knowledge makes the assumption that such knowledge, along with the systems of thought which sometimes dictate its organization, is not without links to, among other things, educational subject matter and methods. So, the students discover the importance of the legacy of Thomas Aquinas, of Christian Aristotelianism, of Latin and so on; they also discover that, for example, the roots of the genre of the dialogue, often included in scenes of debate in a salon or café, or on rambles with friends, are deeply embedded in the tradition of *disputatio* so avidly pursued by the Jesuit colleges. Equally (to give just a brief further example), under the heading of cultural practices, the history of the book and reading allows them to realize that writings in French constituted only a small proportion of printed texts and the contents of libraries. In short, they become aware that the works and authors given to them to read on their courses of study, libertine, Jansenist or philosophical texts, or again dramatic and novelistic fictions, form a minor part of the culture of this time. All the more minor in that only a quarter of the population had access to them, and that they were habitually enjoyed by only a tiny quarter of that quarter … But anybody reading these pages is fully aware of this, although it is always beneficial to remind ourselves of the fact. However, it does seem to me that further benefit is to be had in some additional consideration of two consequences of this historical approach.

By reassessing the preoccupations of the past – what was important, what pertained to a minority of people and what was banal – we become aware of the need to integrate literary history with the history of reading, of publishing, of teaching and so on, and with religious and political history. Moreover, many major texts (for example the works of Pascal, Descartes, Diderot, Rousseau and Montesquieu) were indifferent to the distinctions between disciplines now in use. It therefore seems clear, at least when considering such a period, how detrimental it would be to adopt a limited definition of literature. The term itself in any case was employed at the time as a synonym for 'Letters', and it was only occasionally used with a primary focus on aesthetics. The object of study is therefore defined more as literature in the broader sense of 'Letters', or even – to use the clearest term – as 'the literary'.

The second consequence, and this relates to processes, is that the adoption of an historical approach requires us to engage with categories of practice and thought as they were at the time; in other words, it demands that we make the effort to construct *endogenous* categories, categories which emerge from within the culture. For example, 'libertine' did not designate a formal movement, but was originally a condemnatory term, while casuistry is a technique developed by and necessary to the Church, and so on. For students, the realization that what they read today had minority status at the time of its writing can lead to the avoidance of poorly applied generalizations, and that in itself is a considerable achievement. But it also helps to equip them to question the development of ideas in a different way: which ideas were innovative, and how innovative were they? What was daring, and how daring was it? Which ideas have entered the general pool of acquired knowledge? And which earlier modes of thought have contrived to remain deeply embedded in our culture ever since (in the area of religion, for example)?

Further, an approach which takes account of endogenous categories not only seems unavoidable but also constitutes good practice: it makes students test out a dialectic in which difference is as significant as perceived antecedents and thereby leads them to question the relationship between past and present; for the present can be understood only as the cumulative product of history. Analyses from the perspectives of so-called 'Theories' (post-structuralism, multiculturalism, feminism ...) or others linked to contemporary issues, can be carried out only once this fundamental work is sufficiently advanced, and they should take the form of questions; for, of course, what we perceive as the inherent characteristics of current issues are made up of what is taken for granted, of what is endogenous to ourselves. Indeed, the benefit which accrues to our understanding lies in this confrontation of two endogenous spaces.

These few thoughts will not surprise those who have read my work elsewhere (for example, *La Culture littéraire*): the experience I have evoked here (which despite its limited nature involves direct engagement with the needs of undergraduate students) confirms me in my view that the 'first modernity' – this term is probably more appropriate today than *ancien régime* and 'early modern period' – is in many respects an ideal ground in which to discover that supreme shaper of the present and the past, of similarity and difference, namely, the dialectic which lies at the very heart of humanist scholarship and which is formative in the original sense of the word if we are prepared to engage, there as elsewhere, with both the literary and the endogenous.

Translated by Teresa Bridgeman

15
Literature, Philosophy and Medicine: Strategies for an Interdisciplinary Approach to the Seventeenth Century

Bernadette Höfer

Humanities departments of research universities, among them Harvard University and the Ohio State University, are increasingly prioritizing interdisciplinary courses. Arguments favouring interdisciplinary teaching include the idea that real-world problems are not arbitrarily fragmented into individual disciplinary perspectives and that a single-lens perspective leaves important parts of the problems unaddressed. Those universities that encourage interdisciplinary education have created freshmen seminars, honours courses, general education programmes, different major tracks and international studies majors to generate more comprehensive explanations of the world. The Ohio State University, for example, offers all of the above to allow students to combine one or more areas of study that are closely related. Interdisciplinary teaching allows for the creation of hybrid courses, in which one discipline may dominate but in which other fields are included, in order to provide a broader insight into the material discussed and to foster critical thinking across the disciplines.[1] In this essay, I will focus on a course that addresses the mind/body question in the early modern period. It aims to address questions such as: are mind and body distinct? If so, how do they interact? What exactly is the mind? There is also the question of what to do with feelings, sensations and the classification of what is conscious experience. Insofar as the relation between mind and body concerned seventeenth-century philosophers, literary authors and physicians, my course, entitled 'The Mind/Body Problem in Early Modern French Literature' necessarily crosses lines and seeks interdisciplinary connections. It incorporates new perspectives from literature, philosophy, medicine and cultural studies. Exploring viewpoints from contemporary neuroscientists moreover encourages diachronic comparisons between past and present. Neurobiologists' new perspectives help us to understand trends and themes that have been understated or understudied in literature until now. Their recent insights allow us to see literary texts in a new perspective and can foster a better under-standing of what 'passions' are or create new ways of discussing the self and identity. In support of the approach used here, a vast array of critics and thinkers identify Descartes as being at the origin of modernity's preoccupation with the mind/body problem. The seventeenth-century French philosopher remains the focus of contemporary works in which he becomes the major target of critics, who point out his errors, or the defender of those who credit him for defining mainstream Western thought and formulating clear concepts that aid us in our understanding of ourselves. In addition to Descartes, other important seventeenth-century voices who clearly contributed to the discussion of how mind and body interact must be taken into account. While often excluded from the current debate, they substantiated notions of monistic thinking and attempted to resolve the still unanswered question of how our mental states – beliefs, actions and thoughts – are related to the physical states, events and processes in our bodies.

This course, then, identifies, constructs and clarifies problems that are crucial to the biological and philosophical contexts of the world in which we live and that find their modern roots in dualism and its rejection within the seventeenth century. *Newsweek, Scientific American* or *The New York Times*, for example, continuously review the findings and new debates within neuroscience and reproduce the questions that, so far, have only been answered unsatisfactorily. What characterizes the conscious mind? What makes for an emotion, a feeling? 'How do the processes we call mind emerge from the activity of the organ we call brain?'[2] Do we need to separate 'the brain from the body, the body from the mind, and the brain from the mind'?[3] The last decade has seen yoga and Buddhist mind/body practices, such as meditation and mind training, go mainstream. In 2003, a *New York Times* article asked the telling question: 'Is Buddhism Good for your Health?' What can monks teach the rest of us about the mind/body connection that we have not yet grasped sufficiently? Beyond the popular outreach of these questions, neurobiologists still continue to tackle the difficult question of how to explain the 'mind' as a result of brain action and its relation to physiological stimulus. Numerous questions keep arising of how to describe consciousness as a matter of brain, body and mind. While brain science is still in its infancy, the abstract question of how body and mind work together is rooted deeply within the early modern period and finds its expression in a variety of texts that offer different approaches and solutions. We study the question from a multiplicity of angles: through literary, philosophical, medical and cultural texts of that period. Students in my class perceive how seventeenth-century Europe became the arena for a passionate debate focusing on whether mind and body formed a single substance or whether, conversely, they constituted two distinct substances.

The compelling case for a dialogue between the two eras is that, first of all, scientists, in recent attempts to identify the cogito, invite us to look again at the seventeenth century and to rethink the opposition between Descartes and Spinoza in ways that favour Spinoza's holistic conceptions and cause us to question the Cartesian legacy. The importance of understanding seventeenth-century sources for the contemporary discourse is stressed in prominent neuroscientist's Antonio Damasio two book titles: In *Descartes' Error* (1994), he refutes Descartes' characterization of the human mind as separate and independent of the body, while in *Looking for Spinoza* (2003), he identifies Benedict Spinoza as an important pioneer of neurobiology of the affects. This allows us to study the role of the seventeenth century as a meaningful source for contemporary issues. Secondly, in the wake of the steady reorientation of many departments within the humanities, due to significant findings in disciplines such as neurobiology or the philosophy of the mind, our way of approaching literature has shifted. Discussion groups entitled 'Cognitive Approaches to Literature' flourish all over the United States.

While I focus primarily on seventeenth-century France, the course engages with other fields of the humanities, the arts, cultural studies and, outside the humanities, with early modern medical treatises, as well as with recent neurobiological discourse on the mind/body relationship. I have two goals in this class. Firstly, I want students to study seventeenth-century perspectives on the body/mind relation in terms of the history of thought. I also want them to understand the implicit *dialogue* taking place specifically between the seventeenth and twenty-first centuries through neurobiologists like Damasio or Daniel Dennett who specifically engage with Descartes and his contemporaries and who focus either on the 'error' of early modern voices or on their tremendous insight into the holistic relationship between body and mind. Of course, such an approach should not become anachronistic but only underscore the foundation of early modern views and reveal the impact these views still have on contemporary thinkers. A study of early modern texts can, for example, contribute to a broader understanding of the development of medical thought from the seventeenth century to the twenty-first century and reveal how medical practice and the knowledge attached to it have grown and developed. Difference and similarities in the medical knowledge of the two periods concerned can foster in our humanities students an awareness of the development of a humane medical practice and encourage them to pay careful attention to issues that are still at stake. Above all, the mind/body question is still with us. Students become sensitive to the fact that the same issues remain – namely, how to define the relationship of the mind to the body, how to describe consciousness adequately – and they study the seventeenth century as the beginning of modernity's investigations into mind and body. Secondly, I want to introduce them to early modern canonical texts, together with non-canonical ones, based on the literary curricula within many French programmes that strive to grant familiarity with some of the classics as well as some exposure to the different periods of French literature. Cross-disciplinary teaching can include canonical texts in the syllabus in accordance with the requirements of upper-level courses within a department of French literature.[4] Students read three key literary texts in French in my course: Molière's *Le Malade imaginaire*, Lafayette's *La Princesse de Clèves* and Racine's *Phèdre*, as well as excerpts from Pascal, Descartes and other lesser-known writers.[5] Students read excerpts dealing with contemporary mind/body medicine in English.

According to Raymond Wlodkowski, 'perceived relevance' plays an important role in the students' motivation to learn.[6] In choosing a topic and texts that seem accessible and pertinent to them and that meet the linguistic challenges in the foreign-language curriculum, the key goal is to foster motivation, active commitment to learning and an increased ability to think critically through a comparative viewpoint. Engaging students in this way not only helps them to develop their observational and analytical skills, but also increases their attention, as the content of the course deals with topics that still matter nowadays and that concern the general human condition. Far from being 'foreign', 'strange', 'old', boring and even 'unrelated' to their existence, we can engage in a comprehensive and interdisciplinary approach to teaching the early modern period that shows how seventeenth-century perspectives concerning the mind/body interdependence provide an insight into the question of the self that still matters, as thinkers study the nature of emotions, of the senses, of 'chemical' imbalances (through humoral theories) as important agents of the correlation between body and mind, and the role the body adopts in creating consciousness.

When we are used to teaching literature and culture, such a cross-disciplinary approach might at first seem beyond our comfort zone, bringing us outside our own research areas into primarily literary and cultural texts. The challenge of interdisciplinary teaching is certainly that this kind of course necessitates extensive preparation and research in areas that are unfamiliar to us, and can provoke the apprehension that our students may be more 'knowledgeable' than us in disciplines outside our own. It requires what Lisa Lattuca refers to as 'intellectual humility'.[7] The fundamental intellectual challenge of interdisciplinary courses is summed up by Jean Schwind:

> Interdisciplinarity is difficult for most faculty because of the disciplinary specialization that characterizes graduate education and the epistemological differences that training reinforce. [...] Interdisciplinary teaching and research require that we recognize the limitations of a particular disciplinary perspective in addressing complex questions or problems. It demands that we trespass in fields that we'll never master and borrow methods and concepts that we'll never use with complete confidence.[8]

There is a certain degree of anxiety involved on our part when facilitating the students' encounter with different approaches, terminologies and perspectives outside our specialization areas.[9] Another potential risk could be that we engage in too many things at the same time, while losing the primary focus of a conventional course.[10]

Yet making early modern literature and culture *matter* to our students requires more than an introduction to the period. Students enjoy incorporating their knowledge from other fields, within and outside the humanities, into the French-literature classroom. By 'allowing for comparisons between past and present', we create an engaged classroom in which students actively incorporate their individual interests and strengths. Crossing disciplines fulfils an important condition for active engagement in learning, since each student can bring a different intellectual skill set to class to share with their peers.[11] We may thus make the learning experience meaningful to those also who might not otherwise have explored it. Breaking down existing disciplinary boundaries can also create a learning environment where viable exchanges between students, staff and departments can take place.[12] Ultimately, interdisciplinary teaching and learning have been shown to contribute to the development of key cognitive skills:[13] intellectual synthesis, contextual understanding, critical thinking, capacity for creativity and problem solving, receptivity to new ideas, tolerance of ambiguity, ability to switch perspectives and willingness to challenge assumptions.[14] Last but not least, interdisciplinarity opens up new possibilities for 'learner-centred teaching', a term used by Maryellen Weimer to advocate changes in instruction. A classroom is learner-centred when the balance of power, the responsibility of power, and the purposes and processes of evaluation are shared between instructor and students. Cross-disciplinary courses leave room for collaborative assignments based on the students' interests (students may choose which contemporary aspects of the mind/body debate they wish to focus on), and increased power sharing (with students incorporating their knowledge from other disciplines). According to Weimer, such pedagogy promotes student independence and growth.[15]

To encourage students to become actively involved in understanding and identifying the seventeenth-century investigation into the nature and relationship between mind and body, I organize my course into three units: the first focuses on philosophical conceptions of mind and body in the seventeenth century; the second on melancholy as a key illness that illustrates the mind/body interdependence; and the third on mind/body disorders featured in Lafayette, Molière and Racine's works. The three literary authors identify, construct and substantiate holistic views of the union of body and mind, which make them central thinkers in the history of medicine and philosophy of how to define the self. These authors all subscribe to the inseparability of body and mind. They critically engage with the Cartesian mind/body binary. These explorations of the causes and manifestations of disorders are placed within the context of philosophical, medical and ethical preoccupations about the human constitution and the notion of the 'I'.

The conception of mind/body interaction in the seventeenth century

This course starts by outlining fundamental questions and defining key terms: what is monism? What is dualism? What is the self? How do we understand the mind/body interaction? Excerpts from philosophical and scientific texts serve as an introduction to the topic, as contemporary scholars as well as neurobiologists alike refer back to Descartes, as the starting point of dualism in modernity and as an important contributor to the history of mind/body medicine, as a 'symbol of modern errors'.[16] Students may Google the term 'mind/body problem', investigate the areas and disciplines that are associated with it, and explore the shift from dualism to monism in medical and philosophical thinking. I then introduce them to the starting point of dualism in the 'modern' era[17] through selected passages taken from Descartes' *Meditations* (1641), his

Passions of the Soul (1649) and from his correspondence with the princess of Bohemia, Elizabeth, who launched a thorough critique of the ontological distinction between substances, and probed mind/body interaction as he described it, or rather, failed to describe it. Our discussion centres on his most influential legacy – the so-called 'mind/body problem'. He defines mind and body in such a way that they have no common properties. According to his proposal, the immaterial (rational) mind is entirely distinct from the material body, and the latter does not have the capacity to affirm its existence. The body, a principle of motion, is by its very nature a natural automaton comparable to 'clocks, artificial fountains, mills and other similar machines which, being made by men, nevertheless have the power to move on their own'.[18] Descartes considers the body a free-standing mechanism operating entirely *apart* from the mind but devoid of any self-reflective capacity.

For Descartes, this separation operates only theoretically and he provides an articulation of the interaction between mind and body. The body may affect the mind through the passions. In our reading of *The Passions of the Soul*, we consider how his theory of the six principal passions (wonder, love, hatred, sadness, happiness, desire and joy) conceives of a connection between the two properties. His main thesis is that passions originate in the body and dispose the mind to will an action. Yet, passions are necessarily regulated through the intervention of the will. In addition, for Descartes the body adopts a secondary role in the acquisition of self-knowledge. I point out to students how many of his contemporaries already thought that his theory of the mind/body interaction remained unsatisfying, above all Elizabeth of Bohemia – as is clear from her correspondence with Descartes – and Spinoza. For the Dutch thinker, the body is crucial for the functioning of the human mind. Students discover another seventeenth-century philosopher who conceived of a union of body and mind. In the *Ethics*, Spinoza proposes that mind and body are the manifestations of the same property and that 'the human mind is the idea itself or the knowledge of the human body'.[19]

To give my students a fuller picture of Descartes we set in opposition those thinkers who underscore Descartes' dualistic legacy and a number of current scholars who invite us to rethink Descartes as a non-dualistic thinker. Erec Koch's study on corporeality in the seventeenth century focuses on the central role Descartes grants to corporeal sensibility and argues that 'the body becomes the source and site of passion and sensation, which the mind receives'.[20] There has been a powerful tendency recently to re-evaluate Descartes' findings. Students of this class also learn to perceive critically the agendas of contemporary neurobiologists who often limit themselves to one-sided arguments of Descartes' inter-actionist theory (for example by focusing on the pineal gland as *the* connection point), who counteract the French philosopher's metaphysics with an exuberant materialism, or who repeatedly debunk his results but fail to consider how Descartes initiated a set of key questions about the self in the modern era.

In the context of the opposition between Descartes and Spinoza, students discover the dialogue specifically between the seventeenth and twenty-first centuries. I invite students to explore the affinities between seventeenth-century conceptions of mind/body union and the contem-porary insights of a unified mind and body, and to take into consideration the adequacy of early modern holistic endeavours that showed how the mind arises from the mechanisms of the body. We read excerpts from Damasio's *Descartes' Error* and *Looking for Spinoza*, works that already in their titles point to the contemporary appeal of seventeenth-century thinkers.[21] We examine how neurobiologists crown Spinoza as one of the fathers of current theories because, a pioneer in his time, he discovered that the I's self-understanding is not at all based in our rational thought but rather in the concrete and moment-by-moment experience of the body. Indeed, according to Spinoza's most radical and anti-Cartesian thesis, if there is no body, there is no longer mind. Damasio establishes a new framework for understanding the interdependence of body and mind through an exploration of the role of the emotions and feelings as manifestations of the body/mind interplay, the influence of joy and sorrow on the body-proper and the disruption of our organism by stress, anguish and suffering. Efforts to redefine how body and mind mimic each other in correlated processes reveal theoretical implications of seventeenth-century ideas that have not yet been fully digested or established.[22]

The course then turns to Pascal as a third important and representative philosopher of the era, and to an analysis of passages taken from the *Pensées* (1669). Here, like Descartes, he makes use of the theory of two different substances, explaining that: 'Our soul is cast into the body, where it finds number, time, dimensions' and that 'we are automaton as much as we are mind'.[23] Like Descartes, Pascal also gives preference to the mind as a tool of cognition: 'All our dignity therefore consists of thought. It is by thought that we must right ourselves, and not by space and time, which we could not fill.'[24] We examine, however, how for Pascal, differentiation becomes the basis of a *moral* philosophy and not, as for Descartes, the foundation of a philosophical and scientific epistemology, and analyse how he creates additional binary divisions, between God's grandeur and man's bereft state, between divine purity and human sin, between the pure love of God and concupiscence. We can then investigate how present-day mind/body medicine also places illness in a *moral* context and advocates self-study and self-help. Trends within alternative medicine define the belief in 'the power of positive thinking' and advocate 'laughter treatments' as possible means of patient empowerment.[25]

Melancholy: an illness of mind and body in the seventeenth century

In the second part of this course, we turn to an examination of melancholy as a key illness in the seventeenth century that illustrates the interdependence between body and mind. Medical doctors and thinkers all over Europe, among them Timothy Bright and Robert Burton – the latter having studied medicine (England) – and André du Laurens and Jacques Ferrand (France), took an interest in the ongoing debate about the relation between mind and body and used their own observations of the pathology of melancholy to examine that connection. In these reflections, there is 'a framework in which medicine and the science of the soul, physics and ethics [...] communicate'.[26] At the same time, I encourage students to recognize that most of these medical doctors adopted an exclusively *monist* perspective. In order to expand the way that students think about melancholy as a pathological illness in the early modern period, I expose them to a variety of media, including music, the visual arts and film. The exhibition catalogue on *Mélancolie, génie et folie en Occident* that was organized at the Grand Palais in Paris in 2005 allows students to study iconographical and cultural readings of the history of the mind–body relationship. We outline two perspectives: on the one hand, melancholy as a pathological manifestation that troubles man's reason and that entails mental and physiological symptoms; on the other hand, melancholy as a manifestation of genius. Through presentations, in-class group work and discussion, as well as short papers, students study distinctive characteristics of melancholy: the role of the humours, in particular black bile, the perturbation of reason, the role of the passions (what neurobiologists now call the 'affects') and the imagination, the interdependence of physiological and mental troubles, and love melancholy or erotic melancholy.

I introduce students to the visual arts from the Middle Ages onwards. Here they examine, within the context of the history of medicine and the history of ideas, firstly, the notion of *acedia* (as represented, for example, in Jérôme Bosch's *La Tentation de Saint-Antoine* and Déodato di Orlando's *Saint Jean*); secondly, the idea of four temperaments (through an analysis of etchings by Johan Reinhard); thirdly, Dürer's famous engraving (*Melencolia* I) that combines the idea of melancholy as a manifestation of genius and as a pathological ailment; fourthly, alchemic conceptions of melancholy (as represented, for example, in Wolfgang Kilian, Emblem 4 in M. Geiger, *Microcosmus*); fifthly, the link between melancholy and vanity (as in, for example, Bruegel de Velours' *La Vue*); sixthly, sadness as one of the principal manifestations of melancholy in medieval and Renaissance iconography; and finally, the relation between melancholy and death (as in Georges de la Tour's *La Madeleine à la vieillesse* and Ferdinand Bol's *Le Vieux Savant*). In addition to art, I lead students to consider the links between melancholy and music, both in terms of music as an envisioned cure for melancholy (analysing, for example, Elizabethan music, Bernardo Cavallino's *David jouant devant Saül* and Giovanni Francesco Barbieri's *Le Roi David*),[27] and through an analysis of profoundly melancholic music, such as the works of Saint Colombe and Marin Marais popularized in Alain Corneau's film *Tous les matins du monde* (1991).[28]

Finally, it is important for students to be familiar with the cultural contexts of absolutism, which decried and condemned melancholy. On the one hand, it was associated with the political unrest that found its heyday during the *Ligue* years. On the other hand, melancholy contrasted with the social doctrine of *honnêteté* that prescribed a vigilant self-monitoring of the courtly subject through the use of judgement, understanding, virtue and reason. Illness and death were not tolerated at court and the melancholic was shunned as an outsider. Students may read excerpts from Nicolas Faret's *L'Honneste Homme ou L'Art de plaire à la court* (1630), which describes the new social etiquette that took root in seventeenth-century France. They learn how the courtly subject was expected to practise self-restraint, 'train' his/her body, desires and humours, and follow the demand for moderation and firm judgement, qualities that made the courtier what was called an *honnête homme*. We then study literary voices who undermined the repression of the body, as encountered in dualist philosophy, and who expressed the unresolved tensions between the subject and oppressive socio-political doctrines of that time.

Literary perspectives

Descartes' thesis was also under severe attack in the literary tradition of his times. The seventeenth century marks an important era in which major authors began to question the dominant dualistic conception of their time. The third section of the course focuses on three literary writers who rejected the mind/body dichotomy, its insistence on the primacy of reason, its conviction that autonomous will may successfully subdue and control corporeal function, and the Cartesian disjunction that placed consciousness and affect, thought and feelings, internal experience and external experience in opposition. Molière (1622–73), Lafayette (1634–93) and Racine (1639–99) did not separate internal reality and external space as Descartes did, but perceived the experience of interiority as one in which 'I think' proceeds from 'I feel in my body.' These authors reveal the detrimental consequences of the 'training' of the body, the desires and the passions, through mind/body illness. Illness becomes an 'idiom of distress'[29] that exposes the harmful nature of physiological repression and debunks dualistic perceptions.

In *Le Malade imaginaire*, students notice immediately that the character's hypochondriac melancholy has no marked physical manifestations. The protagonist is ill only in his own mind, in his imagination. Class discussions focus on two principal questions: firstly, the origin of his illness (as Molière visibly detaches himself from humoral theories of melancholy); and secondly, the role of the senses and the imagination, that is, how the imagination brings about the hypochondriac Argan's *real* sensation of *having* a body and of *feeling* it. Students do some basic research into the ambivalent role of the imagination in the seventeenth century: it is linked to delirium and perturbation, but it is also a faculty that can bring about knowledge. Excerpts from John Lyons' book *Before Imagination* could be read to help them understand 'why imagination, as the form of thought that mediates between the body and the intellect, was central and crucial to themes that [were] widely recognized as typical of this period [...]: concealment, disguise, sociability, interiority, and morality'.[30]

They look up current definitions of hypochondria on the Internet and find out that it is considered a psychosomatic disorder. We ask whether in Molière's play this illness is conceived of as a malady of mind and/or body. The answer is based on the study of the role of the imagination in the play. In practice, hypochondria may be related to an overwrought imagination. Yet Molière stresses that the disorder is real, unsettling, even disabling and that the imagination has to be taken seriously as an indicator with real significance, because the patient truly feels ill. The imaginative faculty becomes an important point of connection between body and mind, and it has the capacity to give expression to real anxiety disorders in the play. Through twentieth-century psychoanalytic thought, we can underscore what Molière had already grasped: the link between the hypochondriac's *real* suffering and the imagination, not as a depraved faculty, but as an important connection between mind and body with real content.[31] Through the comic hero's melancholy, the playwright explores how the imaginative faculty can externalize or expel repressed anxiety and how it translates inner distress into a concrete body image.

Lafayette, the second author examined, also conceives of illness as an idiom of distress and debunks the dualistic philosophical and socio-political contexts of her time that elevate the rational and impose corporeal repression. Throughout our reading of *The Princesse of Clèves*, students note that the illnesses of the various characters remain unexplained but are often violent and deadly. They either bring about the death of the character or, if the character survives, lead to withdrawal from mundane life as a form of 'mental' death. Surreptitiously, Lafayette gives us crucial indications for understanding the illnesses and alerts us to the strong link between internal disorder and somatic manifestations of it. Once more, we are confronted with a psychosomatic disorder in which violent fevers and physical illness refer to unresolved inner distress. Lafayette shows us how the mind *can* affect physical disease, situates illness within the cultural and political context of patriarchal regimes, and reveals how the lack of self-determination leads to psychosomatic suffering as a direct result of such 'repression' of the passions.

In Lafayette's fiction, the body also acquires a certain intelligence and a profound intimacy, since it modulates the triggers of the emotions. The body, in other words, is a fundamental principle that records and articulates the emotions. The concordance between Lafayette's ideas and neurobiological research today lies in the conception of a chronological *sequence* running from bodily signals to deliberate mental reaction. The neurobiologist Joseph LeDoux calls that sequence 'the emotional procession' from stimuli to physical and psychic responses. As he puts it:

> First, emotional reactions occur. These overt bodily responses and associated changes in internal body physiology are the advance guard of emotional responsivity. Subsequently [...] a feeling emerges as we become aware that our brain has determined that something important is present and we are reacting to it.[32]

That sequence is central in Lafayette's works when the princess first falls in love with Nemours and the body reveals the growing passion *before* the mind has even grasped it. Students examine how, in the novel, the body maps and transmits the passion before the mind captures it: the 'I feel' precedes the 'I think.'

Finally, the class turns to *Phèdre* to discuss the seventeenth-century conception of love melancholy through the protagonist. A brief staging of Phèdre's appearance on stage can help students to work through the linguistic difficulties caused by the alexandrine and the mythological allusions in the play, and to recognize the physical and mental oppression portrayed via the languishing body. Students become aware of the interplay of mind and body, which is more than just a humoral imbalance and which also does not arise from the Cartesian body-machine.[33] Discussions focus on understanding the passions as an integrated process that unifies body and mind, and on exposing the socio-political conflict underlying the character's illness, since melancholy can be psychodynamic, embedded in the context of absolutism. Above all, Racine demonstrates the interplay and union between physiological and mental processes. The notion of 'I' is grounded in the body and the body expresses the passions. This idea of exact correspondence is also central to current trends within neurobiology. Neuroscientific research sheds light on the central role of the body, which transmits to the mind adequate and verified information about the current state of the organism, allowing the brain to react effectively, and scientists study how feelings are produced through a representation of the body in the brain.[34]

Phèdre has been called a hereditary tragedy in which the sins of the mother come back to haunt the daughter through the vengeance of a 'cruel god': Venus. Racine presents us with a pathology that is transmitted from one generation to the next. Illness *pre-exists* in Phèdre's lineage but is transmitted from *within*: through the blood. Scholars have understood this blood disorder metaphorically, linked to the present/absent gods who impose Phèdre's monstrous desire but watch her silently. To elaborate on this idea, we can understand illness in terms of an archaeological mythology of heredity: 'illness' constitutes the centre of hereditary transmission. We can examine how in addition to a religious preoccupation with the transmission of sin, there is in Racine's play a question of heritage, treated from a mythological angle that places illness at its centre. Another option is to interpret Phèdre's references to blood in biological terms. The importance of blood in the play allows us to read Phèdre's illness within the context of two theories that co-existed in the seventeenth century: the biological understanding of melancholy as stemming from a transformation of blood; and the belief (a precursor to an understanding of 'genetics') in the perversion of blood as a hereditary mark transmitted at birth. Blood was a prominent element in theories of melancholy in Racine's time. Timothy Bright postulated that a change in temperature and an alteration in the melancholic humour could bring about changes in the patient. In addition, the biological view that illness is produced from *within* can be found in seventeenth-century medical theories. In Racine's tragedy, blood, the heart and illness are all evoked in relation to one another. While Racine does not describe the circulatory system directly, he alludes to it through the role that blood plays in causing physical changes.

Alternatively, students interested in cultural and sociological studies can investigate illness as the result of a profound rift or internal division within the subject between desire and the law. What we see in Racine's play is a conflict between forces that appear antagonistic because they cannot be harmoniously united. The portrayal of Phèdre's and Hippolyte's unresolved conflicts can be used to invite the students to think about governmental zones of operation and the fear of alterity in patriarchal regimes. Students can debate how mind/body illness in Racine can be interpreted – to a great extent – as a socially constructed malady and whether tragedy can unveil the anxiety and actions that shaped its course. Although *hamartia* (the tragic flaw) plays a role in Phèdre's and Hippolyte's suffering and death, it is not simply an error in judgment that shapes the protagonists' illnesses. Rather, there remains an unmistakable link between emotional stress and the cultural codes of conduct. In depicting the scotomizing crisis of his characters, Racine, according to one interpretation, highlights the 'internal opacity, [...] anxiety of being, exhausting confusion, and sense of being lost' within patriarchal society in the seventeenth century.[35]

Scholars and teachers face the challenge of constructing courses that increase student motivation and engagement with the early modern period. One way to do so is to pose challenging problems that still seem relevant to us. The mind/body problem, which within modernity is associated with Descartes and which gives rise to various voices and positions, is still a core issue that has no universally accepted solution. Literary texts and scientific investigations alike grapple with how to describe the mental experiences that arise in the brain. This dramatic topic is not solely central in the sciences but is addressed in literary texts as well. The investigation into the relationship between the physical and the mental within literature and science highlights the continuity and interdependence of this question. According to Lilian Furst, students reflect on the fact that literary texts are influenced by the context of their environments.[36] It is precisely by studying the extent to which literature is determined by social, cultural and political factors that we can understand the characters as 'real' 'through our constructive acts of reading', and realize that these characters exemplify 'a common fate under the circumstances of that particular time and place'.[37] Students discover 'another' seventeenth century, which formulated sophisticated conceptions about how the mind is constructed through feelings, imagination, sensations and physiological changes that transcended dualistic thinking. The core concepts voiced in the early modern period can be seen once more in corresponding contemporary beliefs, practices and notions, such as yoga, meditation or holistic medicine, and scientific approaches, including neurobiology of the affects and the philosophy of the mind. At the same time, we approach seventeenth-century texts in a way that offers us a fruitful reorientation of the way we study the early modern period. As Julie Thompson Klein points out, complex questions can 'demand' interdisciplinary perspectives, whose objectives are to answer these complex problems and achieve unity of knowledge.[38] Students in my course gain an appreciation of the truly 'international' scope of the investigation into the relation between mind and body throughout seventeenth-century Europe, a preoccupation that has gained ground in Western medicine and philosophy ever since. Relating the early modern period to current perspectives, approaches and problems, while drawing on a cross-cultural environment, provides students with the opportunity to engage in complex tasks, to integrate different insights and to construct knowledge between disciplines. I have found that students engage deeply with seventeenth-century French literature through this approach and that it has fostered an interest in literature in many students. It allows them to see that literature draws on distinct environments, that it helps not only to shape aesthetic discourses, but also cultural, scientific and philosophical preoccupations, and that the Cartesian attempt to solve the mind/body problem still stubbornly resists – at least partly – our current efforts.

Notes

1. Interdisciplinary teaching and learning can also refer to the team-teaching of connected or separate courses. Based on a thematic unit, several instructors teach a cluster of courses exclusively in their area of expertise, within one integrated course, or pool together their knowledge in linked courses. In this essay, I will deal with the case of a single instructor who teaches a course on early modern literature but who incorporates elements of other disciplines into the syllabus, among them cultural studies, philosophy, the visual arts, neurobiology and the history of medicine.

2. Antonio Damasio, 'How the Brain Creates the Mind', *Scientific American*, 281 (1999), 112–17 (p. 112).
3. *Ibid.*
4. At the Ohio State University we offer topic-based courses that include key literary texts and that adopt a clear interdisciplinary focus, which tends to be primarily historical, theoretical or generic.
5. Course material could include (in excerpts or full text), but is not limited to, Timothy Bright, *A Treatise of Melancholy* (London: William Stansby, 1613); Robert Burton, *The Anatomy of Melancholy*, ed. T.C. Faulkner, N.K. Kiessling and R.L. Blair, introduction and commentary by J.B. Bamborough and M. Dodsworth, 6 vols (Oxford: Clarendon Press, 1989–2000); René Descartes, *Méditations métaphysiques*, ed. Jean-Marie Beyssade and Michelle Beyssade (Paris: Flammarion, 1979); *Œuvres et lettres*, ed. André Bridoux (Paris: Gallimard, 1978); *Les Passions de l'âme*, ed. Pascale d'Arcy (Paris: Flammarion, 1996); André Du Laurens, *Discours de la conservation de la veue, des maladies mélancholiques, des catarrhes et de la vieillesse* (n.p.: Théodore Samson, 1598); Nicolas Faret, *L'Honneste Homme ou L'art de plaire à la court* (Paris: Du Bray, 1630); Jacques Ferrand, *De la maladie d'amour ou melancholie erotique. Discours curieux qui enseigne a cognoistre l'essence, les causes, les signes, & les remedes de ce mal fantastique* (Paris: Denis Moreau, 1623); Marie-Madeleine Pioche de La Vergne Lafayette, *La Princesse de Clèves et autres romans*, ed. Bernard Pingaud (Paris: Gallimard, 1972); Molière [Jean-Baptiste Poquelin], *Le Malade imaginaire*, ed. Georges Couton (Paris: Gallimard, 1999); Blaise Pascal, *Pensées*, ed. Dominique Descotes (Paris: Flammarion, 1976); Jean Racine, *Phèdre*, in *Théâtre complet*, ed. Jacques Morel and Alain Viala (Paris: Gallimard, 1982); Benedict Spinoza, *Ethics*, ed. James Gotmann, trans. William Hale White and Amelia Hutchinson (New York: Hafner, 1949).
6. Raymond J. Wlodkowski, *Enhancing Adult Motivation to Learn: A Comprehensive Guide for Teaching All Adults*, rev. 2nd edn (San Francisco: Jossey-Bass, 1999), pp. 118–20.
7. Lisa R. Lattuca, *Creating Interdisciplinarity: Interdisciplinary Research and Teaching Among College and University Faculty* (Nashville: Vanderbilt University Press, 2001), p. 159.
8. See Jean Schwind, 'Interdisciplinary Learning and Academic Challenge', Center for the Advancement of Teaching and Learning, Elon University, http://org.elon.edu/catl/documents/ID%20and%20challenge.pdf [accessed 17 August 2009].
9. In addition, Julie Thompson Klein draws attention to the fact that interdisciplinary team-teaching is difficult for faculty who are unused to sharing classroom authority. For more information, see her *Interdisciplinarity: History, Theory, and Practice* (Detroit: Wayne State University Press, 1990), p. 78.
10. A number of studies have attempted to determine the benefits and short-comings of interdisciplinary teaching and learning. At first glance, according to Klein, lines between disciplines are blurred and deconstructed which can seem confusing and unfamiliar to students, as they start wondering which discipline they are learning (*Crossing Boundaries: Knowledge, Disciplinarities, and Interdisciplinarities* (Charlottesville: University Press of Virginia, 1996), pp. 24–5). See also Lattuca, *Creating Interdisciplinarity*, p. 251). Jacqueline Anglin states that 'integrating curriculum correctly requires more than

combining two subjects, or turn teaching'. She points out that an integrated course needs to have a bigger design than just integration for the sake of integration. (See 'Develop your own Philosophy', *New Teacher Advocate*, 7.1 (1999), p. 3.) In addition, critics maintain that the lack of systemization and order is a crucial problem of interdisciplinarity, which often falls short of coherence. (See K.C. Barton and L.A. Smith, 'Themes or Motifs? Aiming for Coherence through Interdisciplinary Outlines', *The Reading Teacher*, 54.1 (2000), pp. 54–63). Above all, critics debunk interdisciplinary learning as 'broad studies' that promote a superficial coverage of the material discussed.

Advocates of interdisciplinarity, on the other hand, focus on the positive learning outcomes: it 'aims at helping students make relevant connections, gain deep understandings, generate meaningful transferences, and apply knowledge, skills, and experiences in contextual and practical settings' (Weijun Chen, 'Interdisciplinary Teaching: Integration of Physical Education Skills and Concepts with Mathematical Skills and Concepts', in *Perspectives on Teaching and Learning*, ed. Linda B. Yurichenko (New York: Nova Science Publishers, 2007), pp. 101–20 (p. 102)). It is rooted in constructivism: it views 'learners as active and constructive meaning makers' (p. 102).

11. This can be done in the form of group projects, oral presentations and research projects that empower students to find the information, and integrate and synthesize disciplinary perspectives, thus fostering more active engagement.

12. On this question, see Julie Thompson Klein's *Humanities, Culture, and Interdisciplinarity: The Changing American Academy* (Albany: SUNY Press, 2005).

13. For interdisciplinarity's important cognitive outcomes and positive learning experiences, see Alexander Astin, *What Matters in College: Four Critical Years Revisited* (San Francisco: Jossey Bass, 1992), pp. 186–228 and 423; and Ernest T. Pascarella and Patrick T. Terenzini, *How College Affects Students*, 2 vols (San Francisco: Jossey Bass, 1991 and 2005), II, pp. 177–8, 207 and 647. Astin discusses the relationship between cognitive development and courses emphasizing interdisciplinary approaches in his study.

14. See William Newell, 'Professionalizing Interdisciplinarity', in *Interdisciplinarity: Essays from the Literature*, ed. William Newell (New York: College Board, 1998), pp. 529–63 (p. 538). Interdisciplinarity helps students to 'move developmentally from a clear understanding of the differences between disciplines and their perspectives on a problem to distinguishing the essential characteristics of disciplines – to understanding their discrete domains of usefulness, what kinds of questions they ask, and their rules of evidence'. See also L. Baloche, J.L. Hynes and H.A. Berger, 'Moving Toward the Integration of Professional and General Education', *Action in Teacher Education*, 18 (1996), 1–9 (p. 3).

15. Maryellen Weimer, *Learner-Centered Teaching: Five Key Changes to Practice* (San Francisco: Jossey-Bass, 2002), p. 49. See also *Innovations in Interdisciplinary Teaching*, ed. Carolyn Haynes (Westport, CT: American Council on Education/ The Oryx Press, 2002), p. xvi. For Haynes, interdisciplinary pedagogy is about facilitating student development and requires the promotion of students' interpersonal and intrapersonal learning in order to foster a 'holistic' process of development.

16. Anne Harrington, *The Cure Within: A History of Mind-Body Medicine* (New York: Norton, 2008), p. 21. Neurobiologists mostly leave out earlier considerations of mind/body dualism and fail to refer to Plato, Plutarch or the Stoics as proponents of binary thinking long before Descartes.

17. References to earlier ways of dualistic thinking in Plato, Plutarch or the Stoics could be included also and would allow to help create a bigger picture for students.

18. 'Des horloges, des fontaines artificielles, des moulins et autres semblables machines, qui n'étant faites que par des hommes, ne laissent pas d'avoir la force de se mouvoir d'elles-mêmes.' René Descartes, *Le Monde, l'homme*, ed. Annie Bitbol-Hespériès and Jean-Pierre Verdet, intro. Annie Bitbol-Hespériès (Paris: Seuil, 1996), p. 199. (My translation.)

19. Spinoza, *Ethics*, p. 99.

20. Erec Koch, *The Aesthetic Body: Passion, Sensibility, and Corporeality in Seventeenth-Century France* (Newark: University of Delaware Press, 2008), p. 14.

21. Antonio Damasio, *Descartes' Error: Emotion, Reason, and the Human Brain* (New York: Putnam, 1994) and *Looking for Spinoza: Joy, Sorrow, and the Feeling Brain* (Orlando: Harcourt, 2003).

22. See Damasio, *Looking for Spinoza*, p. 217.

23. 'Notre âme est jetée dans le corps, où elle trouve nombre, temps, dimensions'; 'nous sommes automate autant qu'esprit'. Pascal, *Pensées*, L 233–418 and L 252–82. (My translation.)

24. 'Toute notre dignité consiste donc en la pensée. C'est de là qu'il faut nous relever et non de l'espace et de la durée, que nous ne saurions remplir.' *Ibid.*, L 347–200.

25. See Harrington, *The Cure Within*, pp. 103–38.

26. '[U]n cadre où la médecine et la science de l'âme, la physique et l'éthique [...] communiquent pour le moins, si elles ne s'interprètent pas'. Patrick Dandrey, '"L'Amour est un mal: le guérir est un bien": la nature du mal d'amour au XVIIe siècle', *Littératures classiques*, 17 (1992), 275–94 (p. 278). (My translation.)

27. These examples are all taken from the exhibition catalogue *Mélancolie, génie et folie en Occident*, ed. Jean Clair (Paris: Gallimard, 2005).

28. After studying these different media, students identify and trace the variety of conceptions surrounding melancholy and the domains it affected.

29. I borrow this expression from Lilian R. Furst, *Idioms of Distress: Psychosomatic Disorders in Medical and Imaginative Literature* (Albany: SUNY Press, 2003).

30. John Lyons, *Before Imagination: Embodied Thought from Montaigne to Rousseau* (Stanford University Press, 2005), p. xiii.

31. For example, we could read excerpts from Henri Ey's *Études psychiatriques II: aspects sémiologiques* (Paris: Desclée de Brouwer, 1950) or read Sigmund Freud's 'Mourning and Melancholia', in *The Standard Edition of the Complete Psychological Works of Sigmund Freud*, ed. and trans. James Strachey, 24 vols (London: Hogarth Press and Institute of Psycho-analysis, 1953–74), XIV, pp. 237–58.

32. Joseph LeDoux, *Synaptic Self: How Our Brains Become Who We Are* (New York: Penguin, 2002), p. 206.

33. Solange Guénoun, 'Mélancolie, hystérie ou le refus classique de la division dans *Phèdre* de Racine', in *Discontinuity and Fragmentation*, ed. Freeman G. Henry (Amsterdam: Rodopi, 1994), pp. 55–66 (p. 57).

34. Damasio, *Descartes' Error*, p. 223 and *Looking for Spinoza*, p. 112.

35. '[L]'opacité intérieure, [...] l'angoisse de l'être, la confusion épuisante et le sens d'égarement'. Georges Poulet, 'Racine et la pensée indéterminée', in *Re-lectures raciniennes*, ed. Richard Barnett (Paris: PFSCL, 1986), pp. 127–31 (p. 128).

36. According to Lilian R. Furst, 'novels, short stories, and plays normally show the context of the action, the circumstances that lead to the choice of one course over another, and the motivation for behaviours. Their spatial and temporal expansiveness creates a forum for the portrayal of interpersonal relationships as they develop over a period of days, months, or often years.' See Furst, *Idioms of Distress*, p. 17.

37. *Ibid.*, p. 55.

38. Klein, *Humanities, Culture, and Interdisciplinarity*, p. 44.

16
Teaching Versailles

Henriette Goldwyn

> Dans ce palais charmant dont l'Art et la Nature
> Ont à l'envi formé l'admirable structure;
> Dans ce visible ciel, dans ce séjour des dieux,
> Que du nom de Versailles s'appelle dans ces lieux,
> S'assembla pour un roi du monde la merveille,
> L'élite d'une Cour ici-bas sans pareille.[1]

For many today, the word 'Versailles' inspires awe and wonder, symbolizing as it does a splendid palace, a monument, a memorial (*lieu de mémoire*), a museum, a masterpiece of seventeenth-century French classicism. Teaching a course on Versailles to American undergraduate students is an exciting and challenging task. It involves dispelling popular clichés while building on what students already know. In the imagination of most of my young American students, Versailles is first and foremost a symbol of 'early modern France', a lavish monument associated vaguely with a period predating the French Revolution. For many, it brings to mind images of the Sun King: a monarch who wore wigs and high-heeled shoes, but also ruled by divine right and established a centralized political order epitomized by the magnificence of his château and the geometry of its manicured gardens. For others, it is coloured by the apocryphal tale of a young queen imported from Austria – the Marie Antoinette of Sofia Coppola's 2006 film – who had a shoe fetish and who supposedly advised hungry French peasants to 'eat cake' when they had no bread. Few students have visited Versailles, but most have seen pictures of the hall of mirrors, the garden sculptures or of statues such as Neptune rising out of one of the fountains on his chariot. They have heard of notions like 'divine right monarchy', 'absolutism' or even 'Colbertism' in their History or Political Science courses.

A course on Versailles proved to be an extraordinary opportunity for the French Department at New York University to explore uncharted territories in early modern culture by means of both canonical and non-canonical texts. For many years, 'Versailles' was taught by Guy Walton, the eminent art historian, who still delivers the introductory lecture to my course by explaining the intricacies of Le Vau's plans and designs and how they transformed a modest hunting lodge into one of the grandest and most imitated palaces in the world.[2] Since Versailles is a multifaceted space that signifies power, ceremonial, festivities, intense literary life, religious fervour and controversy, my own approach is mostly literary – focusing on original texts in French concerning life at Versailles and at court – with special emphasis on the political and religious context of the time. Selections from a variety of genres and styles provide students with invaluable insight into primary rather than secondary readings. These primary readings are chosen to underscore the complexities and nuances of a period so far removed from the twenty-first century. It goes without saying that the choice of modern editions is crucial; happily today, a number of critical editions exist whose introductions, notes and bibliographies heighten students' appreciation and provide them with the critical expertise necessary to enjoy seventeenth-century literature. In addition, I invite colleagues working on different aspects of life at Versailles (such as baroque music, dance, fashion, the art of tapestry, cooking) to give guest lectures in order to bring a novel point of view along with many visual elements to a student body with diverse interests.

This is a course open to a wide variety of students, some majors and minors in French for whom the course is required (mostly double majors with history, political science, theatre and performance studies) and some others wishing to take an elective in French and intrigued by the subject matter. Therefore my goal is to bring to life one of the richest periods in French literature, cultural and intellectual life at the court of Louis XIV. The monument becomes the magnificent setting for an extraordinary literary and historical moment that is played out in front of a multitude and reaches its apogee at the height of the reign of Louis XIV. Students are assigned to work in groups to pursue in-depth research on a topic that interests them. The research is written in French and each group presents their research to the class.

I start the course with a close reading of the play *Le Favori* by Madame de Villedieu, analysing genre, style and structure.[3] The choice of Madame de Villedieu reflects the contribution of a whole generation of female writers who influenced seventeenth-century French literary and intellectual life and contributed to the aura of the period; furthermore, she is the only female author of a vivid description (as quoted in the epigraph above) of the 1665 court festivity during which her play was performed by Molière's troupe in the gardens in front of the king and his courtiers.[4] This lively tragi-comedy sets the tone for an examination of the societal transformation underway in the first years of the reign of Louis XIV by illustrating the interplay of self-serving courtiers, such as 'the court chameleon', and the person of the king.[5] In class, we examine how strict etiquette regulates all activities and dominates the life of the sovereign and his entourage, how courtiers vie for attention and recognition from the king, how power dynamics are played out, how the power of the gaze is constructed in this society of appearances, this highly structured space, this world of coded signs. On another level, we analyse how the play can be read as the enactment of a major political intrigue of the period since the fall from grace of the minister, Moncade, is reminiscent of Nicolas Fouquet's disgrace.

The fact that *Le Favori* was performed as one of the many attractions in the gardens of Versailles during a court festivity celebrating the Queen Mother, Anne of Austria, provides an opportunity to introduce the work of André Félibien, architect and court historiographer, who describes in great detail the splendour and glory of the gardens during major royal festivities, elevating them to a work of art. In his *Relation de la fête de Versailles du 18 juillet 1668*,[6] Félibien expounds on the impact of this 'Grand Divertissement Royal' and the visual effect of the garden layout and its arrangements of parterres, terraces and waterworks lined by *bosquets*. He shows how the vision of the monarch, the creativity of André Le Notre, the garden architect, and the labour of thousands of workers sought to improve upon nature, in the development of elaborate gardens around the property. Through the lens of the different events (banquets, ballets, dramatic performances, music and fireworks) that took place during this particular festivity, which was to commemorate and celebrate Louis XIV's conquest of Franche-Comté establishing the peace of Aix-la-Chapelle, Félibien insists on the significance of royal festivities in the pursuit of pleasure and as a source of myth creation.[7] Ritual and regalia are on full display. Behind the rhetoric of representation of the king as the peace bearer and the enchanting descriptions of magnificent waterworks, exotic and intricate flower and fruit arrangements, Félibien interweaves aesthetics and politics and draws the reader's attention to the realities of numerous wars and the cost of such lavish festivities. Excellent supplements to Félibien's *Relations* are Louis XIV's showing of the gardens[8] and Mlle de Scudéry's *La Promenade de Versailles*.

There are many books both in French and in English on life at the château, on the wives and especially the mistresses of the monarch. However, one timeless and entertaining account of the theatre that Versailles was, with portraits of mistresses, courtiers and other key historical figures of the period can be found in, of course, Saint-Simon's *Mémoires*.[9] This text, the one most commonly cited by all those who work on early modern France, provides a vital insight for undergraduates into life at court. It is also a remarkable literary monument which emphasizes for students the importance of the genre of memoirs – the personal ocular testimonial – so cherished and practised by seventeenth-century authors such as Mme de Lafayette, Mlle de Montpensier, Cardinal de Retz and La Rochefoucauld, to name but a few. Even Louis XIV (with the help of court historiographers) dabbled in the genre and left *Mémoires pour l'instruction du dauphin*, a literary legacy to self-fashioning, given that he describes himself to be 'the head of a body of which [the subjects] are the limbs'.[10]

The course goes on to analyse Molière's *Tartuffe*, the first three acts of which were also performed at Versailles in 1664 and enjoyed by the king, although immediately banned. A controversial comedy, it allows students to examine early modern debates surrounding questions of religious hypocrisy and the nature of true devotion. It also provides an opportunity to analyse the key concerns in the controversy that rattled the century between playwrights and various religious groups. Molière tried to placate the authorities by modifying his play and produced three different versions. In the preface to the final and only published version, in 1669, he legitimizes the rights of the playwright and establishes Comedy as a powerful moral and pedagogical tool, referring to it as 'an ingenious poem which corrects men's flaws in an agreeable fashion'.[11] Finally, *Tartuffe* allows students to explore a particular moment considered by many historians to represent the turning point of the seventeenth century: the *Fronde*. It can be useful to examine together Tirard's *Molière* (2007) and Corbiau's *Le Roi danse* (2001) which show interesting vignettes of Tartuffe, or to assign films such as Rossellini's *La Prise de pouvoir par Louis XIV* (1966) for students to view at home.

Depending on the level of the class,[12] I like to end the course with extracts from religious polemical texts, particularly those central to the controversy between Jacques Bénigne Bossuet and Pierre Jurieu on questions of religious and political issues, freedom of conscience and the matter of 'peaceful' conversions.[13] They shed a unique light on a pivotal moment – the Revocation of the Edict of Nantes in 1685 – and introduce students to the epistolary genre used for doctrinal controversy.

Demystifying the difficulties of seventeenth-century French literature – especially original texts – through a course on Versailles has proven to be a thought-provoking journey. It has allowed even the most hesitant student to delve into ideas prominent in early modern France and see how they connect with the present, while simultaneously inspiring some of the more thoughtful students to produce some of the best undergraduate papers in the department.[14]

Notes

1.   In this charming palace whose admirable shape
       Nature and Art together vied to create;
       In this visible heaven, in this seat of gods,
       Which goes by the name of Versailles in these parts,
       For a king of the world was assembled in wondrous show
       The elite of a Court knowing no equal here below.

       Description d'une des fêtes que le Roi a faites à Versailles, in *Nouveau recueil de quelques pièces galantes faites par Mme de Villedieu autrefois Mlle Desjardins* (Paris: Jean Ribou, 1669), pp. 63–82. (Quotation translated into English by Richard Sieburth.) The entire description of the festivity written by Mme de Villedieu is available online (accessed 10 September 2010): http://theatredefemmes-ancienregime.org/IMG/pdf/Description_de_la_fete_du_Favori.pdf.
2. Guy Walton, *Louis XIV's Versailles* (University of Chicago Press, 1986).
3. In addition to a new edition of the play in *Théâtre des femmes de l'ancien régime*, ed. Aurore Evain, Perry Gethner and Henriette Goldwyn (Saint-Étienne: Publications de l'Université de Saint-Étienne, 2007), vol. II, a reading, produced by Aurore Evain, should be available on DVD in 2011.
4. See n. 1.
5. Excerpts from Norbert Elias' *The Court Society* are assigned as secondary reading in order to encourage students to scrutinize further the centralization of power and the relationship between the king and his courtiers. Further secondary readings include work by historians Joël Cornette, Jean-Christian Petitfils, Yves-Marie Bercé and Peter Burke. More recently, Stéphane Castellucio brings to life the seminal role played by the hall of mirrors throughout the century in *Les Fastes de la galerie des glaces: recueil d'articles du 'Mercure galant' (1661–1783)* (Paris: Payot, 2007).
6. André Félibien, *Relation de la fête de Versailles du 18 juillet 1668*, ed. Allen S. Weiss ([Paris]: Mercure de France, 1999).
7. See Marie-Christine Moine, *Les Fêtes à la Cour du Roi Soleil, 1653–1715* (Paris: Fernand Lanore, 2004).
8. *Louis XIV, Mémoires, suivis de Manière de montrer les jardins de Versailles*, ed. Joël Cornette (Paris: Tallandier, 2007).
9. Saint-Simon, *Mémoires I*, ed. Yves Coirault (Paris: Gallimard, coll. Folio, 1990), and *Mémoires II, suivi de Lettre anonyme au Roi et Œuvres diverses*, ed. Yves Coirault (Paris: Gallimard, coll. Folio, 1994). A useful secondary text is Emmanuel Le Roy Ladurie's *Saint-Simon ou le système de la Cour* (Paris: Fayard, 1998).

10. '[L]a tête d'un corps dont ils [ses sujets] sont les membres'. *Mémoires*, p. 45. See n. 8 for full reference.
11. '[U]n poème ingénieux qui par des leçons agréables, reprend les défauts des hommes'. Molière, *Tartuffe*, ed. Françoise Ruller-Theuret (Paris: Larousse, 2006), 'Préface', pp. 25–6.
12. I have taught a variation of this course at MA level, as well as to fourth-year undergraduates.
13. See Bossuet's *La Lettre pastorale de Monseigneur l'évêque de Meaux aux nouveaux Catholiques de son diocèse, pour les exhorter à faire leurs Pâques* (Cologne: chez Pierre Marteau, 1686), and the excellent edition of Jurieu's *Les Lettres pastorales adressées aux fidèles de France qui gémissent sous la captivité de Babylone*, ed. Robin Howells (Hildesheim: Georg Olms Verlag, 1988).
14. Two very useful resources are the CD *Joël Cornette Versailles et la Monarchie de Louis XIV* ('De vive voix', 2006) and the CD-ROM *Claude Villiers raconte Louis XIV et Versailles* (Paris: Arborescence, c. 1996). The official Château de Versailles website is also useful: http://www.chateauversailles.fr.

17
Paradoxical Creativity: Using Censorship to Develop Critical Reading and Thinking

Karolyn Waterson

Many contemporary students consider the early modern period remote or irrelevant. However, triumphs of the human spirit, whenever and wherever they thwart external pressures that would stifle critical thinking, remain perennially galvanizing and pertinent. Furthermore, as Louise M. Rosenblatt observes: 'readers, [...] especially young readers, respond most readily to literature as an embodiment of human personalities, human situations, human conflicts and achievements'.[1] Therefore, analysing creative ways to express dissident thought offers a gateway to lively and fruitful classroom discussions of early modern literature and culture. Initially captivated by the intellectual 'cloak and dagger' atmosphere of ingenious, often humorous defiance of censorship, students become eager to develop the close-reading skills needed to experience 'delight in sheer ingenuity of expression, [...] skill, difficulty-value',[2] before exploring other facets of the early modern experience. Throughout, students are buoyed by at least three optimistic premises that emerge from reviews of censorship. The first is that, wherever there are humans, some will always think critically and wish to communicate their concerns to others. The second is that, faced with censorship, some will always accept the risks of preserving what Marc Fumaroli, paraphrasing Montaigne, calls 'freedom's back room' ('une arrière boutique de liberté').[3] The third is that some critical thinkers will always succeed in winking to readers and posterity so that, like Galileo forced to deny the earth's movement, they will find ways to whisper, in a still audible aside, 'But it does move.'

Given in English or French, permutations of my ice-breaking introduction to the early modern era, via censorship, have opened graduate and undergraduate French literature classes, served as a discussion piece in faculty workshops on pedagogy and furnished the nucleus of guest lectures designed for interdisciplinary study of the early modern era.[4]

The pioneering studies of Georges Couton, Marc Fumaroli, Annabel Patterson, David Pottinger, Leo Strauss and Perez Zagorin, as well as the work of the Paris-based 'Groupe de recherches interdisciplinaires sur l'histoire du littéraire', inform my introduction to the early modern period. A synthesis of these analysts' often-convergent observations, supplemented and inflected by my own, provides the theoretical grounding for my ice-breaker's *Guides*.

In recent decades, the groundbreaking work of such scholars on the functioning and effects of censorship has done much to expand and nuance our understanding of the early modern world. Previously, many concluded that the combined powers of Church and State reduced dissident thinkers to inescapable silence or compliance with official norms. Jean-Paul Sartre's portrait of the seventeenth-century French literary scene typifies this view. In his eyes, the French classical period offers a quintessential example of 'writers' adhesion to the ideology in place' ('l'adhésion des écrivains à l'idéologie constituée'):

> In the seventeenth century, convictions are unshakable, religious ideology has twinned itself with political ideology [...] it is never from a viewpoint *external* to that of the ruling class that one makes fun of ridiculous marquises.[5]

Nonetheless, while recognizing that major figures, such as princes and parliamentarians, could not publicly challenge prevailing norms, Marc Fumaroli holds that they did not 'think any the less, for all that' ('ils n'en pensent pas moins').[6] Thus, as Leo Strauss maintains, it is 'reasonable to assume that earlier ages produced proportionately as many [... people] capable of independent thought as we find today, and that at least some [...] combined understanding with caution'.[7] Moreover, Annabel Patterson is persuaded that early modern Europe witnessed the emergence of 'a highly sophisticated system of oblique communication, of unwritten rules whereby writers could communicate with readers or audiences (among whom were the very same authorities who were responsible for state censorship) without producing a direct confrontation'.[8] As a result, literature often became 'political representation' where 'encoding' was 'accepted' as 'the deference due to political authority'.[9] Functioning within 'a joint project, a cultural bargain between writers and political leaders', and governed by 'a set of conventions [...] as to how far a writer could go in explicit address to the contentious issues of his day', literature had 'a unique role to play in mediating to the magistrates the thoughts of the governed'.[10] In this way, even texts constrained by censorship could contribute to what Marc Fumaroli calls the 'diplomatic' role of creative thought in early modern France where literature's 'vocation' frequently became:

> to bring forth [...] that humanity, that gentleness, that consideration for others that makes social life sociable [...]; to dissipate those opinions that [...] make society difficult, impossible, tragic [...]; to pull back from the brink.[11]

Once censored works were placed under a linguistic, literary and philosophical microscope, and re-examined in the light of such considerations, it became possible to uncover often overlooked but vitally important dimensions of the early modern age when the 'phenomenon of dissimulation [...] was so extensive that it was like a submerged continent in the religious, intellectual and social life of early modern Europe'.[12] What is more, this renewed and more complex perspective deepened our understanding of literature itself, for Annabel Patterson recognizes that: 'it is to censorship in part that we owe our very concept of "literature," as a kind of discourse with rules of its own'.[13]

Pedagogically, my ice-breaking introduction and its utilization in class are informed by approaches to teaching literature that view an author and an active reader as an inseparable tandem. The fundamental writer–reader partnership, whose continuous dialogue creates and recreates a text's meaning, also serves as the matrix for dynamic classroom exchanges, facilitated by instructors' judicious mediation. Thus dialogues between writers and readers are framed by a larger classroom dialogue, and all these exchanges encourage students to probe and interrogate literary works by engaging in 'intense personal activity'.[14] In this context the educator strives primarily to:

> help [students] toward a more and more controlled, more and more valid or defensible, response to the text; [...] contribute to a continuing process of growth in ability to handle responses – linguistic, emotional, intellectual – to literary texts; [help] students to learn to perform in response to a text.[15]

The title of Louise M. Rosenblatt's classic essay, *Literature as Exploration*, and the explanatory subtitle, *Teaching a Response-Centered Literature Curriculum*, given to an enigmatically entitled pedagogical study, *How Porcupines Make Love II*,[16] encapsulate the essence of this orientation. It considers 'the students' response the starting point for all growth in understanding and critical powers',[17] and it capitalizes on the pleasures of discovery and self-discovery to reinforce intellectual curiosity and sustain inquiry.[18] This 'student-and-subject-centered' approach aims to develop readers who are 'careful explorers of themselves [...] and the text'.[19] It seeks to enable students to reap the multiple benefits of what Richard D. Altick calls 'critical intelligence' and 'the philosophic habit of mind' thanks to which 'everything [one] read[s] with close attention to substance and to implication will prove to have more in it than [one] would earlier have suspected'.[20] Cultivating the ability to dissect, in sophisticated and discerning ways, 'the communication of ideas: how they are embodied in language and how [...] they are conveyed'[21] is indispensable to those who strive to become sensitive readers of censored works, where controversial ideas cannot be expressed openly. Furthermore, such a skill set enables students to profit from lifelong advantages that extend far beyond the classroom. As Altick indicates:

> Critical reading involves reading and [...] *rereading*, digging beneath the surface, attempting to find out not only what a writer is saying but also *why* he or she is saying it [...], and what further implications the message may hold. [...] Only [...] practice in criticism and analysis can train [... students] to recognize the pitfalls that await superficial, hasty readers: not only the too-easy acceptance of anything in print, but the deliberate tricks of the manipulator of language [...] Such skills will give [...] control over the material [one] read[s] and [...] may turn out to be the most valuable benefit [of] formal education. Critical reading can permanently improve the workings of [the] mind.[22]

Furthermore, studious scrutiny of the iconoclastic thinking embodied in censored works inevitably leads students to consider the merits of the opposing viewpoints that led to the imposition of censorship and motivated its evasion. Thus students are prompted to extrapolate from such historical debates on conflicting values in order to consider, develop or refine their own views thoughtfully. From the philosophical maturation brought about by 'students' clarification of the choices they participate in through literary works, the values affirmed and denied, and the light that reflection on the work and their response to it throws upon their own value systems'[23] significant benefits can accrue to society as a whole:

> the literature classroom offers something unique – the opportunity to participate directly and imaginatively in value choices, to reflect

on them within an emotionally colored context [...] to think clearly about issues that engage our emotions [...] we need to foster the growth of people who will have the inner strength and the humane values needed to face constructively [...] times of crucial decisions and awesome yet wonderful possibilities [...] teachers of literature can contribute in vital ways to these goals.[24]

In the following pages, I would like to suggest how my ice-breaker can, by appealing to students' curiosity and sense of adventure in the early stages, enable them to reap these benefits while generating broader interest in a purportedly 'dusty' period and making it come alive. The illustrative examples, drawn mainly from my areas of specialization, are primarily representative.[25] Their role is to suggest how easily colleagues can adapt this approach to teaching contexts focusing on other early modern literatures, or other disciplines such as History and Philosophy.

My initiation begins with an introduction to censorship tailored to the subject matter. Then it explores fictitious, early modern 'self-help guides' for authors and readers, which I have written. These guides explicate communicative strategies and complementary perspectives used by authors, striving to circumvent censorship safely, and readers, trying to read, as carefully and thoughtfully as possible, between and around the lines of texts that had to express controversial thinking obliquely. Lastly, hoping the dual but synergistic perspectives of courageous writers and sophisticated readers will have resonated with listeners, I reserve ample time for questions, comments, discussion and suggestions on how the guides might be expanded, modified or illustrated by examples drawn from other thinkers, disciplines, countries or periods.[26]

Although it is beyond the scope of an ice-breaker to examine censorship, which inevitably varied from period to period, and realm to realm, during the entire early modern period, my overview highlights a few of its salient features in pre-revolutionary France and provides a contextual backdrop to classical French literature.[27]

Even though state censorship was instituted in France as early as 1563, the late French Renaissance experienced a brief period of relative freedom from constraint. It also witnessed a struggle for control of censorship, and through it control of thought and investigation, that pitted Parliament, ecclesiastical bodies, the Sorbonne and the Crown against each other. As the seventeenth century advanced, and France became increasingly centralized, the Crown assumed more and more control over censorship. Although enforced, over time, with varying degrees of efficiency and consistency, this state censorship always remained ambitious in scope. Virtually all new printed material was subject, prior to publication, to its 'prophylactic' scrutiny. To be allowed to print a text, an author, printer or bookseller must submit that text to a censorial *examen*. If the text was deemed acceptable, *lettres patentes* were issued giving permission for it to be printed, providing it displayed the names of both author and printer. Moreover, the holder of such *lettres patentes* generally received a *privilège*, which granted the sole right to print, sell and distribute the text for a limited period of time. Obtaining censorial approbation thus proved doubly beneficial; not only did it permit openly printing a text, it also offered financial gain.

Subsequent to publication, conformity with the censor's requirements was also verified, and official approval sometimes revoked. By the mid-seventeenth century, state censorship had become quite effective, particularly in Paris. During the latter part of the century, book shipments to Paris from French provinces or foreign countries, as well as the activities of printers, became subject to very rigorous control. By then it was well nigh impossible to openly publish unorthodox works in Paris, although manuscript or unauthorized copies, most often anonymous or with fictitious authors and frequently published abroad by equally fictitious printers, continued to circulate clandestinely.

By the mid-eighteenth century, censorship was again in considerable flux. Prohibition was exercised both before and after publication, sometimes by more than one authority. Censorial criteria were unstable and increasingly difficult to define. In a context of evolving values, tacit or oral permission to publish was often granted, and condemned works circulated more freely. The monarchy's influence having diminished, parliamentary and ecclesiastical challenges to the State's censorial authority reappeared.[28]

Even when censorship was most clearly codified, approval or rejection of any given work was not entirely predictable. Some censors were incompetent, others highly skilled, still others venal. All had to apply, according to their lights, an *interpretatio rigorosa* or an *interpretatio benigna*.[29] While many focused primarily on ideological concerns, some appear to have been particularly attentive to aesthetic or intellectual ones. At times, some may even have consciously or unconsciously exercised the censorial equivalent of 'benevolent neglect'. Even though the Italian philosopher Vanini was denounced for sorcery and astrology and consequently burned alive in Toulouse, not all his works were censured.[30]

Censorship's impact on the authors of potentially problematic texts ranged widely. In some, it engendered cautious self-censorship. As early as 1637, the playwright Corneille resorted to self-censorship when he suppressed four lines that, though spoken during the initial performances of his *Cid*, were overly sympathetic to duelling, recently banned by royal decree.[31] During the Sun King's reign, it is noteworthy that a play hostile to absolutism, Du Ryer's *Lucrèce*, was neither reprinted nor performed. Even after La Fontaine hid behind a spurious source, the fabulist still found it necessary to cut 19 lines from one fable where they praised royal clemency ambivalently.[32]

The treatment of those who ran afoul of official norms was often severe. During the French Renaissance, Étienne Dolet, a humanist, advocate of religious tolerance and printer, of Rabelais among others, was burned at the stake for atheism and heresy. A mid-seventeenth-century poet knew a similar fate.[33] During the early Enlightenment, six years after the death of Louis XIV, Montesquieu still chose to publish his satirical *Lettres persanes* anonymously, abroad, despite the work's apparent frivolity. In 1734, 19 years after the Sun King's disappearance, Parliament condemned Voltaire's *Lettres philosophiques* as 'likely to inspire that libertinage which is most dangerous for Religion and order in civil society: [...] scandalous, contrary to Religion, good morals and the respect due Authority'. Parliament's ruling also threatened anyone printing, selling or distributing this text, in any manner whatsoever, with corporal punishment.[34] The work was seized, torn up and burned; its publisher was arrested; its author fled Paris to escape imprisonment.[35]

Whether internalized by writers or exerted by external authorities, censorship's influence was all-pervasive, witness the persistent references to it in La Bruyère's *Caractères* alone. In this masterwork, France's most prominent seventeenth-century character writer suggests that it may not be entirely by accident that 'Descartes [was] *born French* and *died in Sweden*' ('Descartes *né Français* et *mort en Suède*').[36] With understatement, La Bruyère expresses frustration at the limitations imposed on critical thinkers: 'a man born Christian and French finds himself constrained in satire' ('un homme né Chrétien et Français se trouve contraint dans la satire').[37] He recognizes that: 'One must remain silent about the high and mighty; [...] it is dangerous to speak ill of them during their lifetime' ('L'on doit se taire sur les Puissants; [...] il y a du péril à en dire du mal pendant qu'ils vivent').[38] Hence the moralist claims to satirize only 'people in general' ('les hommes en général'), although a wink to alert readers characterizes this assertion as 'this most necessary precaution [...] whose consequences one can sufficiently fathom' ('cette précaution si nécessaire [...] dont on pénètre assez les conséquences'), for it allows one to protest against 'any [...] censorship' ('protester contre [...] toute censure').[39] Such recurrent allusions make readers curious to learn if La Bruyère, despite his forethought, will dare to circumvent the constraints he chafes against.[40] They also attest to censorship's role in shaping classical French culture and offer insights into its functioning under the *ancien régime*. For instance, one character mocks platitudinous writers who insist on seeing themselves in print at all costs and simultaneously confirms that the Crown and the Church were censorship's most sensitive topics:

> Such a man suddenly and without having given it any prior thought, takes up paper and pen and says to himself, I'm going to write a book [...]. He would write readily that the Seine flows through Paris, that there are seven days in the week, or that the weather is rainy; and since this text is neither against Religion nor the State [...], the censor approves it, and it is printed.[41]

Following such a perusal of censorship, my 'self-help' guides, *On Writing around Censorship: An Author's Guide* and *On Reading around Censorship: A Reader's Guide*, bring students to the heart of the matter. Classroom presentations and discussions revolve around an analysis of the advice in the two *Guides*, each one printed in a different colour, both using fonts that evoke the early modern period.[42] The *Author's Guide* offers 15 suggestions, the *Reader's Guide*, 12. In both, the first six recommendations are co-ordinated, so that the approach advocated for readers becomes the corollary of the subterfuge, bearing the same number, suggested to authors. Throughout the review of the *Guides'* recommendations and the exploration of their interpretive implications, contextually appropriate examples illustrate significant authorial winks, nods and nudges so as to spur students to develop the analytical skills of alert and discerning readers.[43]

In the *Author's Guide*, the initial, overarching recommendation advises: 'Express yourself simultaneously in two different ways. For the general public, use an exoteric mode; for an initiated elite, sensitive to the slightest interpretative wink, nod or nudge, use an esoteric mode' (A1).[44] Consequently, the corresponding number in the *Reader's Guide* advises: 'Watch carefully for signals of an esoteric meaning and interpretative clues' (R1). After urging writers to use two communicative levels, one could add that, hopefully, the general public, for whom the author writes in an exoteric mode, will include those censors who were rather inattentive, rushed or obtuse. It is also worth pointing out that, in the esoteric mode when extreme caution is required, authors should be content to formulate a key idea in a way that is just a bit different from official wisdom, just different enough to orient readers to an iconoclastic perspective. Here, the devil will indeed remain 'in the details'.

After readers have been urged to become hypersensitive to shifts in meaning or potential gaps between the exoteric and the esoteric meaning of a work, textual case studies, such as the revealing anomalies in La Bruyère's chapter on the monarchy, illustrate the process. The first edition of his *Caractères* entitles this chapter 'On Sovereignty' ('Du Souverain'). Later editions subtly but significantly shift the focus by changing the title to 'On Sovereignty or the Republic' ('Du Souverain ou de la République'). Because no seventeenth-century French writer could discuss sovereignty without extolling the reigning monarch, La Bruyère does insert some apparent praise of Louis XIV into this chapter. However, he sprinkles his text with numerous caveats that undermine the theoretical justification for divine right absolutism. As soon as he speaks of 'a king who deserves to be king' ('un Roi qui mérite de l'être'), or adds the proviso, 'if the king is a good one' ('[un] Prince [...] s'il est bon Prince'), it becomes implicit that some monarchs are unworthy of divine sanction. Humbling asides – often expressed in interrogative, conditional or exclamatory modes – emphasize the difficulty of any ruler's task: 'How many gifts from Heaven does one need to reign well!'; 'Would I want to be King?' ('Que de dons du ciel ne faut-il pas pour bien régner!'; 'Voudrais-je régner?'). Throughout this chapter both Sovereigns and Subjects are capitalized. And because La Bruyère, unlike very many early modern writers, carefully verified all typographical detail, this unconventional symmetry deliberately elevates the status of Subjects. Another particularly revealing capital letter appears in a different chapter when La Bruyère fiercely denounces peasants' dire poverty. Almost in passing, he notes that, because peasants work outdoors, their skin is 'badly burned by the Sun' ('[ils sont] tout brûlés du Soleil'). Here the totally unexpected capitalization of 'Sun' instantly suggests to observant French contemporaries and informed modern readers the Sun King's responsibility for grinding, agrarian poverty.[45] Such deliberate idiosyncrasies signal to readers that, when La Bruyère seems to be applauding royalty, he is more likely advocating what should be, rather than adulating what actually exists.

With respect to religion, La Bruyère's provisos can also be quite telling. Since a superficially glaring statement of orthodoxy lauds all kings who banish heresy, it could be, and often is, taken to support Louis XIV's revocation of the Edict of Nantes that gave Protestants religious freedom. Nonetheless, to what was a platitude in seventeenth-century France, the moralist attaches a qualification: heresy should be banished from the realm 'if it appears there' ('s'il s'y rencontre'). He thus opens the door to an alternative interpretation of his views on Protestantism, informed by a holistic reading of the *Caractères* that bears in mind how this work defines authentic Christianity and how it criticizes late seventeenth-century French Catholicism.[46]

The second set of co-ordinated recommendations counsels authors negatively: 'Don't express dissident thinking in what you state loudly and clearly or repeat frequently' (A2).[47] Critical thinkers may have to trumpet conventional views they do not hold; they may need to put this veil over an objectionable T-shirt.[48] Logically then, the corresponding advice to readers becomes: 'Don't be too quick to accept, at face value, thoughts which authors express most often, most openly, most vigorously' (R2). An eighteenth-century English text provides a guideline for evaluating proclamations of orthodoxy as it differentiates exoteric from esoteric discourse:

> the one open and public, accommodated to popular prejudices and the Religions establish'd by Law; and the other private and secret, wherein, to the few capable and discrete, was taught the real Truth stript of all disguises [...] While liberty in its full extent is more to be wish'd than expected, and thro human weakness people will prefer their repose, fame or preferments, before speaking of Truth, there is nevertheless one observation left us, whereby to make a probable judgement of the sincerity of others in declaring their opinion. 'Tis this. When a man maintains what's commonly believ'd, or professes what's publicly injoin'd it is not always a sure rule that he speaks what he thinks: but when he seriously maintains the contrary of what's by law establish'd, and openly declares for what most others oppose, then there's a strong presumption that he utters his mind.[49]

It being dangerous to emphasize one's real thought, how can thinkers express it? The third set of recommendations complements the second by advising writers to: 'Scatter controversial ideas around, and be brief and subtle about it' (A3). Annabel Patterson finds that:

> In a work of oblique sociopolitical import any markedly topical allusions will tend to be widely scattered throughout the text, so that they appear to be random shots at local irritations, rather than a sustained and coherent attack on a government or a court.[50]

The moralist genre's fragmented discontinuity lends itself perfectly to this strategy. No censor could be expected to note every unacceptable allusion in La Rochefoucauld's 504 maxims or La Bruyère's more than 1000 characters. In his late seventeenth-century *Dictionnaire historique et critique*, Bayle usually placed his most trenchant analyses in voluminous notes or marginalia. Similarly, during the Enlightenment, the *Encyclopaedia* often inserted its most controversial commentary into the notes casual readers tend to skip. A variant of this technique submerges a few gripping sentences, which arrest the alert reader's attention and express true convictions, in long or deliberately boring texts.[51] La Bruyère delights in abruptly juxtaposing massive textual accumulations to lapidary denunciations, producing 'whiplash', 'boomerang' or 'guillotine' endings. In his chapter 'On Fashion', one character contains two grossly disproportionate paragraphs. The first devotes 27 lines and 31 infinitives to an ironic outline of 'the most wonderful effort of piety in our time' ('le plus bel effort de la dévotion du temps'). The second paragraph offers a scathing one-liner that demolishes false piety by defining a 'pious person' as 'one who, under an atheist King, would be an atheist' ('un dévot est celui qui sous un roi athée, serait athée').[52] Expecting that nonconformist thinking will tend to be dispersed, to avoid attracting attention, an esoteric audience must consequently: 'Be alert to multiple, though perhaps subtle hints pointing in the same direction. Alone none may be conclusive; together, they create a strong presumption' (R3).

The fourth pair of recommendations enjoins authors to: 'Use irony imaginatively, in as many forms as possible, and hope your contemporaries and posterity won't overlook it' (A4). Then it directs readers to: 'Tune antennae to every possible shade of irony' (R4). This advice being relatively accessible, it is possible to advance quickly to the next set of recommendations that appeals strongly to students' ludic sense. It encourages authors to: 'Be "incompetent". Use "mistakes" creatively to "let slip" dissident commentary or orient readers to alternative interpretations of surface meaning.' To this end, it identifies some particularly useful devices such as 'ambiguity, pseudonyms, weird and wonderful expressions, inaccurate summaries of what one has already said, contradictions, structural flaws, the absence of clear organizational principles' (A5).[53] In other words, write badly the better to alert readers to your intentions, remembering that, as Leo Strauss puts it:

> A careful writer of normal intelligence is more intelligent than the most intelligent censor [...] For the burden of proof rests with the

censor [...] he must show that certain literary deficiencies [...] are not due to chance, but that the author used a given ambiguous expression deliberately, or that he constructed a certain sentence badly on purpose.[54]

Examples of this strategy abound. When the Clown of Shakespeare's *Twelfth Night* is asked, 'Art not thou the Lady Olivia's fool?', he indignantly retorts, 'I am indeed not her fool, but her corruptor of words.'[55] Any professional 'corruptor of words' might easily confuse terms appropriate to humans with ones reserved for things or presumably inferior life forms. Thus his language could satirize by 'innocently' reifying victims. La Bruyère uses this technique in a comparison between ordinary people ('le peuple') and the elite ('les Grands'). Here images that incorporate dehumanizing terms related to trees reduce the high and mighty to unsavoury vegetation where 'malicious and corrupted sap hides beneath the bark of politeness'.[56]

Montesquieu's notebooks show he was pleased to be considered absent-minded, for this perception emboldened him to become purposefully 'negligent' in ways that would have caused him grief, had he not benefited from this reputation.[57] Similarly, France's great fable writer, La Fontaine, cultivates a misleading but highly visible, self-deprecating, authorial persona, implying he is merely an entertainer, magically bringing plants and animals to life before readers' wondering eyes. Using phrases like 'I don't know which one' ('je ne sais pas lequel'), or 'if memory serves' ('si j'ai bonne mémoire'), he emphasizes his inability to be precise. Once shielded by this carefully crafted reputation for ineffectiveness, he allows himself to take liberties that would put obviously competent writers at considerable risk. For example, he questions the wisdom of the Sun King's international policies. Nonetheless, he only does so after wondering if the insignificant, 'light and graceful verse' in which he takes such an audacious step is truly worthy of attention. Constantly exploiting his 'shortcomings', La Fontaine opens the second fable of his third book with a *mea culpa*: 'I should have begun my work with Royalty' ('Je devais par la Royauté / Avoir commencé mon Ouvrage'). Although prevailing norms would indeed have him do so, the fabulist never does. Instead, he draws attention to a 'slip' that immediately sets the irreverent tone of a fable where left-handed praise of royalty serves primarily as a foil for satirical depiction of aristocratic idleness. Furthermore, an analogy between kings and stomachs is required to establish some degree of royal superiority. Seventeenth-century semantics does give 'stomach' nobler connotations than 'chest'; notwithstanding, the royal digestive system still runs the risk of remaining, for many readers, just another body part.[58]

While La Fontaine's feigned modesty readily concedes that he lacks the Herculean strength required to attack vice, the supposedly 'weak' poet never stops doing so quite effectively throughout his *Fables*. The poet also makes exceptionally good use of impertinently discordant combinations that tend to 'inadvertently' reshuffle the social hierarchies to which his seventeenth-century French audience was extraordinarily sensitive. In the context of a debate about Descartes' notion of animals as mere machines, La Fontaine allows a serpent, so vividly associated with intrinsic evil in biblical mythology, to represent the entire animal kingdom. Then, in a fable where the human/animal dichotomy also replicates society's aristocratic/plebeian cleavage, he makes an 'inept' attempt to clarify a 'clumsily' ambiguous reference to 'the perverse animal'. Instead of disculpating humans/nobles, this effort actually renders the supposedly incorrect attribution of 'perversity' to human/aristocratic exploiters more credible. 'It's serpents I mean, / And not humans, one could easily be mistaken.' ('C'est le serpent que je veux dire, / Et non l'homme: on pourrait aisément s'y tromper'). Consequently, the fabulist's anamorphosis not only criticizes social inequities in pre-revolutionary France, it also raises questions, with unsettling implications for religious orthodoxy, about the human species' place in the universe.[59]

In one of his characters, La Bruyère boldly castigates the absurd pretensions of aristocrats who profess to be Christian. Nonetheless, instead of revering their biblical namesakes, these nobles arrogantly scorn the Apostles when they conclude they can best assert their superiority by abandoning baptismal names in favour of allegedly more prestigious pagan ones:

> We've already altogether too much in common with the people by having the same Religion and the same God; how can one allow oneself to be called *Peter, John, James*, like Merchants or Workers? [...] For us Great Ones, let's take pagan names, let's get baptized with names like Hannibal, Caesar or Pompey, they were great men [...]; or let's be baptized Hector, Achilles, Hercules, they were all demi-gods; [...] and who will prevent us from calling ourselves Jupiter or Mercury?[60]

This text offers an opportunity to challenge students to dig deeper and identify the 'lapse' that enables a strategically absent-minded moralist to hazard extending his satire to the pinnacle of the privileged caste.

Alert readers will notice how, by being a 'poor' writer, La Bruyère allows himself to get 'carried away' when talking about ancient gods and 'lets slip' a code name for Louis XIV (Jupiter). Those paying close attention to linguistic detail will also note how prudently the author prevents his 'inadvertent' clue from closing the final enumeration where it would have coincided with the end of a rhythmic group. Had the word 'Jupiter' appeared here, this 'slip' would have attracted dangerously disproportionate attention by receiving, in its last syllable, the primary accent that French prosody places on the final syllable of rhythmic groups.

Poor writing and deliberately inverted or fuzzy logic – what Jean Lafond calls 'madness that is the accomplice of reason' ('une déraison complice de la raison')[61] – may well create dissonance capable of leaving any censor wondering what an apparently foolish author truly meant. However, watchful readers should, conversely: 'Consider such "mistakes" to be by strategic design and take very seriously any allusions to the possibility of a "mistake" whenever unquestionably competent authors commit gross errors' (R5).

Surrounding whatever is expressed, silence deserves equal scrutiny, since it is often far from 'golden' in texts examined by a censor. Consequently, the final pair of twinned recommendations invites authors to: 'Let ideas become conspicuous by their absence' (A6). When Fénelon was elected to the French Academy, the distinguished, but dissident, cleric had to make an acceptance speech. Normally it would have gone to great lengths to glorify Louis XIV. Because Fénelon's did not, his less-than-hyperbolic praise spoke volumes and contributed to his exile from the seats of power. As Annabel Patterson observes, 'the institution-ally unspeakable makes itself heard inferentially, in the space between what is written or acted and what the audience, *knowing what they know*, might expect to read or see'.[62] Thus it is incumbent upon readers to: 'Be attentive to what is not said' (R6). Marc Fumaroli cautions those who read classical French authors that 'what they allow to be published must be read with acute sensitivity to silence' ('ce qu'ils laissent publier doit être lu avec un sens aigu des silences').[63]

When the two *Guides* diverge, one might turn initially to recommen-dations addressed solely to authors. The first states that: 'To more safely express an unorthodox viewpoint, present a venerable authority, preferably from antiquity, as your ostensible source, inspiration and model. It's not really necessary to imitate the model, just be sure to claim that's what you're doing' (A7).[64] In this way, La Bruyère used Theophrastus, whom he barely imitated, as both a pretext and a shield. Likewise, La Fontaine maintained that he merely put sentiments from various ancient fables into contemporary, French verse.

In the biological realm, Konrad Lorenz would probably call the eighth recommendation to writers the 'pecking order strategy'. 'To attack some-one more powerful than yourself, lavish outrageous praise on another contemporary even more powerful than your satirical target. Seek, or at least imply you have, the more powerful contemporary's patronage' (A8). Both Molière and La Bruyère used this tactic when they praised members of the royal family, often in ambiguous or coded ways, in order to attack lesser nobles or powerful institutions with some degree of impunity. For example, when opponents excoriated Molière's *École des femmes* (*School for Wives*) for offering a libertine attack on the principles of Christian marriage and the type of education girls received in convent schools, Molière parried by composing a *Critique de l'École des femmes*. However, since the *Critique* was likely to provoke an equally hostile reception, he astutely deflected anticipated condemnation by dedicating it to the Queen Mother, Anne d'Autriche, who was equally renowned for her staunch defence of piety and her passion for the theatre.[65]

Authors will also find it advantageous to: 'Tell tales that happened "long ago" and "far away"; any resemblance to contemporaries becom-ing purely coincidental' (A9). Following the ban of Molière's explosive attack on religious hypocrisy, *Tartuffe*, the playwright continued to treat other sensitive topics in his usual manner. Nevertheless, he set many new satires, such as *Dom Juan* or *George Dandin*, abroad or in French provinces, leaving spectators to decide if this distancing was a substantive change or a transparent defence.

In addition to using venerable authorities as a pretext, authors should: 'Use history, preferably ancient history, as a template for local or contemporary events. Invite readers to make connections with con-temporary issues by swearing there are no such links' (A10). Molière's *Amphitryon* illustrates how easily the past suggests parallels with the present. In ancient Greek mythology, Jupiter wished to seduce Alcmena, still very much in the honeymoon phase of her relationship with her husband, Amphitryon. To succeed, the chief Olympian had to compliment a mere mortal by disguising himself as Amphitryon, and the latter had to try to accept this extraordinary dishonour as flattering. When Molière's troupe performed *Amphitryon*, Louis XIV was courting one of his many mistresses, the Marquise de Montespan, to which the Marquis de Montespan, like Amphitryon, was disinclined to acqui-esce. In Molière's play, Jupiter's prestige is definitely tarnished so that, despite *Amphitryon's* popularity with Parisian audiences, it was coolly received at court.[66] In such circumstances, declarations of authorial innocence are usually quite revealing. Georges Couton calls them 'those denials which confirm' ('ces démentis qui confirment').[67] Similarly, Annabel Patterson sees 'the disclaimer, [as] denying, and therefore implying'; accordingly, 'disclaimers of topical intention are not to be trusted, and are more likely to be entry codes to precisely that kind of reading they protest against'.[68] Close inspection of texts subject to censorship demonstrates that they teem with characters who express contentious ideas by denying they meant what they said. In a court-room setting, it is: 'Objection!'; 'Sustained: the jury will ignore that question.' However, once the jury of readers has heard the question, it is more than enough.

Iconoclastic thinkers can also protect themselves if they: 'Let characters who need not be taken seriously express potentially explosive material' (A11). Authors gain much freedom by exploiting paradoxically wise fools, court jesters, drunkards, peasants, servants, children who see that the emperor has no clothes. In *Amphitryon*, it is a servant who makes the T-shirt's abrasive comments,[69] and Molière's contemporary, Scarron, shrewdly characterized the playwright as 'an all too serious buffoon' ('un bouffon trop sérieux'). Erasmus exploited 'praise' of folly, preferred by Folly itself, in order to include, within his wide-ranging satire, scathing denunciations of corruption and venality within the seats of temporal and spiritual power. In the same way, by letting a fox speak for him, La Fontaine was able to make disparaging remarks compa-rable to those La Rochefoucauld felt compelled to suppress, despite the considerable privilege he enjoyed as a Duke and Peer of the Realm. In the latter's *Maximes*, self-censorship cautiously replaced specific, powerful targets, 'ministers' and 'princes', with innocuous generalities, 'men' and 'young people'.[70] On the other hand, La Fontaine can allow a wily canine, admiring a sculpture, to quip: *'Lovely head, said-he; but no brain. / How many great Lords are Busts in this way?'*[71] In England, Falstaff was a dismal role model: he drank too much, womanized, fled danger while claiming others' victories. Nevertheless Shakespeare gives him an exceptionally persuasive, iconoclastic challenge to traditional notions of honour.[72] After scrutinizing numerous eloquent purveyors of paradoxical wisdom, Leo Strauss concludes there is 'good reason for our finding in the greatest literature of the past so many interesting devils, madmen, beggars, sophists, drunkards, epicureans and buffoons'.[73]

Because using less-than-prestigious genres is analogous to evading the censorial spotlight by making a less-than-prestigious character one's spokesperson, authors are counselled to: 'Use minor literary forms as vehicles for non-conformist thought' (A12). Classical French poetics places Molière's farces, La Bruyère's characters and La Fontaine's fables in this category, allowing the fabulist to delight students as he mischievously combines multiple defensive manoeuvres. Ostensibly, La Fontaine wrote for children, in a neglected genre. He also hid behind venerable ancient sources and self-diagnosed incompetence. In this way, he may well have put censors in the impossible position of having to explicate his insinuations in order to silence his subtle fusion of critical commentary and infectious frivolity. La Rochefoucauld's 326th maxim posits that 'ridicule dishonours more than dishonour' ('le ridicule déshonore plus que le déshonneur'), and modern French still affirms that 'ridicule kills'. An absolute monarch may say 'I am the State,' but dare he even think 'the tyrannical lion, the brutal eagle, the bloodthirsty wolf, Jupiter – they're all me – and therefore this children's book must be burned?' Recognizing how this would look, Louis-the-Great settled for shunning his realm's troublesome fabulist.

Another useful subterfuge and its variant advise authors to: 'Claim to be refuting unorthodox thinking, but articulate or summarize it well, then refute it weakly or clumsily; or put your message in the mouth of a character you pretend to criticize' (A13). Molière does both in his theatrical treatment of the Don Juan theme, which would almost certainly have been banned, as *Tartuffe* had been, had he not withdrawn it after a few performances. Throughout Molière's *Dom Juan*, the playwright seems to deprecate his freethinking protagonist. However, he lets this iconoclast articulate nonconformist opinions brilliantly, and he delegates the defence of orthodoxy and received wisdom to an incoherent, poorly reasoning servant.[74] An eighteenth-century censor's explanation of why he rejected a poorly written text, despite the author's pious intention of using it to combat deism, lucidly confirms the inherent dangers of anaemic defences: 'I find his work useless, even harmful, for to defend religion feebly is to expose it indiscreetly.'[75]

Should all else fail, authors need not hesitate to: 'Blame unacceptable interpretations of texts on misguided readers' (A14) and 'Exploit rhetorical devices including particularly useful ones such as irony, paradoxical praise, paralipsis, antonomasia, anamorphosis, and ambiguity' (A15). One striking example of anamorphosis – which offers a portrait that, viewed from one angle, shows one subject, but viewed from a different angle, exposes another subject – illustrates the effectiveness of rhetorical resources:

> Eight or ten thousand men are like currency with which a Sovereign
> buys a victory; if he makes it cost less, if he economizes on men,

he resembles one who bargains and who knows better than another the price of money.[76]

Seemingly, La Bruyère commends a warrior-king who sacrifices as few soldiers as possible. However, viewed from a lexicological angle, his text becomes so peppered with commercial terms that its king looks and acts like a merchant. Consequently, this text portrays an abrogation of noble title, through the practice of a then demeaning occupation, and this anamorphosis fortifies the denunciations of the Sun King's militarism that permeate the *Caractères*.

Advice offered to readers alone prompts them to: 'Evaluate carefully the impact of restrictive phrases such as "sometimes"' (R7). 'Sometimes' can appear to diminish the importance of a problem by presenting it as an isolated case. Nonetheless, if insightful readers recognize that the text refers to a generalized problem, they will translate 'sometimes' as 'almost always'. Conversely, 'sometimes' may imply 'almost never', especially when a text lauds something much needed, but in very short supply. In La Fontaine's fables, the wolf is habitually the incarnation of 'might makes right'. Nonetheless, a lone wolf, 'filled with humanity', contemplates becoming vegetarian. Likewise, nature's absolute animal monarch, the lion, is ordinarily a threat to his subjects. Yet a single lion magnanimously spares a rat and, 'on this occasion', proves he has 'the right royal stuff'.[77] Such rare moments, when the wolf, the lion or Jupiter are admirable, do not necessarily rehabilitate their species or rank. Rather, the exception proves the rule, hints at what could or should be, and gives greater relief to the shortcomings of the majority who do not use power benevolently.

The *Reader's Guide* also reminds students to: 'Be sure to take into account the context of a text's genesis, its nature and its structure' (R8).[78] Molière's *The Middle-class Aristocrat* (*Le Bourgeois gentilhomme*) offers a case in point. Like The Grand Magic Circus' 1981–82 poster that pasted an image of Molière's ridiculous protagonist into an official portrait of Louis XIV, or the 1982 film by Roger Coggio that inserted nearly subliminal flashes of the Sun King into ordinary footage, many suggest a loose parallel between Molière's social climber and Louis XIV. Each had just one lifetime to transform himself into an aristocrat or a Sun King. Furthermore, Louis-the-Great, having recently taken offence when the Sultan's envoy seemed insufficiently impressed by his regal splendour, instructed Molière to include a Turkish component in his comedy. Molière had to comply. Still, he did not, as one might antici-pate, disparage the culture deemed to have snubbed Louis XIV. In his satire, Turkish elements are far less intrinsically comic than a theatrical in-joke; for just as the protagonist's foolish vanity necessitated the Turkish play-within-a-play, so Louis XIV's easily wounded pride was the genesis of the entire comedy.

Scrupulous respect for texts also obliges readers to: 'Remove nothing from the text; consider everything the author wrote as potentially relevant' (R9).[79] Understandably, but regrettably, contemporary editors frequently drop voluminous, introductory material if such letters, prefaces and prologues appear outdated, tedious or superfluous. However, early modern writers, hoping censors might skim through this material, often used it to provide interpretive clues to their esoteric audience. A 1682 royal decree, stipulating that all introductory material must be subjected to as much censorial scrutiny as the main text, attests to this subterfuge's success in France.[80] The seldom-performed prologue to Molière's *Hypochondriac* (*Le Malade imaginaire*) offers a richly ambiguous encomium. Through its initial lexical choices and syntax, it prompts perceptive spectators to hear, in hyperbolic praise of LOUIS' exploits, a parody of Corneille's very well-known and often mockingly quoted battle narration from *Le Cid*. Next a competition seeks, ostensibly, to determine who can best extol France's victorious monarch. More subtly, its polysemy mimics equally grotesque flattery ridiculed in the comedy's second act. *Sotto voce*, the contest offers posterity a satirically exonerating apology for the reluctant sycophancy no early modern writer could entirely elude.

To illustrate readers' recommendations 8 and 9, in a way that is especially close to students' experience during the 'late modern period', what may well be the most commonly read French-language book on any campus, Saint-Exupéry's *Le Petit Prince*, often proves quite valuable. If one were to ask how many students read it, many hands would go up. If one then asked who also read its dedication to Léon Werth, the man Saint-Exupéry calls his 'best friend', far fewer hands would go up. Finally, even though nearly everyone who did read the dedication found it exceptionally charming, very few, if any, hands would go up if one inquired who took the trouble to uncover the identity of the author's best friend or consider its implications for an analysis of the text.

Saint-Exupéry wrote *Le Petit Prince* in 1943, when he was safe in New York. Where was his 'best friend' in 1943? In occupied France where the dedication describes him as 'hungry, cold and very much in need of consolation'.[81] More importantly, who was Léon Werth? An outspoken, freethinking intellectual and social critic, with controversial, anti-conformist views. Most importantly in Nazi-occupied France, Léon

Werth was the son of a Jewish father. Simply learning a bit about the dedicant immediately gives this 'children's book' an additional interpretive dimension and makes it resonate within a heightened metaphorical framework.

The last three recommendations to readers emphasize the intellectual responsibilities of those who seek to read conscientiously around censorship. 'Try not to read between the lines when it would be more accurate to read the lines alone' (R10). 'Even when reading between the lines, make the author's explicit statements your starting point' (R11).[82] 'Recognize that, although certainty isn't always possible, readers of texts written in an age of censorship, when non-conformist thought could not be expressed directly, have a responsibility to read between the lines, and to do so as judiciously as possible' (R12).[83] Both Annabel Patterson and Leo Strauss underscore the obligations of conscientious readers. The former concludes it is essential to '*combine* a practical recognition of the indeterminacy of the text in a culture governed by censorship with an equally pragmatic recognition that behind each text stood an author, whose intentions it was the reader's responsibility to try to discern'.[84] The latter asserts that:

> If an able writer who has a clear mind and a perfect knowledge of the orthodox view and all its ramifications, contradicts surreptitiously and as it were in passing one of its necessary presuppositions or consequences which he explicitly recognizes and maintains everywhere else, we can reasonably suspect that he was opposed to the orthodox system as such, and we must study his whole work all over again, with much greater care and much less naïveté than ever before.[85]

Such meticulous and thoughtful scrutiny of works censored during the early modern period affords students many catalysts for intellectual growth. Precisely because 'censorship [...] predictably creates sophisticated audiences',[86] negotiating one's way through censored texts leads students to become as mentally nimble as those who, in earlier generations, wrote censored texts or understood how to read them perceptively. For their pains, students learn how to follow in the footsteps of their highly skilled predecessors. As Couton puts it:

> Seventeenth-century people were trained in an intellectual discipline which kept them from being satisfied with obvious meaning, and instead led them to search for realities hidden behind appearances with, very probably, the idea in mind that those meanings which

required the greatest subtlety to be uncovered were the best. Truth had to be earned.[87]

Studying how censorship functions, and how writers evade it, constantly prompts learners to enhance their reasoning and critical thinking abilities, refine their judgement, and become capable of analysing complex phenomena such as philosophical or literary discourse. It also trains tomorrow's thinkers to recognize the value of probing received wisdom and, whenever it is found wanting, of examining it further, judiciously, in order to acquire new insights into canonical subjects. For example, it behoves students who encounter praise of a powerful, early modern monarch, to pause and ask not only if, but equally how, they can determine the author's intentions with reasonable probability. Is the commentator grinding out compulsory homage, sincerely applauding royalty, or giving coded praise to an ideal but fictitious monarch which the actual ruler's regal vanity would readily accept as genuine?

For those who undertake reading around censorship, 'the process of [...] reading' and the 'steps to understanding' are 'no less important than the understanding achieved'.[88] Learning how to approach censored texts, in particular, and how to read them with astute sensitivity, making informed and fine but crucially important distinctions, necessitates the immediate acquisition of investigative and exceptionally well-disciplined close-reading skills. Subsequently, these valuable transferable skills facilitate, enhance and accelerate the acquisition of benefits derived from the study of literature in general. And they continue to serve post-modern students well, throughout life, in many other contexts. Tellingly, Annabel Patterson insists that: 'one of the main objectives of [... her] study of [censorship] is to break down the barriers between academic discourse and "real" issues'.[89] As Rosenblatt argues:

> When we are helping students to better techniques of reading through sensitivity to diction, tone, structure, image, symbol, narrative movement, we are also helping them to make the more refined responses that are ultimately the source of human understanding and sensitivity to human values.[90]

And, as Altick puts it:

> An unfailing mark of truly educated people is their insistence on weighing all aspects of an issue, on avoiding oversimplification and unwarranted generalization, on applying the tools of critical analysis

to the materials presented to them. Their responsibility as citizens and members of society [...] obligates them to be critical readers and thinkers.[91]

Another equally compelling reason to study or teach the early modern period and its censored texts is the wish, indeed the need, to better understand the world that emerged from this era and is still nourished by its heritage. The student who acquires the 'emotional and intellectual and esthetic maturity necessary for appreciating the great works of literature [...] grows also into partnership in the wisdom of the past and the aspirations for the future, of our culture and our society'.[92] Consequently, when discussing early modern censorship, it is important to establish a link to present-day censorship and its even more insidious variant, self-censorship, lest students conclude that these intellectual scourges disappeared with the early modern era and will never confront them. In my Canadian context, I could draw attention to Val Ross' *You Can't Read This*, a history of censorship written in 2006 for older children and adolescents. Or I might refer to 2007's *Censor This!*, the Canadian Broadcasting Corporation's series of interviews, news coverage and documentaries examining facets of contemporary censorship.[93] Or I might indicate that the University of Toronto's Massey College is currently sheltering a *scholar-at-risk*.[94]

In the future, the works of iconoclastic, early modern thinkers will still afford critical readers and thinkers many rich veins to be explored. An excerpt from André Gide's *Journal* suggests just how rewarding thoughtful reading between and around the lines can be and issues a challenge that remains particularly pertinent to today's educators and their successors:

What an astonishing anthology one would get [...] if it brought together and made prominent the revolutionary element of all great writing from the past. It seems that schooling tames the classics; they appear moderate, subdued, softened, inoffensive; familiarity blunts their sharpest weapons. One does not read them *well* unless one restores their cutting edge.[95]

Notes

1. Louise M. Rosenblatt, *Literature as Exploration*, 4th edn (New York: MLA, 1976), p. vii.
2. D.P. Walker, 'Esoteric Symbolism', in *Poetry and Poetics from Ancient Greece to the Renaissance*, ed. G.M. Kirkwood (London: Cornell University Press, 1975), pp. 218–32 (pp. 220–1).

3. Marc Fumaroli, 'Interview', *Le Figaro littéraire*, 20 February 1997, p. 4. All translations are my own.

4. Following one such guest lecture, given to the Early Modern Studies Programme of Kings College in Halifax, Nova Scotia, many students remained in the Senior Common Room for several hours, continuing to probe questions raised by this talk.

5. 'Au XVIIe siècle, les convictions sont inébranlables: l'idéologie religieuse s'est doublée d'une idéologie politique [...] ce n'est jamais d'un point de vue *extérieur* à la classe dirigeante qu'on moque les marquis ridicules.' Jean-Paul Sartre, *Situations, II* (Paris: Gallimard, 1948), pp. 133, 135, 140.

6. Marc Fumaroli, *Le Poète et le roi* (Paris: Éditions de Fallois, 1997), p. 33.

7. Leo Strauss, *Persecution and the Art of Writing* (Westport, CT: Greenwood Press, 1973), p. 26.

8. Annabel Patterson, *Censorship and Interpretation, with a New Introduction* (Madison: University of Wisconsin Press, 1984), p. 53.

9. *Ibid.*, pp. 17, 16, respectively.

10. *Ibid.*, pp. 8, 12, 16. Likewise Jean-Pierre Cavaillé infers that the libertines' evasion of censorship was designed not only to protect themselves and communicate with an initiated, esoteric audience, but also to 'test the narrow limits of public tolerance' ('sonder les limites étroites de la tolérance publique'). *Dis/simulations: religion, morale et politique au XVIIe siècle* (Paris: Champion, 2008), pp. 18–19.

11. '[D]égager [...] cette humanité, cette douceur, cette attention à autrui qui rendent sociable la vie sociale [...]; dissiper ces opinions qui [...] rendent la société difficile, impossible, tragique [...]; diverti[r] de l'abîme'. Marc Fumaroli, *La Diplomatie de l'esprit* (Paris: Hermann, 1994), pp. xv–xvi, xxv.

12. Perez Zagorin, *Ways of Lying* (Cambridge, MA: Harvard University Press, 1990), p. 14.

13. Patterson, *Censorship and Interpretation*, p. 4.

14. Rosenblatt, *Literature as Exploration*, p. v.

15. *Ibid.*, pp. 281, 282–3, 279, respectively. See also Alan C. Purves, Theresa Rogers and Anna O. Soter, *How Porcupines Make Love II* (New York: Longman, 1990), p. 56.

16. See n. 15 above.

17. Rosenblatt, *Literature as Exploration*, p. ix.

18. See the comments of M.P. Schmitt and A. Viala, *Savoir-lire*, 5th edn (Paris: Didier, 1982), p. 3.

19. Purves, Rogers and Soter, *Porcupines*, pp. 48, 52.

20. Richard D. Altick, *Preface to Critical Reading*, 6th edn, rev. by Andrea A. Lunsford (New York: Holt, Rinehart and Winston, 1984), pp. xiii–xiv, xviii.

21. *Ibid.*, p. xi.

22. *Ibid.*, pp. xiii–xv.

23. Rosenblatt, *Literature as Exploration*, p. xiii.

24. *Ibid.*, pp. xiii–xiv.

25. Key pedagogical considerations, specific to my context, guided the choice of examples to be included in this corpus. My selection features a sub-group of classical French thinkers whom students encounter in their programme at the time when an introduction to the early modern period is especially useful. The corpus largely excludes critics who published abroad or with real

anonymity, as well as those who circulated their works through clandestine networks, often in manuscript form. Such sacrifices and risks gave this latter category of nonconformists the licence to use relatively ordinary writing strategies. As a result, their opposition to the status quo could be as immediately visible as it is in the title of the *Sighs of Enslaved France Yearning for Freedom* (*Soupirs de la France esclave qui aspire après la liberté*), which was printed abroad, anonymously, and attributed to Michel Le Vassor. Conversely, most of my *Guides'* authors remained in France, moved in courtly circles, published openly and signed their works. Consequently, they were obliged to express heterodox views by using precisely those indirect writing strategies that lead students to develop highly sophisticated analytical skills. Finally, while early modern censorship repressed both political and religious deviance, examples of political dissent predominate in the *Guides* because, at the introductory level, contemporary students readily grasp hierarchical considerations, understand challenges to secular authority or abuses of power, and quickly discover motivating parallels within their own experience. On the other hand, many of the early modern era's doctrinal controversies, such as the exact nature of Christian grace, however vitriolic they were at the time, often appear obscure and inaccessible to present-day students who, for the most part, have known little other than a largely secular, multicultural society, mediated by ecumenism.

26. As sessions end, the audience is invited to add examples of writing or reading around censorship encountered in other contexts. Representative contributions include: experiences of censorship in countries from which participants had emigrated; parallels between computer treatment of language and linguistic devices used to circumvent early modern censorship; the esoteric import, addressed to the gay community, of Oscar Wilde's *The Importance of Being Ernest*.

27. The studies by R. Birn, H.-J. Martin, I. Moreau, D. Pottinger, cited below in notes 28–30, in addition to Alain Viala's *Naissance de l'écrivain* (Paris: Minuit, 1985) provide the foundation for this brief summary and constitute a valuable resource for further examination of early modern French censorship. For an excellent, analytical evocation of the ideological climate that gave rise to it and the intellectual horizons of those who defied it, see Jacques Prévot's introduction to *Libertins du XVIIe siècle*, 2 vols (Paris: Gallimard, 1998), I, pp. ix–lxx.

28. Raymond Birn, *La Censure royale des livres dans la France des Lumières* (Paris: Jacob, 2007), pp. 65–94.

29. Isabelle Moreau, *'Guérir du sot': les stratégies d'écriture des libertins à l'âge classique* (Paris: Champion, 2007), pp. 250, 257–9.

30. Henri Jean Martin, *Livre, pouvoirs et société à Paris au XVIIe siècle*, 2 vols (Geneva: Droz, 1999), I, p. 441; Moreau, *'Guérir du sot'*, p. 154. For an example of a censorial blunder that is particularly remarkable in its historical context, and ironically ecumenical in a contemporary context, see David T. Pottinger, *The French Book Trade in the Ancien Régime, 1500–1791* (Cambridge, MA: Harvard University Press, 1958), p. 73.

31. *Le Cid*, ed. Georges Forestier (Paris: Société des Textes Français Modernes, 1992), pp. 27–8, n. 1.

32. *Fables*, ed. Georges Couton (Paris: Bordas, 1990), 'Le Milan, le roi et le chasseur'. All subsequent references to the *Fables* refer to this edition and indicate

only the individual fable's title. On 'Le Milan, le roi et le chasseur', see also Georges Couton, *La Politique de La Fontaine* (Paris: Les Belles Lettres, 1959), pp. 132–4.

33. See the account of the fate in 1662 of Claude Le Petit in Bernard Teyssèdre, *L'Art au siècle de Louis XIV* (Paris: Librairie Générale Française, 1967), p. 32.

34. '[P]ropre à inspirer le libertinage le plus dangereux pour la Religion et pour l'ordre de la société civile: [...] scandaleux, contraire à la Religion, aux bonnes moeurs et au respect dû aux Puissances'. Voltaire, *Lettres philosophiques*, ed. Raymond Naves (Paris: Garnier, 1964), n. pag.

35. Voltaire, *Mélanges*, ed. Jacques Van Den Heuvel (Paris: Gallimard, 1961), p. 1323.

36. La Bruyère, *Les Caractères*, ed. Louis Van Delft (Paris: Imprimerie Nationale, 1998), 'Des Biens de Fortune', 56. All subsequent references to *Les Caractères* refer to this edition and indicate the chapter title and the character number.

37. 'Des Ouvrages de l'Esprit', 65.

38. 'Des Grands', 56.

39. 'Préface', p. 130.

40. Of both La Bruyère and La Fontaine, Marc Fumaroli finds that 'one cannot under-estimate their courage, [...] or their extraordinary subtlety in speaking the truth without overly endangering themselves' ('on ne peut sous-estimer ni le courage, [...] ni l'extraordinaire subtilité à dire la vérité sans trop s'exposer'). 'Interview' (see n. 3 above).

41. 'Tel tout d'un coup et sans y avoir pensé la veille, prend du papier, une plume, dit en soi-même, je vais faire un livre [...] il écrirait volontiers que la Seine coule à Paris, qu'il y a sept jours dans la semaine, ou que le temps est à la pluie; et comme ce discours n'est ni contre la Religion ni contre l'État [...], il passe à l'examen, il est imprimé.' 'De la Chaire', 23.

42. Colleagues who would like to receive a pdf file of the *Guides* for photocopying and classroom use are invited to send a request to: Karolyn.Waterson@Dal.Ca.

43. A simple, home-made mannequin representing Molière can provide a graphic prelude. Initially Molière's stand-in wears a T-shirt bearing an impertinent excerpt from his comedy *Amphitryon*:
    'Coming from a nobody, / All speech is nonsense. / Were a Notable speaking, / His words would be exquisite.' ('Tous les discours sont des sottises, / Partant d'un homme sans éclat; / Ce serait paroles exquises / Si c'était un grand qui parlât.') At this point, I invite the audience to imagine Molière wanting to express such sentiments during a performance at Louis XIV's court. Once students realize the playwright would be well advised to make his text less conspicuously audacious, a student volunteer slips a semi-opaque, poet's shirt over the T-shirt's impudent verse. I then point out that this is precisely what writers had to do when they submitted their works to a censor: the author's dilemma being how to let the real message shine through the prudently protective veil; the reader's challenge becoming how to get at the T-shirt's message and what value to place on its more or less transparent camouflage. (See Molière: *Œuvres complètes*, ed. R. Jouanny, 2 vols (Paris: Garnier, 1962), II, *Amphitryon*, II.1. ll. 839–42). All subsequent references to Molière's theatre refer to this edition.

44. Excerpts from both *Guides* are signalled by A for the *Author's Guide*, R for the *Reader's Guide*, and the number of the recommendation within each *Guide*.

45. 'Du Souverain ou de la République', 16, 29, 35, 34, respectively; 'De l'Homme', 128.

46. 'Du Souverain ou de la République', 35. For a more detailed analysis of this thorny question, see Karolyn Waterson, 'La Bruyère ou l'art de commenter l'histoire entre les lignes', in *Littérature et histoire au XVIIe siècle*, ed. Gérard Ferreyrolles, *Dalhousie French Studies*, 65 (2003), 112–20 (pp. 113–16).

47. See also Strauss, *Persecution and the Art of Writing*, p. 17.

48. See n. 43 above.

49. John Toland, *Clidophorus*, cited in Annabel Patterson, *Reading Between the Lines* (Madison: University of Wisconsin Press, 1993), pp. 7–8. See also Zagorin, *Ways of Lying*, p. 295.

50. Patterson, *Censorship and Interpretation*, p. 71.

51. See also Strauss, *Persecution and the Art of Writing*, pp. 24–5.

52. 'De la Mode', 21.

53. See also Strauss, *Persecution and the Art of Writing*, p. 36. On the genealogy of the strategy of dissimulation by 'feigned stupidity' ('la bêtise feinte'), see Cavaillé, *Dis/simulations*, pp. 27–30.

54. Strauss, *Persecution and the Art of Writing*, pp. 25–6.

55. *The Riverside Shakespeare*, ed. G. Blakemore Evans, 2 vols (Boston: Houghton Mifflin, 1974), I, *Twelfth Night*, III.1. All subsequent references to Shakespeare's theatre refer to this edition.

56. '[I]ci se cache une sève maligne et corrompue sous l'écorce de la politesse'. 'Des Grands', 25.

57. Montesquieu, *Œuvres complètes*, ed. Daniel Oster (Paris: Seuil, 1964), p. 854.

58. Respectively, 'L'Aigle et le Hibou', 'Le Meunier, son Fils et l'Âne', 'Le Pouvoir des Fables', 'Les Membres et l'Estomac'.

59. Respectively, 'Le Bûcheron et Mercure', 'L'Homme et la Couleuvre'.

60. 'C'est déjà trop d'avoir avec le peuple une même Religion et un même Dieu; quel moyen encore de s'appeler *Pierre, Jean, Jacques*, comme le Marchand ou le Laboureur? [...] Pour nous autres Grands, ayons recours aux noms profanes, faisons-nous baptiser sous ceux d'Annibal, de César et de Pompée, c'étaient de grands hommes [...]; sous ceux d'Hector, d'Achille, d'Hercule, tous demi-Dieux; [...] et qui nous empêchera de nous faire nommer Jupiter ou Mercure?' 'Des Grands', 23.

61. Jean Lafond, 'Avant-propos', in Jules Brody, *Du Style à la pensée* (Lexington, KY: French Forum, 1980), pp. 13–14.

62. Patterson, *Censorship and Interpretation*, p. 71.

63. Fumaroli, 'Interview'. See n. 3 above.

64. See also Patterson, *Censorship and Interpretation*, p. 65.

65. For La Bruyère's approach, see Maurice Lange, *La Bruyère: critique des conditions et des institutions sociales* (Paris: Hachette, 1909), pp. 24–5, 27. For an analysis of how Naudé, Cyrano and La Mothe Le Vayer used a similar strategy, see Moreau, '*Guérir du sot*', pp. 184–7.

66. Antony McKenna posits that Molière's Jupiter, far from prefiguring the Sun King, represents instead a divine impostor whose failings throw doubt on the solidity of that divine truth which underpins Cartesian philosophy ('En Marge d'*Amphitryon*', in *Autour de Cyrano de Bergerac*, ed. Patricia Harry, Alain Mothu and Philippe Sellier (Paris: Champion, 2006), pp. 257–64). Yet both interpretations of Jupiter's role portray a dominant, hierarchical figure

who abuses extraordinary power, and they need not necessarily be mutually exclusive. Should both subtexts function simultaneously, on different levels, they would render *Amphitryon* an exceptionally disturbing comedy.

67. Georges Couton, *Écritures codées: essais sur l'allégorie au XVIIe siècle* (Paris: Aux Amateurs de Livres, 1990), p. 105.
68. Patterson, *Censorship and Interpretation*, pp. 118 and 65, respectively.
69. See n. 43 above.
70. *Maximes*, ed. Jacques Truchet (Paris: Bordas, 1992): respectively, p. 19, n. 2; p. 67, n. 1.
71. '*Belle tête, dit-il; mais de cervelle point.* / Combien de grands Seigneurs sont Bustes en ce point?' 'Le Renard et le Buste'.
72. *The Riverside Shakespeare*, II, *Henry IV*, Part I, V.1.
73. Strauss, *Persecution and the Art of Writing*, p. 36.
74. See especially III.1.
75. 'Je juge son ouvrage inutile, nuisible même, car défendre faiblement la religion, c'est l'exposer indiscrètement.' Quoted in Birn, *La Censure royale*, p. 112.
76. 'Les huit ou les dix mille hommes sont au Souverain comme une monnaie dont il achète une place ou une victoire; s'il fait qu'il lui en coûte moins, s'il épargne les hommes, il ressemble à celui qui marchande et qui connaît mieux qu'un autre le prix de l'argent.' La Bruyère, 'Du Souverain ou de la République', 25.
77. Respectively, 'Le Loup et les Bergers', 'Le Lion et le Rat'.
78. See also Patterson, *Censorship and Interpretation*, pp. 55–8.
79. See also *ibid.*, p. 56.
80. Martin, *Livre, pouvoirs et société*, II, p. 691.
81. '[C]ette grande personne [...] a faim et froid. Elle a bien besoin d'être consolée'. Saint-Exupéry, *Œuvres* (Paris: Gallimard, 1959), p. 407.
82. With respect to R10 and R11, see also Strauss, *Persecution and the Art of Writing*, p. 30.
83. For a fuller appreciation of the typical complexities of reading and writing between and around the lines, see Jean-Pierre Cavaillé, 'L'Art d'écrire des philosophes', *Critique*, 55 (1999), 959–80.
84. Patterson, *Censorship and Interpretation*, p. 56.
85. Strauss, *Persecution and the Art of Writing*, p. 32.
86. Michael Holquist, 'Corrupt Originals: The Paradox of Censorship', *PMLA*, 109 (1994), 14–25 (p. 14).
87. 'Les gens du XVIIe siècle sont formés à une discipline intellectuelle qui est de ne pas se contenter du sens évident, mais qui les porte à chercher des réalités cachées derrière des apparences, avec sans doute très ordinairement l'idée que les sens qui ont demandé, pour être dégagés, le plus grand effort de subtilité sont les meilleurs. La vérité se mérite.' Couton, *Écritures codées*, p. 175.
88. Peter Scotto, 'Censorship, Reading, and Interpretation: A Case Study from the Soviet Union', *PMLA*, 109 (1994), 61–70 (p. 61).
89. Patterson, *Censorship and Interpretation*, p. 5.
90. Rosenblatt, *Literature as Exploration*, p. 290.
91. Altick, *Preface to Critical Reading*, p. xvii.
92. Rosenblatt, *Literature as Exploration*, p. 291.
93. On the Canadian Broadcasting Corporation's Radio One and Two, 18–27 February 2007.

94. Ramin Jahanbegloo, a Canadian-Iranian philosopher, currently at the University of Toronto where he is a Professor of Political Science and Research Fellow in The Centre for Ethics. He is the author of numerous books, in English, French and Persian, including *Penser la nonviolence* (Paris: UNESCO, 2000), *Iran: Between Tradition and Modernity* (Lanham, MD: Lexington Books, 2004), *The Clash of Intolerances* (New Delhi: Har-Anand, 2007) and *The Spirit of India* (Toronto: Penguin, 2008).

95. 'Quelle étonnante anthologie ne ferait-on pas [...] qui grouperait et ferait ressortir de tous les grands écrits du passé l'élément révolutionnaire. Il semble que le travail scolaire soit d'apprivoiser les classiques; ils paraissent tempérés, assagis, adoucis, inoffensifs; leurs armes les plus acérées, l'accoutumance les émousse. On ne les lit pas *bien* sans leur redonner du tranchant.' *Journal, 1889–1939* (Paris: Gallimard, 1951), p. 1243.

18

T-shirt Day, Utopia and Henry VIII's Dating Service: Using Creative Assignments to Teach Early Modern History

Carole Levin

It is the last day of the semester in my course on Tudor and early Stuart England and some of the students have produced creative final assessments which they are presenting to the class. Perhaps the most creative of all is a PowerPoint presentation called 'Henry VIII's Dating Service'. The student uses this format to cleverly provide information about, and an interpretation of, many of the people we have studied over the course of the semester; the format also provides a welcome laugh and release of tension for students who are feeling under stress as the semester is ending, they are finishing their final papers and preparing for their final exams. Henry VIII explains that he has had a lot of experience, and had he had this dating service perhaps he would not have had to go through six different wives. There are men seeking women, women seeking men, men seeking men and some seeking everyone. One of those who provides a hearty recommendation for the service is the astrologer Simon Forman, who boasts that he has never 'haleked' – Forman's code for intercourse – so frequently or successfully until he signed up. While this is very amusing, it also cleverly analyses sexual and power relationships in early modern England. As well as producing the PowerPoint presentation, the student wrote an essay about the process involved in doing the project, which all students who do creative projects are required to do.

I teach a range of courses that deal with early modern history, from ones that are aimed at first-year university students to ones open only to the most advanced graduate students. As well as survey courses on subjects such as Western civilization to 1715, Roman Britain to 1688 and the history of European women, I offer a range of more specialized classes. One is a course introducing students to doing research that focuses on Henry VIII and his court. I also teach a course for advanced Honours students from a variety of specializations in their final year called 'Historical and Literary Retellings' that centres on early modern topics. My advanced undergraduate courses that are also open to graduate students are on Tudor/early Stuart England; medieval and early modern history through biography; and on women on the margins and issues of identity, a course called 'Saints, Witches, and Madwomen'.

In my classes, students read a wide range of texts that include primary historical and literary sources and modern historical interpretations. They write in-class essay exams, out-of-class analytical essays on assigned readings and do research essays. But, depending on the level of the class and its theme, the students also have a variety of creative assignments that allow them to think through and make the material their own. Frequently I offer my students the option to do a creative project as part of their final assessment. Since they, at that stage, have already had a series of exams and written a number of papers, this allows them to examine the material in a very different way. I then use the last day or two of class to have the students present these creative projects to the entire class. This assignment helps the students in reviewing the material, and allows them to develop a sense of pride in their work. These creative assignments are often the ones to which they devote the most time, think most deeply about the material and find the distant past of the early modern period easier to comprehend. In these brief pages, I discuss a number of creative assignments that I have successfully used to teach early modern history; I indicate what the students were able to accomplish and provide some examples of students' work.

One of the assignments that I use in many of my classes is 'T-shirt day'. It is always the day before a break when students want to extend their holiday and cut their last classes. Since I insist my students come to class – and sometimes there is an in-class writing assignment that day – I also want to give my students something fun that gives them more of a chance to be invested in the material. I tell my students that if they wear a T-shirt that somehow reflects a theme of the course each will get an extra point. There are 100 points in the class, and this allows a student to have one extra one. While some of the students buy a T-shirt, most of them make them, with elaborate images and quotations. I take photographs of them in their T-shirts and post them on my office door for the rest of the semester. Though I usually dress carefully and professionally when I teach, on 'T-shirt day' I too wear a T-shirt that represents a theme of the class. Since the students know that much of my research is on Elizabeth I, a number of them create clever and beautiful Queen

Elizabeth T-shirts. In one instance, in my European women's history class, one male student's T-shirt read 'Real men take women's history with Dr Levin.'

I teach an introductory class for history students on how to do research. This class is co-taught by a number of faculty members who teach individual seminars on research focusing on a topic from their area of specialization. I decided mine would be on Henry VIII and his wives. I start the course with an assignment I call 'Words, Words, Words'. I find obscure words that were used in the sixteenth century but are not used today. Each student gets a different word and then has to look it up in the *Oxford English Dictionary* and find all the meanings of the word used in the sixteenth century. Then each student must write a sentence for each definition that in some way relates to Henry VIII, his wives or his court. Regularly, throughout the semester, we devote some time at the beginning of class to this exercise: students bring in words they find in the *OED* and we put them on the board. The students read several different modern studies on Henry VIII and his wives and discuss the various interpretations the authors present. In the class, each student does a paper that involves use of such research tools as the *Letters and Papers of Henry VIII* and Early English Books Online. They do an early draft, a second more finished draft and a final version. I read all the drafts but each student also reads and critiques one other person's draft at each stage.

However, in addition to this major project I assign two other short essays linked to an in-class activity, as a way for them to have a different experience with the early modern. I do this after each of their drafts is due. The first is Utopia Day. My students read Book II of Thomas More's *Utopia*. Each student chooses one of the following topics discussed in Utopian society and writes a brief essay critiquing it. The topics include: treatment of the mentally incompetent, education, health care and hospitalization, euthanasia, the criminal justice system, the class system, marriage customs, poverty and how to deal with it, family structure, the significance of clothing styles and wearing jewellery, sexual relations between those who are unmarried, the reasons for political intervention in another country's affairs, choosing a trade or profession, responsibility to self or to the state, women's status. The day the essay is due, students have to come to class as either Utopians or anti-Utopians. If they come as Utopian, they have to wear a black, white or grey T-shirt with no slogans on it, blue jeans and no jewellery or make-up. Anti-Utopians must dress with wild abandon and wear bright and garish colours and much jewellery. The Utopians and the Anti-Utopians sit across from each other and debate aspects of Utopian society. It is interesting to see which students choose to be Utopians or Anti-Utopians and how they marshal their arguments.

After their second draft is due, we have our 'press conference in purgatory'. Students volunteer or are assigned to be Henry VIII, his wives and certain members of his court, or they are assigned to be reporters interviewing them. Each reporter works for a different magazine or newspaper that I have invented, which include: *Official Tudor News*; *Henry VIII Gossip Rag*; *Women's Wear Royalty*; *Queens Rule!*; and *Tudor Sports Illustrated*. The students who are part of the court write a short essay about the person they are representing. The reporters write a short essay describing themselves as reporters, the nature of their magazine or newspaper, and the questions they will pose. The students also have the option of dressing up for this class as either reporters or Henry VIII and his court. I find that students enjoy this assignment and it works well after the labour devoted to the serious draft of their research essay.

I also teach an undergraduate Honours course called 'Historical and Literary Retellings' that centres on early modern topics. The last time it ran, I taught units on fairy tales, several Shakespeare plays and Queen Elizabeth I. For the unit on Elizabeth, the students had to create a retelling of the sixteenth-century queen. A range of projects was produced. One of the most unusual and imaginative was a comic strip of Queen Elizabeth being interviewed on the TV show *Actor's Studio: Royalty Edition*. The student cleverly demonstrated her knowledge of Elizabeth's policies and her courtships through this medium. As she wrote in her 'process essay', 'I thought it would be interesting to put Queen Elizabeth in a modern setting and [to] discuss her past exploits in a comedic way.' She explained that, 'To see her various unguarded reactions to the common conceptions and misconceptions of her courtships was the real aim of the storyboard,' as was showing Elizabeth as an independent woman 'who put the needs of her country before her own needs'.

As I mentioned earlier, the students in my classes read widely from a range of texts, and write analytical essays and research papers as well as taking in-class essay exams. They do traditional serious study and produce excellent research and analytical essays, often having worked on them in multiple drafts. But I find that the creative projects that I also assign to them provide an alternative style of learning that they greatly appreciate and enjoy. For some of these students, these projects allow them a different way to understand the past.

19
The Importance of Boredom in Learning about the Early Modern

Ceri Sullivan

Putting my foot in it to an eminent Dryden scholar ('Gosh, not as sexy as Marvell, is he?'), I tried to atone by a fantasy sketch of a Hollywood production of *The Conquest of Granada*. Professor X hummed crossly.

He was quite right to do so, because I was (apart from, yet again, letting mischief interfere with courtesy and career) making Dryden into 'one of us', as Mrs Thatcher would say. So this essay will celebrate the ethical and scholarly value of boredom, of alienating the reader, in studying early modern literature. Attending to an initially rebarbative text (not, of course, one of Dryden's) has three advantages. First, the text shows how truly other a culture can be, demanding we follow its co-ordinates not our own. Boring texts are the antidote to cultural narcissism. Second, paying attention without interest is a sophisticated mental skill, which asks for persistence, dispassion, discipline, clarity and exertion – in a word, maturity. Third, the pain rapidly turns into pleasure. Intimate knowledge of a period, an understanding of how and why issues are represented in the way they are, is delightful. It is not just sado-masochistic to enjoy mastering the details of a text.

You will notice the mingling of scholarship and ethical questions in each of these three points. Literature is a joyful subject to study because saying something interesting about it depends on character and experience as much as ability. Newman's idea of a university – Arnold's sense of literary criticism, looking for the best that is known and thought in the world – voice this for our discipline.[1] But early modern pedagogy was beforehand. The Renaissance grammar schools and universities were the first to make thought experiments about the experience of the *whole* of another culture. A brief period of birching and boredom over, and Latin acquired, the schoolboy was put to translate works dealing with topics ranging between classical hydraulics, metempsychosis, property statutes, poetic metre, seduction techniques, stoicism and the rest. Only classics and literary studies find out how the whole of society works – and the Renaissance did it first. Boundlessness is the point, an oxymoron which laughs at the bullet points of learning outcomes, and is mulish when asked to give syllabi which list ideas, not texts.

What are the implications of all this for teaching? We need the following in the classroom:

- Text-based, not theme-based, introductory courses to the period. Themes filter out what we are not interested in. Texts, especially with solid historicist footnotes, stubbornly retain it, as, to take a random example, has been a tradition in Milton scholarship in the Longman and new Oxford editions.
- More reception history, to show that the things we find opaque were gripping to their listeners. Donne's intricacies in 'Air and Angels', for instance, were not merely invented to torture little children.
- A wider view of the canon, to include texts of interest to early modern readers judged entirely on records of circulation, either in manuscript or print. This inevitably excludes texts chosen solely because they were written by groups now recognizing themselves as groups on the basis of a shared identity, so claiming a new visibility and importance (women, gays, Muslims), unless they were widely heard, seen or read in the past. This will give a far clearer impression of the particular hegemonies of early modern England than setting up victim-support groups based on ascribed identities of authors. Early modern England would not have seemed virtually normal to us. Celebrate or deprecate differences in identity politics between then and now, but do not hide them as differences between today's mainstream and minority culture.
- Ceasing to teach gobbets from selected texts (a covert form of themed teaching), or at least press publishers to work towards print-on-demand for selected texts. Let the students skip if they must, but put the choice of what to read and what to omit back onto them, so they understand the consequences to the parameters they are setting (that is, they see that how they choose to know is also what they will know). They need to feel frustrated that they have not read it all, not comfortably at ease that they have covered the 'important' points. Our discipline loses its point when it is reified in this way.
- Validate all approaches against the specific verbal evidence of the texts. Thus wanting to – and being able to – read texts in detail, alone, is *the* skill. 'Read it again, and closer!' should be our cry when dealing with Renaissance sentences that can be hypotactic, tightly

concise, polysyllabic, or whatever. Push students to go to primary research aids, particularly the etymological sections of the *Oxford English Dictionary*, even while acknowledging all understanding gained is always partial. Thus also, since the medium is the message, both in physical text and in words used, resist sole dependence on modernized texts. Use Early English Books Online, rather than a modern anthology such as the Norton, and take students to the university archives to handle material.

- Profit from the fact that 20-year-olds now are more visually than verbally literate. The drama of the early modern period is its glory, and is also the mode which responds best to being visualized using new techniques, such as the English Subject Centre's Globe on Second Life, the National Theatre's live productions screened across the UK by the cinema chain Vue, or YouTube clips of student productions. This is the area where the students guide me.
- Abandon the distinction between research and teaching in favour of the Renaissance term 'learning'. In this model no one is right. Classes are rhetorical tussles to persuade others of the interest one takes in a text, and the seminar leader wins at the moment she loses an argument to a student.
- Deplore the arrogance of our twenty-first-century colleagues when they claim literary theory all for themselves. Just snap 'Ramism, Euphuism, pathos, quantitative verse, mimesis, tropes' at them. See if they can be anything like as concrete and engaging, about who is doing what to whom in which words, as the master theory of our period, rhetoric. Hah!
- Above all, politicize our classes. Early modern texts are an antidote to the realism of the novel (the genre students most often read independently), an antidote to conservative comfort reading. Tudor–Stuart writers show how representation is always interested: 'Look at how I say is what I say, and what I do to you in saying it this way.'

That all should put the fear of the Renaissance back into the heart of the easy-access, make-it-relevant, tick-box co-ordinators of learning outcomes.

Note

1. J.H. Newman, *The Idea of a University*, ed. I.T. Ker (Oxford: Clarendon Press, 1976); M. Arnold, 'The Study of Poetry', in *The Complete Prose Works of Matthew Arnold*, ed. R.H. Super, 11 vols (Ann Arbor: University of Michigan Press, 1960–77), IX, pp. 161–88.

Part 4
Performing the Early Modern

20
Teaching French Seventeenth-century Theatre: Saying is Believing

Henry Phillips

In teaching seventeenth-century French theatre, why not choose a method that begins with the materiality and practice of the text? Jacques Copeau comments in respect of Molière: 'To understand a play and to stage it as it is written, one need simply know how to read the text and to cede to its movement.'[1] This is a simple but not so simple injunction. What is the sense in a modern context of 'as it is written'? How exactly do we give ourselves over to the text? What follows is not meant to be a manual, but a framework that justifies a particular classroom approach to teaching classical theatre, combining in a symbiotic way the teachings of French theatre practitioners and the work of scholars who appear on our bibliographies. It is above all centred on active learning.

The importance of Copeau's remark lies above all in the true meaning of reading ('lire') for a man of theatre, since reading becomes reading aloud (a practice whose absence is commonly deplored among the young). In reading aloud, two types of materiality coincide, the signs for identifying meaning in the way the text is written and the actualization of those signs through vocalization, which may in itself, at this basic level, generate meaning. If we begin by inviting students to read aloud and to reflect actively on what they hear, both essentially participatory processes, the classroom becomes a stage, indeed a laboratory where critical positions can be put to active test. Moreover, students, especially in group work based on performance, can claim a good degree of ownership of the learning situation. What is in any case essential is to move on from the emphasis on classical theatre as the literary theatre of the canon to classical theatre as a living art with which we can have direct contact beyond that of silent reading.

Louis Jouvet as pedagogue is a good guide for the classroom. In the verbatim accounts of his classes at the Paris Conservatoire, he exhorts his pupils to concentrate on diction as the platform for understanding characters rather than expression. One assumption for our students to test therefore is the precise way in which diction can relate to meaning. For Jouvet, 'the actor deems it necessary to give meaning to his lines, whereas the *text* carries enough meaning in itself'.[2] Equally, Jouvet warns against 'acting' too soon: 'one shouldn't rush to perform the text, one should speak it'.[3] Diction remains the priority before the revelation of 'the feelings that the text evokes in you'.[4] Such a position may not only be valid theatrically: it also means that teachers and students need have no qualms about the absence of prior dramatic experience. Experience derives first and foremost from vocal contact with the text. Copeau's words may surprise but also comfort: 'No need for erudition, not even for a detailed analysis.'[5] Instinct can lead us to 'the original *spirit* [of the text] and the meaning of the true tradition'.[6]

On the other hand, erudition need not be the enemy of the theatrical but a close collaborator. Recent research offers specific challenges for teaching through performance. The *presence* of the text in class through performance can become an engagement with an approach highlighting the historical when our attention is brought to the pronunciation and rhythms of the alexandrine as originally conceived, at least in the much-informed opinion of Georges Forestier and the productions of Eugène Green. Jouvet's foregrounding of the importance of diction can, for example, be tested when the pause length attached to the full stop, comma, colon and semi-colon of original editions is contrasted with the punctuation of modern editors.

Developing awareness of the particularities of seventeenth-century verse through reading lines aloud, leads to an enhanced appreciation in theatrical practice of playwrights' use of the art of rhetoric. The opening words of the title of Michael Hawcroft's book on Racine's language, *Word as Action*, point again, along with Peter France's *Racine's Rhetoric*, in the direction of materiality and actualization.[7] Anaphora is a figure easily identified on the page. What is less easy to identify is its actual force for the listener and the speaker. Again, saying, listening and hearing, in other words learning through performance, offer insights beyond the silent act of reading or 'disembodied' analysis.

This interaction of history and practice emerges strongly through Forestier's argument in his work on Corneille and Racine that seventeenth-century writers were unconcerned with the metaphysical concept of the tragic and employed their art in the production of effects, especially through the choice of subject and the articulation of the action, perhaps the 'mouvement' referred to by Copeau. All else, like heroism and politics, is entirely subordinate to what, according to Forestier, Racine promotes as 'the fundamental importance of the action, meaning the way in which the facts are organized so as to move the spectators in the writing of a tragedy'.[8] Teachers and students taking the place of the practitioner (or in this particular case, as with rhetoric, the audience) gives life to scholarly insight rather than suggesting it as simply corroborative or authoritative in its own right.

In his writings, Antoine Vitez suggests the value in the classroom of active reflection on the presence of the text through performance and its inescapable historical status. He challenges 'the oft-repeated stupid declaration [...] that works should be staged *as they were written*'.[9] Vitez reminds us that in the theatre we are in the presence of an historical consciousness which is not our own: the theatrical event acts as the translation in the present of a text from the past. Vitez states therefore as a *theatrical* position that: 'The issue is to make the public understand that time has past, while bearing this historical perspective in mind ourselves, and to show the past in the strangeness of the objects rediscovered onstage.'[10]

In these circumstances, the student may ask whether the force of diction allows us to get closer to seventeenth-century characters or to construct them as different. French theatre practitioners employ different and highly discussable emphases. For Copeau, 'The most beautiful eternity is that of a voice which is alive, one which, three hundred years on, continues to address the audience directly, to speak to them, to move them.'[11] Theatre is a meeting point. Vitez's promotion of 'strangeness' ('étrangeté') makes the performance, and study, of a classical play primarily an encounter promoting a process of differential self-identification. Comprehending fully the relation of classical theatre to the present means that in the practice of the classroom students must articulate to some degree their own apprehension of present and historical selves.

So, an approach through voice and the materiality of the text fruitfully combines the historical with the 'here and now'. The classroom is the site of reflection on the parameters of scholarly debate when applied to texts representing a particular history within a living tradition. Through the framework of performance-centred learning provided in class, students must engage with the need to balance scholarly debate and the generic specificity of classical theatre. After all, the text is the first to ask us the questions and, in the transition from page to stage, to demand the answers. In the end, as Vitez puts it: 'A dramatic work is a mystery which the theatre must solve.'[12] Discuss.

Notes

1. 'Pour comprendre une comédie et la représenter comme elle est écrite, il suffit d'en savoir lire le texte et d'en suivre le mouvement avec docilité.' Jacques Copeau, *Registres II: Molière*, ed. André Cabanis (Paris: Gallimard, 1976), p. 212.
2. 'L'acteur croit nécessaire de donner du sens à ses répliques, alors que le *texte* a assez de sens en lui-même.' Louis Jouvet, *Tragédie classique et théâtre du XIXe siècle* (Paris: Gallimard, 1968), p. 40.
3. '[I]l ne faut pas commencer à jouer trop tôt le texte, il faut le dire.' *Ibid.*, p. 43.
4. *Ibid.*: 'les sentiments que le texte te fera éprouver'.
5. 'Pas besoin d'érudition, pas même d'analyse approfondie.' Copeau, *Registres II*, p. 64.
6. *Ibid.*: 'l'*esprit* original et le sens de la vraie tradition'.
7. Peter France, *Racine's Rhetoric* (Oxford University Press, 1965) and Michael Hawcroft, *Word as Action: Racine, Rhetoric and Theatrical Language* (Oxford University Press, 1992).
8. '[L]a primauté de l'action entendue comme organisation pathétique des faits dans l'élaboration de la tragédie'. Georges Forestier, *Passions tragiques et règles classiques: essai sur la tragédie française* (Paris: Presses Universitaires de France, 2003), p. 246.
9. '[L]a perpétuelle stupide affirmation [...] selon laquelle il faudrait monter les œuvres *telles qu'elles sont écrites*'. Antoine Vitez, *Le Théâtre des idées*, ed. Danièle Sallenave et Georges Banu (Paris: Gallimard, 1991), p. 293.
10. 'Il s'agit de faire comprendre au public que le temps s'est écoulé en prenant nous-mêmes conscience de cette perspective historique et de montrer le temps passé dans l'étrangeté des objets que l'on retrouve.' *Ibid.*, p. 194.
11. 'La plus belle éternité, c'est celle d'une voix qui, trois cents ans passés, ne cesse pas de s'adresser directement aux hommes, de leur parler, de les toucher, vivante [...].' Copeau, *Registres II*, p. 15.
12. 'L'œuvre dramatique est une énigme que le théâtre doit résoudre.' Vitez, *Théâtre*, p. 125.

21
Teaching Early Modern Spectacle through Film: Exploring Possibilities, Challenges and Pitfalls through a French Corpus

Guy Spielmann

While research on the history of drama as a branch of literature can be conducted largely through texts, the history of spectacle relies on images of all kinds – sketches for sets and costumes, playhouse blueprints, frontispieces, paintings and engravings, and so on – which must necessarily be used in any course that covers more than literary analysis. Unfortunately, a teacher whose background does not specifically include theatre and stagecraft history may find locating and selecting such documents challenging; interpreting them in a manner that is both accurate and appealing may prove near impossible. Therefore, recreations of stage shows featured in motion pictures offer an enticing, ready-made alternative to primary visual resources, because they help students gain an immediate, vivid sense of what spectacle events of the seventeenth and eighteenth centuries looked and sounded like.

However, relying on cinema for sources raises its own problems, which may not be immediately apparent. In the following pages, I would like to lay out a number of principles and guidelines that an instructor can follow in deciding which films are appropriate, and how they could best be exploited in teaching. For purposes of coherence and brevity, I will limit myself exclusively to the French domain, with the understanding that the principles discussed here, *mutatis mutandis*, would apply to other national traditions as well, with adjustments according to the current status of a particular dramatic corpus in its native setting. In order to avoid excessive abstraction, I discuss specific titles that prove most useful – or that raise serious problems; where applicable, I have indicated a precise timeframe (in hours, minutes and seconds) so that the sequences being analysed may be retrieved easily on the VHS tape or DVD of the film (full publication data appears at the end of this essay).

231

Those who teach French theatre will therefore be provided with a useful starter list of titles in various categories.

The first issue that we face is methodological, because film is a medium, not a genre. Films set in the early modern period are considered to fall under the 'historical' heading when the main purpose is to recreate a particular event or era, or under the 'costume drama' category when the focus is on a fictional or semi-fictional plot (such as the innumerable adaptations of novels by Alexandre Dumas or Jane Austen). These clearly delineated boundaries, however, are too often blurred in practice for us to assume that even self-described historical films provide a particularly accurate depiction of historical events. Moreover, what we may call 'theatre films', far from constituting a single homogeneous category, should be classified into three broad types whose characteristics differ significantly:

1. films that are directly based on early modern drama, that is, whose script is adapted from a stage play;
2. films dealing with a person or event that is somehow linked to drama or spectacle; for instance, a playwright or actor (Molière in two eponymous films and Shakespeare in *Shakespeare in Love*,[1] composer Henry Purcell in *England my England* and opera singer Carlo Broschi in *Farinelli, il castrato*);[2]
3. films that are set in the early modern period, with no particular concentration on drama or spectacle, but which include relevant scenes: the erotic ballet in *The Libertine*,[3] the king's banquet in *Vatel*, the staging of Racine's *Esther* by the pupils at the orphanage in *Saint-Cyr*, brief sequences occurring at the Paris opera in *Jefferson in Paris* and *Dangerous Liaisons*.

As we will see, close examination of these various types of films sometimes yield counterintuitive conclusions, inducing us to keep an open mind as to where the best source material can be found, pedagogically speaking.

Films directly based on early modern drama

The primordial factor in selecting a film (or parts thereof) for teaching purposes is the scope of the course and the instructor's range of expertise. When dramatic literature alone is concerned, and the goal is limited to illustrating a play-text in order to make it more lively, perhaps more accessible for students, one tends to look first for films that appear to deliver a 'straight' performance, without added layers of meaning. But even if the filming itself remains relatively unobtrusive – as in a video capture, where one or more cameras are set to record a live performance with a minimum of editing and visual effects (zooming, panning, fade-ins and so on) – the *mise-en-scène* never is. Non-specialists frequently believe that there is a kind of default setting to staging a play, and in some countries a venerable institution (such as the Comédie-Française or the Royal Shakespeare Company) is considered as *de facto* purveyor of 'standard' productions.[4] In fact, while these productions do tend to reflect a somewhat conservative vision, they are anything but neutral, even though they may refrain from putting forward a particularly provocative interpretation. Such films are well suited to teaching if performance *per se* is not studied in class, or if the point is merely to show in very general terms how a text can be brought to stage, without delving into the complexity of multiple interpretations, or into technical issues.

Let us for example compare three filmed versions of Molière's first real comedy, *Les Précieuses ridicules* (1659): one released by the Comédie-Française in 1998, the 1999 production by Macha Makeïeff and Jérôme Deschamps,[5] and a new staging at the Comédie-Française under the direction of Dan Jemmett, first presented at the Vieux Colombier playhouse in 2007 and broadcast on French TV (France 3) in 2009. The earliest version, directed by Jean-Luc Boutté, seems to avoid taking a controversial or radical stance on any aspect of the production: period costumes are used, but not to the point of fastidious authenticity, and the set combines elements of realism, abstraction and stylization. The actors deliver their lines in a declamatory style, but only insofar as the script dictates it (though written in prose, the seventeenth-century French text includes many archaic words and phrases). Boutté follows stage directions exactly, with the exception of two odd bits of stage business (at one point, the actors start to play with giant translucent balloons; a servant rushes in the room every time Mascarille cries out 'Au voleur!' while reciting his improvised poem). The performance is lively and entertaining enough, but it does not let us see and hear anything about the play that we cannot grasp from attentively reading the text alone – unusual restraint in an age when directors tend to revisit stage classics in the most idiosyncratic ways. In any case, such a self-consciously 'standard' approach makes the play extremely accessible to a general audience, without suggesting that this is the way Molière's troupe would have played *Les Précieuses ridicules* in 1659.

By contrast, Makeïeff and Deschamps opted for choices that purport to be unconventional. As they point out:

> While retaining great respect towards the text and its construction, we significantly move away from the traditional manner in which this play is generally staged. What people choose to emphasize, most of the time, is a kind of a prowess in diction: Molière's elegance is overly emphasized as if to make excuses for the fact that *Les Précieuses ridicules* is not as great a play as those to follow. It is therefore presented as a kind of salon conversation, an exchange of ideas about the mores of the time. In fact, it is a really brutal confrontation, where characters speak to one another with extreme violence.[6]

However, restoring this violence and allowing the actors to improvise was not supposed to compromise authenticity, quite the contrary in fact:

> We believe that these idiosyncrasies are probably close to the acting style of Molière's troupe, at least in spirit, and even if the outcome is undoubtedly not exactly the same, three centuries apart.[7]

Be that as it may, the Deschamps-Makeïeff production differs from the Comédie-Française version mostly by what is *added* to Molière's dialogues and stage directions: not much is actually *changed*, and the first half of the performance hardly fulfils the promise of subverting tradition. This is most evident, by contrast, in the high point of the play (scenes 7–12), a visit to the would-be fashionable girls by two valets posing as noblemen, the Marquis de Mascarille and Vicomte de Jodelet, which is enriched here with a number of unscripted sight gags and *lazzi*. Molière wrote this latter part for an already famous farce player, Julien Bedeau (whose stage name was Jodelet); unsurprisingly, it is also the part that best lends itself to improvisation, as when the actor (Olivier Saladin) stretches a simple, mechanical gesture – putting his sword back in its scabbard – into a comic routine lasting several minutes.

Finally, the 2007 *mise-en-scène* by British director Dan Jemmett provides a clear example of a strongly 'interpretive' direction that preserves only Molière's text (and proves that even the Comédie-Française occasionally commissions non-standard productions). In a setting reminiscent of a dingy 1960s music hall (with incidental music to match), actors in clownish outfits and make-up dance and prance frenetically around the stage, delivering their lines with deliberate disregard for their actual meaning – much of which is lost anyways out of the seventeenth-century context. While the main characters are supposed to be in their twenties at most, Jemmett cast veteran actors in their fifties and sixties, and turned the maid Marotte, a mere bit part in the script, into a kind of master-mind figure who seems to be running the show. Alone, this production has no documentary value on early modern performance, nor does it bring out any theretofore hidden shades of meaning; but a comparative study of all three versions could prove useful in establishing criteria of relative (in)fidelity to period staging. For instance, we must note that the Boutté version was shot without an audience present and shows much greater reliance on purely cinematographic means of expression, such as multiple angles of vision, heavy post-production editing or background music; from a performance perspective, then, this suppos-edly more 'neutral' version is less authentic than the others.

Even within this first category, we must obviously distinguish between (and draw students' attention to) three dimensions pertaining to the film director, the actors and the stage director respectively:[8]

- a *technical* dimension: how was the film made? Did the director attempt to mostly recreate a theatrical experience (each spectator sees the whole stage at once, from a fixed spot), or did s/he fully exploit the possibilities of film (multiple vision angles, close-ups, panning and so on)?
- a *performative* dimension: how do actors act out the script, say their lines, move and gesture according to stage directions, whether internal or external to the dialogues?
- an *interpretive* (or aesthetic) dimension: how did the stage director express his/her own vision of the play, beyond what the script indicates?

Choosing a film of one type over another depends on pedagogical purpose rather than on intrinsic quality; in a literature class, the Boutté version would be most suitable, while the Deschamps-Makcïeff version would work well in an introduction to early modern performance. Exploiting the Jemmett version would require of students a solid background on seventeenth-century French drama, because the deliberately radical directorial options only make sense in light of previous familiarity with standard approaches and audience expectations: the show was widely praised in the French media for its refreshingly iconoclastic take on a well-known classic.

The major works of Molière provide a uniquely rich corpus for com-parative analysis, since two (or more) versions of *L'École des femmes* (*School for Wives*, 1662), *L'Avare* (*The Miser*, 1668), *Le Bourgeois Gentilhomme*

(*The Bourgeois Gentleman*, 1670) and *Le Malade imaginaire* (*The Imaginary Invalid*, aka *The Hypochondriac*, 1673) are currently available on DVD, reflecting a wide range of approaches. Beyond the most salient aspects (blocking of a particular scene, acting styles, choice of sets and costumes and so on), I suggest analysing the overall artistic scheme reflected in the film: biases, viewpoints (aesthetical, political or other), idiosyncrasies and any fundamental choices that reveal a director's thinking about how the play should look and sound – a method that must include a critical examination of coherence and consistency in such decisions, in order to help students better realize that no version can possibly be 'authentic' or 'authoritative'.

On the other hand, a director's importance should not be overstated in film, by contrast to a stage show, for which the *metteur-en-scène* gets most of the credit. One remarkable feature of the above-mentioned plays, beside their literary fame, resides in their usability as 'vehicles' for star actors (whose bankable status often allows the production to be filmed at all), because they all involve a strong leading *caractère* – Molière's specialty. The role of the director may then become quite secondary, as choices are dictated by a pre-existing public image that must be accommodated. The late beloved comedian Louis de Funès most probably picked *L'Avare* (1980), for instance, because the part of Harpagon perfectly conforms to his established screen persona of a vociferously dictatorial, hyperkinetic man in a position of authority (CEO, police inspector, family patriarch). As a result, several scenes have a feel of *déjà vu* for French viewers, and de Funès dressed in black cassock and ruff, feverishly pawing through a chest full of gold coins, irresistibly brings to mind an identical scene from an earlier film, *La Folie des grandeurs* (1971).[9]

However, de Funès, who also co-directed, was keenly aware that his status as star of popular, commercial films might induce critics to think that he was defiling a national monument – in those days, films made from classics almost always featured resident actors from the Comédie-Française – and he therefore took extraordinary measures to demonstrate his deference towards Molière's work. Not only did he scrupulously follow the text and stage directions, but he also had enlarged reproductions of pages from the *Petit Classiques Hachette* edition of the play – the kind used in French schools, where *L'Avare* was (and remains) standard reading – plastered on the walls of Harpagon's drawing room, as if to assert the seriousness of his purpose and affirm his respect for a hallowed dramatic masterpiece. This highly unusual treatment of decor offers a perfect example of the need to carefully take into account the background of each production before analysing it. In order to rationalize such a heavy-handed approach to establishing scholarly credibility, we must reckon with the almost religious devotion that the French lavish on key cultural figures like Molière, and the importance of formal education in that country, which explains why the greatest screen comic of his day felt such insecurity when tackling a canonical play.

By contrast, no such accreditation seemed indispensable when Michel Serrault took on the part in a 2007 film, perhaps because he had already played it on stage some 20 years earlier. In the making-of featurette included in the DVD version, he even comments that the point was to 'have fun with the play', and that a made-for-TV production should not be overly theatrical, concluding that taking liberties with Molière is not 'sacrilegious'.[10] This difference in attitude could be attributed to the fact that Serrault, at 79 (he had been in films with de Funès in the 1960s), was considered a legitimate theatre veteran; but a general shift in attitude provides a more likely justification. Nowadays, stand-up comedians such as Jean-Marie Bigard and Smaïn, no bona fide thespians by any means, may take on Molière's greatest roles (*Le Bourgeois Gentilhomme* (2006) and *Les Fourberies de Scapin* (1999) respectively) without much compunction about debasing a national treasure, even though neither outrageously modernized adaptations contribute much to our appreciation or understanding of classical drama.

Nevertheless, a comparison between the two versions of *L'Avare* is likely to yield very different results than a contrastive study of the *Précieuses ridicules* as sketched above. Although both are filmed plays rather than live performance captures, their production styles stand distinctly apart: the 1980 set is prim and brightly coloured, while the acting remains close to what it would be on stage, while the nearly monochromatic 2007 version, shot in a decrepit house, features dishevelled actors wearing rags and speaking their lines in as naturalistic a tone as verse allows. Manifestly, this is not so much a case of stark difference in interpretation, as of changing aesthetic trends and standards over the years. In order to cover the full spectrum of what filmed theatre looks like (still within the Molière corpus), I would suggest screening features which represent a range of solutions: at one end, *L'École des femmes* directed by Didier Bezace and recorded live at the 2001 Avignon Festival against the cyclopean stone walls of the Popes' Palace, with a minimalist set; at the other end, Planchon's *Dandin* (1987) which comes closest to a non-theatrical approach to filming a play, at least for the French domain: perhaps because of the aforementioned reverence towards canonical French authors, no Molière film comes close to the kind of daring yet highly successful transposition that Loncraine, Luhrman and Almereyda

managed with *Richard III*, *Romeo and Juliet* and *Hamlet*.[11] Somewhere in
the middle lies Christian de Chalonge's *Bourgeois Gentilhomme*, a made-
for-TV feature starring yet another popular film comedian, Christian
Clavier.

In the 2001 *École des femmes*, one is immediately struck by the vocal
delivery – on the cavernous, open-air stage of the medieval Popes'
Palace, actors virtually have to scream in order to be heard – and the
paucity of movement, also justified by the size of the space (although
the film itself does resort to close-ups). While Molière and his group did
perform outdoors (notably at Versailles), they never had to work in such a
setting, which was invented in the twentieth century: in the 1660s, there
would have been fewer spectators, who would have sat or stood near the
stage. At the other end of the spectrum, Planchon, who had previously
directed a highly interpretive stage production of *George Dandin* (a Marxist
reading that turned Molière's light comedy into a tragedy about class
struggle), decided to write his own script, even adding some characters
(a coven of witches). He shot the film on location with numerous out-
door scenes, as if to subdue the theatrical dimension of the work, at
least to a degree that French audiences find acceptable when it comes to
early modern plays. De Chalonge's *Bourgeois* is another example where
stage and screen director are one and the same; while staying extremely
faithful to Molière's text, de Chalonge also erased the play's theatricality
under lavish production values: sumptuous costumes, multiple settings
in an actual, beautiful château, the action being somewhat arbitrarily
located in various rooms (including the kitchen, the stables and the
surrounding gardens[12]), and the cinematography correspondingly sleek.
Unfortunately, some crucial aspects of this *comédie-ballet* are completely
lost in the process. The famous finale, a mock 'Turkish ceremony' meant
to dupe the hero into letting his son marry according to his wishes, is
supposed to be funny because the audience, unlike the credulous father,
can plainly tell that the ritual is a ridiculous masquerade. De Chalonge,
however, brings such technical refinement to his production that the
Turkish ceremony looks quite authentic – excessively so in fact: with
live elephants and a dozen extras in beautiful costumes, it could not
possibly be a makeshift trick pulled together at the last minute by the
hero's hapless son and his valet. As a result, it is not in the least funny,
nor is the rest of the play: even Clavier, an actor known for his manic
characterizations in slapstick screen farces, comes off as unusually serious
and self-possessed.

Whatever their qualities or flaws, none of these productions can be
deemed 'reconstructive', that is none shows a play in the way it would

originally have been staged (as far as we know), and none therefore helps us teach a class about early modern performance. Is there, in fact, such a film?

One is tempted to place in the 'reconstructive' category a live taping of Molière's *Bourgeois Gentilhomme* as directed by Benjamin Lazar at the Théâtre le Trianon in Paris (2004), which features a candle-lit stage and 'baroque diction' according to the theories of Eugene Green;[13] but while enthusiasts have saluted this kind of effort as a major step towards a historically correct rendition of seventeenth-century theatrical spectacle, others have pointed out that this is just another contemporary, subjective vision with no particular claim to authenticity. Indeed, even if we subscribe to Green's tenets on baroque gesture and pronunciation, and even if the extended musical sequences, candle lighting and single-backdrop set do approximate period staging better than most other productions, frequent close-ups in the film reveal a number of definitely modern touches (make-up, costume details, hair, props, dance moves) that make it impossible to consider this as a mere re-enactment of the 1670 show, especially since an absolutely central element is missing: the 1670 audience.

No simple and easy solution exists: each and every choice materialized through *mise-en-scène*, acting and stagecraft should be carefully questioned in relationship to available evidence: the texts themselves, any period iconography that pertains to the topic, but also witness accounts and other documents. Moreover, the staging of a play and the filming of it are to be considered as separate issues, neither of which can ever be considered self-evident, unproblematic or neutral: both must be treated as objects to be investigated, rather than as surrogate primary sources of sorts.

Films related to spectacle

On a second level, we need to show greater diffidence towards our natural proclivity for filmed performance, and consider the advantages of films *about* spectacle. As a matter of fact, there seems to be a self-imposed, binary choice in what 'theatre films' depict: either a single play in its entirety (such as those examined above), in which case the original conditions of performance are usually all but ignored, or the context in which a play was initially produced, in which case we see only bits and pieces of a show, the focus being usually on the actors and on the preparatory phases of play production, with varying degrees of concentration. Ariane Mnouchkine's and Tirard's *Molière*, while they seemingly belong to the same genre (the so-called 'biopic'), demonstrate opposite approaches: the first is a mostly linear retelling of Molière's entire life story in a very earnest tone, with an implicit claim to historical truth-fulness, while the second focuses on a particular episode, most likely fictitious, and presented in the guise of a lighthearted romantic comedy (much like *Shakespeare in Love*).[14]

In both we find only snippets of performance, which may feel unsatis-fying if one expects a film about a prolific playwright and/or actor to deal mostly with his life in the theatre. However, quality comes before quantity when the purpose is to give our students a sense of what an early modern show could be like: in Mnouchkine's lengthy, slow-moving *Molière*, for instance, there is relatively little acting, but some worthwhile educational sequences such as the first appearance of the still-unknown, newly minted Troupe de Monsieur at court (part 2, 30:00–39:00). Under a thick layer of garish make-up, standing still on stage, Molière and Armande Béjart recite the text from Corneille's *Nicomède* in a fright-ful drone that is literally putting the royal audience to sleep. While Molière seems unaware that his performance is at issue (backstage, he wonders aloud why such beautiful verse by Monsieur Corneille is so unfavourably received), his comrades persuade him to quickly switch gears in the comic afterpiece, *Le Docteur amoureux*, a farcical play dur-ing which the actor, wearing a *commedia dell'arte* mask, launches into an extended *lazzo*. This improvised part has him panting and yelping like a dog, begging the king to intervene in the character's favour – in reality, begging the king to let the troupe settle in Paris. All's well that ends well as the young Louis XIV wakes up from his torpor and laughs good-heartedly.

Tirard imagines a comparable scene, but in a rather different context: on the makeshift stage of a rustic inn, Molière attempts to perform a tragedy, wearing make-up and a costume similar to his accoutrement in Mnouchkine's version. His ineptitude at tragic acting causes a different reaction from the unsophisticated crowd in the tavern: they jeer and throw food at him.[15] Though Molière stoically continues to recite his lines, the show is abruptly interrupted when a party of tax officers and soldiers come to arrest him for unpaid debts – a mishap that inspires the comedian to put on an impromptu farcical scene to poke fun at the lawmen (10:00–12:30). Both scenes make the (documented) point that Molière never managed to succeed in playing serious parts, though he persisted in trying for a long time; together, they illustrate the extremely disparate conditions in which he performed, from the stilted ambiance at court to the hubbub of a provincial public house, all of which helps underscore the fact that 'theatre', in the early modern period, was often an activity quite different from what we usually experience today.

We find an excellent rendition of this reality, paradoxically enough, in a film that does not make any claims to historical accuracy, being based on a late nineteenth-century play that conjured up a definitively subjective vision of the seventeenth century: Rappeneau's *Cyrano de Bergerac* (1990).[16] The film opens with a long sequence (0:2:00–0:14:00)[17] set in the hôtel de Bourgogne playhouse in 1640, as Baro's tragi-comedy *Clorise* is about to be performed. The scene is depicted in much greater detail than what the play-script requires, or what a stage production would allow: some people are trying to sneak in without tickets; in the pit, spectators converse loudly, eat, drink and play cards, while pickpockets get busy. Fops saunter onstage to sit in the chairs located there (a local custom since 1637), making sure to draw attention to themselves. Smoky candles are lit in huge chandeliers. The stage is set for a pastoral play, and the *tapisserie* (a painted backdrop) is raised to reveal the actor Monfleury costumed as Phaedo. As he starts speaking his lines, Cyrano interrupts him, and provokes a scuffle that stops the show; other actors (Bellerose and Jodelet) intervene in a vain attempt to end the commotion. Although the story is quite fanciful overall, and this particular incident was imagined by Rostand, the main characters involved are all historical, and every detail of the scene as filmed by Rappeneau is well documented.

One of the potential pitfalls of using cinema for teaching theatre lies in films that make performance from another era look and sound familiar to contemporary audiences. Another biopic revolving around Molière's troupe provides the best (or worst) example: Vera Belmont's *Marquise*, which focuses on Marquise-Thérèse de Gorla, an actress more celebrated for her beauty and shapely figure than for her talent. This supposedly feminist reinvention of history imagines Marquise to have been a brilliant but undiscovered thespian, who languishes as a bit player until Jean Racine, still only a rising star himself, gives her the opportunity to blossom into a great tragic actress, Molière's opinion notwithstanding. Although Belmont's interpretation of this historical episode is, by and large, a figment of the scriptwriter's imagination, the most pernicious aspect of the film resides in a consistently anachronistic depiction of acting; in the climactic scene (1:21:30–1:23:00), Marquise reveals her purportedly superior abilities by speaking Racine's verse (from *Andromaque*) in a breathless whisper and with a body stance that can only work a few inches away from a camera lens and a microphone – in other words, in the typical manner of a late twentieth-century screen performer. Yet Molière is so impressed that he blurts out 'I did not know that it was possible to perform tragedy in such a naturalistic manner,'[18] which sounds like a second-degree humorous punchline, considering that, indeed, no one at the time acted this way. In an earlier rehearsal scene (1:14:00–1:19:00), Marquise's partner, the illustrious Floridor (played by the illustrious Georges Wilson), is taken aback by her 'common' delivery, remarking dryly that they 'are not on the Pont Neuf' (a favourite location for street shows by strolling actors and mountebanks), and pointing out that tragic verse should not be spoken like 'a woman's words hastily jotted down'.[19]

In the finale (1:52:00–1:53:00), an aging and ailing Marquise, who has been replaced by a younger actress, suddenly bursts on stage at the hôtel de Bourgogne towards the end of a performance, launches into an impassioned monologue about the difficulty of acting – and drops dead. Racine steps in, scoops her up in his arms and carries her away as the audience silently watches. There is absolutely nothing historical about any aspect of this scene; but the main difference between a film like this and *Cyrano* is that there is no perceptible irony or distance, as *Marquise* bills itself as a serious drama with a message, on the plight of women and on theatrical art. Because most of today's viewers are likely to identify with the kind of naturalistic acting presented here as an innovation of the 1670s, the only way imaginable to use such a film in a course would be to have students determine why virtually every aspect is wrong where theatre is concerned – a good exercise to verify if they have understood and retained information about the style and conditions of performance at the time.

Figuring out the strengths and weaknesses of a film proves more difficult when it was made with the benefit of scholarly expertise, such as Corbiau's *Le Roi danse*, based on Beaussant's authoritative monograph on Lully, and thus promising unprecedented documentary value. Because *Le Roi danse* arguably offers more and better performance scenes than any other film about early modern France it should also come under closer scrutiny, thus providing excellent opportunities to exercise students' inquiry skills. In the re-enactment of the 1653 *Ballet de la nuit*, for instance (7:45–13:40), the stage machinery and the king's costume of the rising sun (known through a famous coloured engraving) are faithfully rendered, but the narrator who provides a running commentary to the audience is a complete aberration. A *ballet de cour* had a libretto that spectators would read before or during the performance, and deciphering its allegories and emblems was an intellectual amusement much prized by the upper classes: having these enigma explained would have been humiliating and insulting. In the scene featured on the poster, the young king, stripped to the waist and wearing full-body gold-hued make-up, performs alone a difficult dance routine in the Versailles gardens, while Molière provides a narration (1:07:00–1:09:00); when he nearly falls and badly twists his ankle, an onlooker quips 'It looks like the state is about to collapse!'[20] While this makes for a powerfully dramatic scene, and certainly does not seem out of place in a film devoted to the well-documented importance of dancing for Louis XIV, *everything* about it is erroneous.

On the other hand, the initial performance of *Le Bourgeois Gentilhomme* at Chambord is quite convincingly recreated and, although we only see a few minutes of it (1:11:00–1:15:00), this sequence makes a better pedagogical document than a whole 'reconstructed' performance like Lazar's *Bourgeois*, if only because we get to see the audience, and a room in which the royal family alone occupies the main floor. Such scenes provide useful reminders of the various configurations that 'theatre' could take: *Tartuffe* acted in the Versailles gardens in front of the court and without sets in *Le Roi danse*, or Racine's musical tragedy *Esther* performed for the king and Madame de Maintenon by the young girls of the Saint-Cyr institution (in both *L'Allée du roi* and *Saint-Cyr*) on a very rudimentary stage.

It would be tedious to list here all the anachronisms and inconsistencies in *Le Roi danse*; suffice it to say that Corbiau's earnestness of purpose (he also made *Farinelli* and a documentary about Versailles) and Beaussant's patronage did not yield a film that rises indisputably above the rest in terms of historical accuracy, regardless of its other merits. Better than *Marquise*, to be sure, but very far from being usable as an unmediated document.

Films including elements of spectacle

Beyond the blatant choice of films adapted from plays or entirely devoted to a figure of the stage, we must find less obvious instances of spectacle events featured in films that do not deal primarily with theatrical experience, and/or that may not hold great cinematographic value. Joffé's *Vatel*, for instance, weaves a ludicrously implausible love story around a famous incident: the suicide of François Vatel, who served as chef, steward and master of revels to the powerful Prince de Condé. Hoping to regain the king's favour (lost through his participation in the uprising of the *Fronde* in the 1650s), Condé invited the monarch and his court to a lavish three-day party at his estate in Chantilly.

Focusing on this exceptional fête, Joffé beautifully recreates its various components, showing us not only what the courtiers saw – *trompe-l'œil* sets with movable parts, ballets with African boys in exotic costumes, flying cherubs, fireworks and spectacular displays of food – but also how the show was managed backstage (0:22:30–0:26:30). During one of the banquets, a singer comes down in a flying gondola by dint of a machine that uses horse power; but the animals, scared by the fireworks, buckle uncontrollably and cause a stage hand to be crushed to death (1:02:48–1:07:54). While the incident is somewhat overly dramatized in order to highlight Vatel's caring attitude towards his assistants, it is quite verisimilar: operating theatrical machinery was hazardous and injuries were not uncommon.

Although most films about Louis XIV include scenes of revelry, none dwells as much as *Vatel* – and with comparable production values – on the details of those court festivals that hold crucial importance in the development of performing arts in baroque Europe. As such, this otherwise mediocre film offers an ideal complement to studying the texts and iconography relating to the epoch-making *Plaisirs de l'isle enchantée*, the week-long extravaganza that Louis XIV organized in Versailles early in his reign (1664), and that no filmmaker has yet endeavoured to portray on a large scale.

Valuable sources may not be directly related to spectacle at all, like Merchant Ivory's *Jefferson in Paris*. When the future US president, then ambassador to France, discovers how the royal family lives (0:33:49–0:36:03), we hear his voice-off commentary as Louis XVI and Marie Antoinette are seen eating:

> I meant to impress on my daughter the vainglory of such spectacle [...] Daily life at court is still ruled by an etiquette so rigid that the most private pursuits of the king and queen are converted into public ceremony. It is like watching actors, fantastically painted, bewigged and bejeweled, disporting themselves on a stage. The leading actress, though never a popular one, is the queen.

This astute observation provides a useful template for studying as performance episodes of court life featured in other films about the *ancien régime*: Companéez' TV mini-series, *L'Allée du roi*, Planchon's *Louis, enfant roi*, Rossellini's *La Prise de pouvoir par Louis XIV* (*The Rise of Louis XIV*, 1970: see for instance the long sequence that shows the king eating alone, while a large crowd watches [1:16:18–1:23:15]) or Coppola's *Marie Antoinette* (which presents the setting from an almost reverse angle, sympathetically to the queen) – films where theatre proper does not get much screen time.

Jefferson in Paris turns out to be more bountiful than most, however. We are treated to a re-enactment of Marie Antoinette's acting in a pastoral play at the *hameau* in Versailles, and to a street performance witnessed by Jefferson's valet, James Hemings, a graphically obscene puppet play satirizing the queen as a latter-day Messalina engaged in a sexual romp with her husband's debauched brother, the comte d'Artois (0:36:03–0:36:37). The highlight is undoubtedly a sequence when Jefferson attends the Paris opera (0:46:07–0:51:20): when he enters the box of his host, the eccentric British artist Richard Cosway, he is asked to take a bow towards the room, receiving a round of applause as if he were on stage. An old woman requests that he sit by her, 'while everyone yawns at the ballet'. Indeed, spectators appear to be watching one another much more than they do the actual performance of *Dardanus* (a 1784 opera by Antonio Sacchini and Nicolas-François Guillard); a party of Middle Easterners seems particularly curious of the goings-on around them. Interest for the show finally perks up when the main character makes his entrance, descending from the skies on a flying machine. Whereas men in the pit jeer at the actor, calling him a dwarf, women respond enthusiastically and, at the end of his aria, a muddle of booing, clapping and shrieking covers the music. A hysterical female spectator, parting the crowd, rushes towards the stage, calling out to the actor, in French: *'Dardanus! Dardanus! Dardanus! Amenez-le moi, je veux l'embrasser! Je veux monter au ciel avec lui!'* (Dardanus! Bring him to me, I want to kiss him! I want to ascend to the Heavens with him!) The rambunctious audience, at times inattentive and at times vigorously responsive, is particularly well rendered, and so is the musical performance, delivered by the leading French baroque orchestra, *Les Arts Florissants*, with cameos by director William Christie and counter-tenor Jean-Paul Fouchécourt. In addition to the flying apparatus, we catch a glimpse of cloud and wave effects, as well as some fine dance moves by *La Compagnie Fêtes Galantes*. All in all, this is perhaps the richest spectacle scene in any film about early modern France – although it is neither French nor centred on performance.

This quality appears clearly through a comparison with very similar scenes in Stephen Frears' *Dangerous Liaisons*,[21] the first of which includes an excerpt from *Iphigénie en Tauride* by Christoph Willibald Gluck and Nicolas-François Guillard (1779) (0:15:00–0:16:00). Although the Marquise de Merteuil exclaims 'Monsieur Danceny is one of these *rare* eccentrics who come here to listen to the music!' and spectators are shown observing one another, the audience is far too quiet and focused on the show, while the performance itself raises a number of issues: the female lead, as she sings the aria 'O Malheureuse Iphigénie!' from Act II.6, moves around the stage (opera singers, for reasons of acoustics and visibility, were virtually bound to remain in the proscenium area) and behind three-dimensional columns, the like of which were not used until late in the nineteenth century. As for the flames coming out of large copper craters on stage, they would have been unimaginable in an early modern playhouse, where accidental fires were a dreaded occurrence (most French theatres of the period burned down at some point). Superficially, this looks like a convincing recreation, but, like in the open-air solo performance in *Le Roi danse*, almost every detail is wrong. A second, shorter scene at the opera (0:27:00–0:28:00) raises a different issue: someone knowledgeable about baroque music will recognize a famous aria, 'Ombra mai fu', from the opening of *Serse* by Georg Friedrich Händel and Silvio Stampiglia (1738), and the staging is credible enough – but this particular opera was never performed in Paris in the eighteenth century ...

Because historical films always pose a problem of authenticity, we need to teach our students how to systematically approach such depictions with a critical stance, by triangulating textual and iconographic evidence from the period with filmic representations. Our aim should be to determine what belongs to reliable recreation, to educated guessing and to artistic licence – all of which can contribute to the filming of one single sequence. Authenticity must also be assessed against commonsensical assumptions: the scandalously erotic ballet arranged by Rochester for King Charles II in Dunmore's *The Libertine* is closer to historical reality than many of the dance sequences in *Le Roi danse*, even though the latter may appear more plausible to the untutored eye. It should also be remembered that, in addition to country-specific materials, some excellent illustrations of early modern spectacle can be found in films that do not necessarily come to mind as likely sources. In Terry Gilliam's *Adventures of Baron Munchausen*, for example, a hapless group of actors puts on a play about the exploits of the legendary baron, using various items of stage machinery (wave rolls and a sea monster that devours the hero) that are splendidly recreated. Jean Renoir's *The Golden Coach*, based on a nineteenth-century play set in South America, includes a presentation of traditional *commedia dell'arte* far more engaging than what can be found in educational documentary films.[22]

Mostly, we have to encapsulate in our pedagogical programme the essentially subjective vision that films convey. Rossellini made his *Prise de pouvoir par Louis XIV* without a single scene including spectacle, but Corbiau treated a more or less similar topic in *Le Roi danse* on the premise that Louis considered spectacle as an indispensable component of his political takeover. Planchon falls somewhere in between in *Louis, enfant roi*, but in this case the narrative is strongly coloured by the director's Marxist reading of history. Analysing these various interpretations of the same events, or all five versions of *Le Bourgeois Gentilhomme* currently available on film, does not allow us to conclude which is 'best' or 'more authentic': it gives us food for thought in our continuing attempt to understand – and teach – the reality of early modern spectacle, and reminds us that this understanding remains inevitably shaped by our own subjectivity.

Notes

1. *Shakespeare in Love*, dir. John Madden, script by Mark Norman and Tom Stoppard. USA, Universal, 1999. DVD: Miramax, 1999. (Joseph Fiennes as Shakespeare.)
2. *England my England*, dir. Tony Palmer, script by John Osborne and Charles Wood. UK, Channel Four Films, 1995. DVD: Warner Music Entertainment, 2007. (Tony Ball as Henry Purcell.) *Farinelli, il castrato*, dir. Gérard Corbiau, script by Marcel Beaulieu, Andrée Corbiau and Gérard Corbiau. France, K2 SA, Canal +, France 2, 1994. DVD: TF1 Video, 2009. (Stefano Dionisi as Carlo Broschi.)
3. *The Libertine*, dir. Laurence Dunmore, script by Stephen Jeffreys, based on his stage play. UK/Australia, Isle of Man/First Choice/Odyssey, 2004. DVD: Weinstein, 2006. (Johnny Depp as John Wilmot, earl of Rochester, John Malkovich as Charles II.)
4. On the cover of the VHS tapes and DVDs issued by the Comédie-Française, the term '*mise-en-scène de référence*' is explicitly used. In 2008, a 19-DVD set 'Comédie-Française – Collection Molière' was released by Éditions Montparnasse.
5. Under the name 'Les Deschiens', the Deschamps-Makeïeff company rose to fame in the 1990s through a series of popular satirical skits aired on the French TV channel Canal +.
6. 'Entretien avec Jérôme Deschamps et Macha Makeïeff', *Les Précieuses ridicules*, Press Kit, Théâtre national de l'odéon, 9–28 December 1997, p. 3. Translation mine. 'Cela veut dire que tout en conservant un grand respect pour le texte et sa construction, nous nous éloignons beaucoup de la façon dont on monte la pièce généralement. Ce qui est mis en avant, le plus souvent, est une sorte de prouesse de diction; on privilégie l'élégance de Molière comme pour s'excuser que les *Précieuses* ne soit pas une aussi grande pièce que celles qui vont suivre. Elle est alors présentée comme une conversation de salon, un échange d'idées à propos des mœurs du temps. En réalité, c'est un véritable affrontement, brutal, où les personnages se disent des choses d'une extrême violence.'
7. *Ibid.* 'Avec ce parti-pris nous sommes en effet probablement proches du jeu des acteurs de Molière, au moins dans l'esprit. Cela ne se traduit sans doute pas exactement de la même façon, à trois siècles d'écart.'

8. The French language has two words for 'director' depending on the medium: *réalisateur* (film) and *metteur-en-scène* (stage).
9. This film also happened to be adapted (though quite loosely) from a play, Victor Hugo's *Ruy Blas*.
10. *L'Avare et moi*, dir. Frédéric Andrei (2006).
11. *Richard III*, dir. Richard Loncraine, UK, United Artists, 1995. DVD: MGM, 2000. (Ian McKellen as Richard III, recast in a fictitious fascist state in the 1930s.) *William Shakespeare's Romeo + Juliet*, dir. Baz Luhrman, USA, Twentieth Century Fox, 1996. DVD: 20th Century Fox, 1996. (Leonardo di Caprio as Romeo and Clare Danes as Juliet, recast in a contemporary Latino gang war setting.) *Hamlet*, dir. Michael Almereyda, USA, Double A/Miramax, 2000. DVD: Miramax, 2001. (Ethan Hawke as Hamlet, recast in the contemporary New York City corporate world.)
12. This particular approach was famously pioneered by Marcel Bluwal in a made-for-TV movie of Molière's *Dom Juan* (ORTF, 1965; DVD: INA, *Les Grandes Fictions de la télévision*, 2008).
13. Eugene Green, an American-born director and filmmaker working in France, has proposed in *La Parole baroque* (Paris: Desclée de Brouwer, 2001) a system for pronouncing early modern French and English poetry and drama, earning a small but devoted following in some intellectual Parisian circles, in spite of considerable criticism from the scholarly community.
14. In fact, Ariane Mnouchkine's film is adapted from the *Novel of Monsieur de Molière* by Russian writer Mikhaïl Boulgakov (1933), which was censored under Stalin, and eventually published in an expurgated edition in 1962. Boulgakov himself liberally borrowed from the first biography of Molière by Jean-Léonord Le Gallois de Grimarest, *La Vie de Molière* (Paris: Jacques Le Febvre et Pierre Ribou, 1705).
15. In Mnouchkine's version (0:1:00–0:2:00) we also see Molière catch some rotten fruit in the face when he performs tragedy in the provinces.
16. It is based on Edmond Rostand's play *Cyrano de Bergerac* (1897).
17. Act I, scenes 1–3, and beginning of scene 4 in the play.
18. 'Je ne savais pas qu'on pût jouer si naturellement la tragédie.'
19. 'La scène n'est pas sur le pont Neuf! [...] Sont-ce vers, ou des paroles de femme hâtivement notées?'
20. 'On dirait que l'État vacille!'
21. Script by Christopher Hampton, based on his 1985 eponymous stage play, itself a dramatization of Pierre-Ambroise-François Choderlos de Laclos' 1782 novel, *Les Liaisons dangereuses*.
22. *The Golden Coach* [aka *Le Carrosse d'or/La carrozza d'oro*], dir. Jean Renoir, script by Jean Renoir and Jack Kirkland, based on a stage play by Prosper Mérimée, *Le Carrosse du Saint-Sacrement*. USA/France/Italie, Delphinus/Panaria/Hoche, 1952. DVD: Criterion, 2004.

Films referenced

L'Allée du roi. Directed by Nina Companéez. Script by Nina Companéez, based on the eponymous novel by Françoise Chandernagor. France, Ciné Mag Bodard/France 2, 1996. (4-part TV series). DVD: Sony Pictures Home Entertainment, 2003. (Dominique Blanc as Mme de Maintenon, Didier Sandre as Louis XIV.)

L'Avare by Molière. Directed by Louis de Funès and Jean Girault. France, Les Films Christian Fechner, 1980. DVD: Studio Canal, 2007. (Louis de Funès as Harpagon.)

L'Avare by Molière. Directed by Christian de Chalonge. France, Jourd'hui Mitchell Productions/France 3, 2007. DVD: Sony Pictures Home Entertainment, 2007. (Michel Serrault as Harpagon.)

Le Bourgeois Gentilhomme by Molière. Directed by Christian de Chalonge. Script by Gérard Jourd'hui, Pierre Leccia and Christian de Chalonge. France, France 3/JM Productions, 2009. Aired on TV (France 3), December 2009. (Christian Clavier as M. Jourdain.)

Le Bourgeois Gentilhomme by Molière. Directed by Martin Fraudreau. Stage direction by Benjamin Lazar. 2004 live performance at the Théâtre le Trianon in Paris. DVD: Alpha/Abeille Musique, 2005. (Olivier Martin as M. Jourdain.)

Le Bourgeois Gentilhomme by Molière. Directed by Alain Sachs. 2006 live performance at the Théâtre de Paris. DVD: TF1 Vidéo, 2006. (Jean-Marie Bigard as M. Jourdain.)

Cyrano de Bergerac. Directed by Jean-Paul Rappeneau. Script by Jean-Claude Carrière and Jean-Paul Rappeneau. France, Caméra One/Centre National de la Cinématographie (CNC)/DD Productions/Films A2, 1990. DVD: Fox Pathé Europa, 2000. (Gérard Depardieu as Cyrano.)

Dandin. Directed by Roger Planchon. Script by Roger Planchon, based on Molière's *George Dandin*. France, Les Films du Losange/CNC/Antenne 2, 1987. VHS SECAM: Fil A Film, 1996. (Claude Brasseur as George Dandin.)

Dangerous Liaisons. Directed by Stephen Frears. Script by Christopher Hampton, based on his eponymous play. UK/USA, Warner Bros./Lorimar, 1988. DVD: Warner Home Video, 1997. (Glenn Close as Mme de Merteuil, John Malkovich as Valmont.)

L'École des femmes by Molière. Directed by Don Kent. Stage direction by Didier Bezace. 2001 live performance in the Palais des Papes courtyard at the Festival d'Avignon. France, Arte/La Compagnie des Indes/Théâtre de la Commune, 2001. DVD: Sony Pictures Home Entertainment, 2008. (Pierre Arditi as Arnolphe, Agnès Sourdillon as Agnès.)

Les Fourberies de Scapin by Molière. Directed by Jean-Luc Moreau. 1994 live performance at the Théâtre du Gymnase in Paris. VHS: Warner Home Video, 1999. (Smaïn Fairouze as Scapin.)

Jefferson in Paris. Directed by James Ivory. Script by Ruth Prawer Jhabvala. USA, Merchant & Ivory/Touchstone, 1995. DVD: Walt Disney Video, 2004. (Nick Nolte as president William Jefferson.)

Louis, enfant roi. Directed by Roger Planchon. Script by Roger Planchon. France, Les Films du Losange, 1993. DVD: Universal Pictures, 2000. (Louis Mansion as young king Louis XIV.)

Le Malade imaginaire by Molière. Directed by Christian De Chalonge. France, France 3/JM Productions, 2008. Aired on TV (France 3), February 2008. DVD: France télévisions Éditions, 2009. (Christian Clavier as Argan.)

Marquise. Directed by Véra Belmont. Script by Marcel Beaulieu and Véra Belmont, dialogues by Gérard Mordillat, based on the eponymous novel by Jean-François Josselin. France, Stéphan/France 3/AMLF, 1995. DVD: Fox Pathé Europa, 2002. (Sophie Marceau as Marquise du Parc, Bernard Giraudeau as Molière.)

Molière. Directed by Ariane Mnouchkine. Script by Ariane Mnouchkine. France, Les Films 13/Les Films du Soleil et de la Nuit/Antenne 2/RAI, 1978. DVD: Bel Air Classiques (Harmonia Mundi), 2004. (Philippe Caubère as Molière.)

Molière. Directed by Laurent Tirard. Script by Laurent Tirard and Grégoire Vigneron. France, Fidélité Productions/France 2 Cinéma, 2007. DVD: Sony Pictures Home Entertainment, 2008. (Romain Duris as Molière.)

Les Précieuses ridicules by Molière. Directed by Georges Bensoussan. Stage direction by Jean-Luc Boutté. France, France 3 Vidéo, coll. 'Comédie-Française', 1998. DVD: Éditions Montparnasse, Collection Molière, 2008.

Les Précieuses ridicules by Molière. Directed by Don Kent. Stage direction by Macha Makeïeff and Jérôme Deschamps. VHS: Studio Canal, 1999. (This tape includes two live performances of the show at the Théâtre de l'odéon in Paris, with slightly different casts).

Les Précieuses ridicules by Molière. Directed by Vincent Bataillon. Stage direction by Dan Jemmett. 2008 live performance at the Théâtre du vieux colombier. France, France 3, 2009. Aired on TV (France 3), February 2009.

La Prise de pouvoir par Louis XIV. Directed by Roberto Rossellini. Script by Philippe Erlanger and Jean Gruault. France, ORTF, 1970. DVD: MK2, 2004. (Jean-Marie Patte as Louis XIV.)

Le Roi danse. Directed by Gérard Corbiau. Script by Ève de Castro, Andrée Corbiau and Gérard Corbiau, based on *Lully ou le musicien du soleil* by Philippe Beaussant. France/Belgium/Germany: K-Star & France 2 Cinéma, 2000. DVD: France Télévisions, 2001. (Benoît Magimel as Louis XIV, Boris Terral as Jean-Baptiste Lully.)

Saint-Cyr. Directed by Patricia Mazuy. Script by Patricia Mazuy, based on the novel *La Maison d'Esther* by Yves Dangerfield. France, Les Films du Camélia/Canal +/France 2, 2000. DVD: Universal Pictures, 2001. (Isabelle Huppert as Mme de Maintenon, Jean-Pierre Kalfon as Louis XIV.)

Vatel. Directed by Roland Joffé. France/UK, Légende/Gaumont/Canal +, 2000. DVD: Miramax, 2001. (Gérard Depardieu as Vatel, Julian Sands as Louis XIV.)

22
Relevance and its Discontents: Teaching Sofia Coppola's *Marie Antoinette*

Amy Wygant

The Modern Language Association of America reported in 2007 that fewer than 7 per cent of all graduates of foreign-language programmes go on to complete advanced study to PhD level.[1] Those choosing to concentrate on the early modern period will be but a percentage of that small percentage. The question then arises: if those of us who teach early modern history and literature to undergraduates in French departments are not mainly engaged in inspiring, replicating and passing on a taste for academic scholarship at the highest level, if that corresponds indeed to only a small proportion, in terms of outcome, of the work that we do in the classroom, then what is the point of our teaching?

The response to this question generally falls back on the value of the humanities in general, and of languages and history in particular, for the life project of citizenship. However, Lisa Jardine and Antony Grafton long ago exploded the historical basis of this notion.[2] In 1986, they argued that it was not anything like intrinsic value which led to the replacement of medieval scholasticism by humanistic teaching in the fifteenth and sixteenth centuries. Instead, this sea-change was due to the fact that the model of culture offered by the humanists fostered an unquestioning attitude towards authority that governments found convenient. The new purveyors of culture allowed a new elite to recognize its own members with an easily established seal of superiority.[3] Humanistic teaching was founded upon the gap between the claim that it offered 'training for life', and the reality of classroom activity which did not seem to match up to the fervour of this ideal, open as it has ever been, to cite a nineteenth-century charge, to accusations of being 'mere chatter'.[4] This has led, according to Grafton and Jardine, to 'a long history of evasiveness on the part of teachers of the humanities, which has left them vulnerable to charges of non-productiveness [and] irrelevance to society'.[5] When the early humanists were successful in delivering 'training for life', so this argument goes, this was attributable to personal charisma, not the curriculum.[6] Teaching in the humanities has as a consequence been subject to a certain mystification from that day to this, and any doubts that this continues to be the case in 2010 may be laid to rest by consulting 'Why Study the Humanities in 60 Seconds'.[7]

In this essay, I would like to bring together this deeply felt claim that our teaching provides 'training for life', and the accusation that it is, to cite Grafton and Jardine's term, 'irrelevant', and I would like to bring them together around Sofia Coppola's film, *Marie Antoinette* (2006). It will be my argument, firstly, that the film succeeded in triggering the anxieties of academic historians about exactly that gap identified as constitutive by Grafton and Jardine with respect to the teaching of the humanities. An account of the thread concerning the film on H-France, the discussion list of the US-based Society for French Historical Studies, will serve as an instance of this anxiety. Secondly, I will argue that the film itself stages a scenario of learning and cross-cultural competence through its powerful images of eating and loving, and that, with help from psychoanalytic insights into the idioms of learning, teachers of the early modern period can hope, at least, not to share the ultimate fate of the famous French queen.

First, some critical pressure must be brought to bear on the notion of 'relevance' and its pedagogical history. Relevance is generally considered to be a good thing. It fills up classrooms and auditoria, it creates a cosy sense of comfort, and it certainly seems to enthuse students. But the word 'relevant' is etymologically not, as we might assume, a cousin of 'relate' (derived from the Latin *referre*, to bear or carry again), but instead belongs to the same family as 'relieve' (derived from the Latin *relevare*, to raise again). The *Oxford English Dictionary* lists no fewer than ten possible meanings for 'relieve', but the first will serve as a convenient point of departure: 'To raise (a person) out of some trouble, difficulty, or danger; to rescue, succour, aid or assist in straits; to deliver from something troublesome or oppressive.'[8] Accordingly, when we sense that spirit that we call 'relevance', the idea that it reduplicates us, that we feel 'affectively involved or connected with someone or something' according to the *OED*,[9] is an accretion to the word's deep meaning; it is a facet of the ungovernable, unpredictable erotic. There is a second, quite directly opposed, deep meaning of the word, which would point to the ability of relevance to succour us, deliver us and set us free from trouble and oppression.

Could students be encouraged to develop a resistance to relevance as affective connection, a certain wariness in its alluring presence and an understanding of its structure, while, at the same time, profiting from the film's deep fascination with the past? One way beyond this seeming contradiction is a return to the thinking of etymology and an insistence upon the problem posed by the etymon: is there a relevance that can emerge from the film that would be closer to the liberation promised by *relevare*, than to the rank seduction promised by *referre*? This potentially useful doubleness is at the heart of the discontents of relevance, I would say, with reference to the usual translation of Freud's late meditation on what makes us happy, and on hunger and love, *Das Unbehagen in der Kultur* as *Civilization and its Discontents*.[10] But if a pedagogical strategy that takes account of the psychoanalytic scenario is required, it must be acknowledged that that account is profoundly pessimistic about the possibility of liberation. According to Freud, freedom is not terribly interesting: it has very little to do with *Kultur*, 'civilization', whose existence depends precisely upon the restriction of individual liberty. Civilization and the claim of individual liberty may well be irreconcilable, he repeatedly suggests, not least in his essay's final sentence, added in 1931. Where, then, does this leave the liberation promised by relevance as a tool for investigating the past?

A brief look at the history of relevance suggests that, from having an older, quite neutral meaning simply of something pertinent to the matter at hand, it became the buzziest of pedagogical buzzwords in the 1960s and 1970s, and, for that era now two generations past, it served as the battle cry of a highly charged relevancy politics. Lately, for the survivors of those battles, it has assumed a fuzzy, unquestioned and unexamined positive value in the classroom.[11] This is a history which certainly merits further investigation. But if teaching of the early modern period aims to be relevant, the relevance for which it must hope can take this step towards demystifying the classroom practices of humanities teaching: not to attempt to produce affective connection, the eros of which will forever be unresponsive to teaching, but instead, and beyond Freud, to produce healing, relief and freedom. Coppola's *Marie Antoinette* can serve as a useful laboratory for this classroom activity of the humanities. Firstly, that activity can alert students to the strategies of a sly and witty version of relevance which bodies forth all of the charms of seduction in its successful attempt to foster precisely an affective connection; and, secondly, it can suggest that the film's engagement with history can lead to a more interesting and complicated 'liberation relevance'.

It is instructive to observe the reactions of academic historians who were first confronted in 2006 with this double possibility presented by the film. Coppola's film biography of the doomed French queen was, as was widely acknowledged – and indeed claimed by its creator – modern, populist and popular. Its curious 1980s soundtrack of Bow Wow Wow and The Cure, its portrayal of the fierce fashion strategies of the court of Versailles, and its incorporation of twenty-first-century French luxury goods (macaroons from Ladurée, Veuve Cliquot) spoke successfully to twin mass-cultural obsessions with fame and dazzle. Historians, that is, did not foster or create its affective relevance; it was a *fait accompli* by the time that they began to consider possible use of the film in the class-room. This congruity of focus claimed by the film's product environment and soundscape between Antoinette's time and ours put pressure on affective relevance by foregrounding its assumptions. Coppola's Antoinette speaks, acts and reacts 'just like' a twenty-first-century Californian teenager, while enjoying the same consumer resources, when she finds herself – by definition 'unlike' any post-revolutionary Californian teenager – in the position of becoming initially Dauphine and subsequently Queen of France. How, the historians asked, in the face of this aggressive yet winsome foregrounding, could the film be incorporated into a university seminar whose concern is with historical criticism? Indeed, should it be taught at all?

Unsurprisingly, the Coppola film became a flashpoint for a debate about teaching methodology on 'H-France'.[12] Initiated by Judith Miller's posting (29 May 2006) expressing deep reservations about the film's apolitical stance and its 'deep roots in American narratives' – what Coppola did was, according to Miller, to 'transplant an American junior high school to Versailles' – the thread comprised some 22 postings before petering out about a week later. While some agreed with Miller's concerns about the film's lack of historical breadth and repetition of clichés which were derived, apparently, largely from the Antonia Fraser biography,[13] the main concern on this side of the debate was that students would be led astray, that is, factually misinformed. David Bell's comment (29 May) placed the film beyond history, and the problem, according to him, was that its reality was false. The threat to pedagogy and the accusation that Coppola was not just a bad historian, but also a bad teacher, followed immediately: 'Films like this scarcely deserve to be called "historical" in any real sense. Nothing wrong with that. The problem is that our students so often take it for the reality.' The criticism of the film on this side of the debate, then, could be characterized negatively as pedantic, but also positively, in its respect for the very notion of the historical fact, as philological.

However, another point of view emerged with the posted comment of a University of North Carolina postgraduate student whose undergraduate teaching load was a heavy one. 'The historical community may look down on the popularization and simplification of history at the hands of Hollywood', wrote Max Orwe on 1 June, 'but we do so at the risk of our students and frankly, at the future of the historical profession as a whole.' In this assessment, then, far from being a desperate threat to academic life as we know it, both history and pedagogy depend upon the film. Its value, according to Orwe, was its potential role as an opening, precisely, into history as a discipline, and as a tool to be used to capture the history department's percentage of undergraduates bound for PhD programmes. 'Perhaps a small number of people', he argued, 'will be fascinated enough to learn more, overcome the stereotypes, and even think of becoming historians – all because of a movie that their future colleagues condemned as a disservice to the field.'

The all-important and familiar humanist move from pedagogy to the life project of citizenship was made in a posting by Daniel Becker. Such a film, he claimed, might be a crucible of contemporary citizenship: 'We can either dismiss these ideas, alienate our students, and lose them, or we can pick up their ideas, run with them, and help them to develop into a historically informed civic mindset.' The historians of the list, then, found themselves on the horns of a dilemma. Venitta Datta from Wellesley College articulated the problem most succinctly in a posting on 8 June: 'I want to pull students in and still keep my vow never to teach [...] "disco history".' No movement beyond the ancient claim that the humanities somehow offer training for life, no elaboration of philology beyond its insistence on the fact, no freedom from the pedagogical dependence upon undependable affect, was offered.

It is indeed unsurprising that this powerful and uncomfortable debate took as its focal point the Coppola film, and there are two reasons for this. Firstly, the film provides a particularly provocative index to a broader discussion of modern popular-culture lenses on the past. This affective version of relevance can restrict itself to surface analogy. When we read up, for example, on one of the favourite topics of the mass-market press, namely how to find a husband and what to do with him subsequently, a comment of the sort, 'Marriage isn't a passion-fest; it's more like a partnership formed to run a small, mundane and often boring not-for-profit business,'[14] might make us think of that great anti-romantic, Norbert Elias. His account in *The Court Society* of the daily life of the marriage partners in a great Parisian *hôtel* in the early eighteenth century maps point for point onto the 'business' of marriage, and may suggest its 'relevance' to this subset of our contemporary concerns.[15] On the H-France discussion list, the issue of the popular-culture lens emerged again in another intense strand of postings at the end of April 2008, on the subject of Graham Robb's *The Discovery of France*,[16] a mass-market success similarly decried both for its sloppiness and for its attractiveness,[17] and called now not 'disco history' but 'knight-errant research' and 'bicycle history', referring to the author's preferred means of transport through the French countryside.[18] The Coppola film re-emerged in the context of this later debate, with one posting observing that 'the discussion of popular history versus academic history has probably reached its nadir here. It would appear that straight "true" history is not of much interest to the general public.'[19] In this formulation, then, the 'true' is of little interest. It lines up with 'academic' and 'straight' to be accused of irrelevance, and it is defeated when opposed to the popular successes of the books the public loves and buys, and the films that it loves and watches.

It is not just academic historians who are apt to pose the grand questions about the popular-culture lens. The visual arts critic of *The Sunday Times*, Waldemar Januszczak, has asked, '[i]s this what we should be looking at in our museums?',[20] referring to the 2008 James Bond exhibit at the Imperial War Museum, London, which included the bikini that Halle Berry wore in *Die Another Day*. This would be fine, Januszczak noted, if the Imperial War Museum were an outpost of the entertainment industry. But in setting it up in 1917 specifically to commemorate the First World War, the British government failed to mention, anywhere, Halle Berry's bikini. Januszczak concluded that the Imperial War Museum is 'chasing [...] after the moronic modern audience' and that 'the continuing collapse of cultural values [...] leaves us unable to tell the difference between Kylie's dresses and the rightful terrain of a museum', referring to the 2007 exhibit at the Victoria & Albert Museum of a selection of the stage costumes of Kylie Minogue.

Nevertheless, we have a responsibility to become automatically suspicious whenever complaints about the decline and fall of culture are advanced, and, in any case, *The Sunday Times* played exactly the same game as did the Imperial War Museum when it accompanied its criticism of the inclusion of Halle Berry's bikini with a full-colour image precisely of Halle Berry in said bikini. A sense of what might more fundamentally be at stake in this otherwise boring circularity was provided by one of Januszczak's central observations: 'Popular culture is ruthless, unsparing and voracious. Not content with taking over cinemas, newspapers, televisions, shopping streets and bookshops, it wants also to control everywhere else.' This means that the problem, in a word, is eating. We are to fear, firstly, that we could be devoured by voracious popular culture, and, secondly, that other people will, precisely, lap it up, and this must be denounced, even if an image of Halle Berry's bikini is required in the first place to attract their attention to the denunciation. The connection between the two is apparent: the problem of eating is always, and for very good Freudian reasons, accompanied by the problem of sex.

There is another reason why Coppola's film's ignition of a broad discussion about the teaching of history was predictable enough. As I hope to have argued so far, it provides a particularly provocative example of a purveying of history through anachronism, be it post-punk music or Converse trainers, which in fact appear in one of its scenes. But additionally, I would claim that the Coppola film collapses the life of Marie Antoinette in France into the two concerns of eating and sex, and so becomes a paradigm of learning and teaching. It is a film, that is, about the very possibility of pedagogy.

The problem of learning was not addressed in so many words by Freud, but it is safe to assume that, as with other aspects of mental life, learning, as a secondary process activity, is underpinned by primary process fantasy, a logic unto itself characteristic of the non-rational.[21] If you are mugged by a person in a green shirt, for example, secondary process thinking will suggest that you avoid muggers in future. Primary process logic, however, will make you, otherwise unaccountably, avoid green shirts. There is a reason that this logic was called 'primary' by Freud, for its powerful, frequently hidden motivations lead us into and out of all kinds of life decisions about what to incorporate and what to disgorge which we fondly believe to be rational. A psychoanalytic theory of learning would hold that it is not possible for us to escape the influence of primary process fantasy. So, in order to open up to new experience, we must represent that experience as a finding again of that which we once found pleasant in fantasy. Of course, what the primitive pleasure-ego enjoys, looks for and finds again is the breast. This is why metaphors of food and eating seem so unaccountably powerful and pertinent when used to describe the learning process. We take in ideas 'in one gulp', 'devour' books, display a 'hunger for knowledge' and so on. And it is why, I would argue, Coppola's film of an Austrian princess whose entire project could be said to be learning to be French, the acquisition of Frenchness, is otherwise so unaccountably focused on food. From the scenes of titbits, champagne and chocolate set to Bow Wow Wow's 'I Want Candy' soundtrack, to images of the strictly formal table of the two French monarchs, to images of Marie Antoinette encouraging her little daughter to gather eggs from the nests of pet chickens in her famous *hameau*, one of the film's determining strategies for the portrayal of learning to live as French is ingestion. If the film takes the trouble to cause its heroine to deny ever uttering the infamous 'Let them eat cake' comment, this only underlines the importance of cake more generally.

The second fantasy that underpins learning is the notion of learning as a kind of loving. In Freudian terms, this is an advance of sorts from the primitive oral stage to the later stage of genital organization of the developing mental apparatus. And it is a familiar scenario that a problematic transference focused on a charismatic teacher will function in the student to produce learning of the highest order. Lacan was at pains, furthermore, to show that the transference, and indeed all love, is a transference to and between knowledges, unconscious though they be.[22] In language, why else do we speak precisely of a 'love of learning'; in our mental life, why else develop a 'passion' for study, or an 'obsession' with a subject area? This has serious implications, both practical and ethical, for the teacher, and perhaps the most moving accounts of teaching describe an almost alchemical mobilization of this powerful force.

Passion and its subsequent productivity is much in evidence in the Coppola film, for its other great theme, apart from eating, is certainly loving. Antoinette's main mission at the French court was, of course, dynastic: she was charged with becoming pregnant and producing an heir to the throne. Famously, however, her marriage remained unconsummated for a number of years: first a daughter and, subsequently, the dauphin of France appeared only quite late in the day. Her strategy in the face of this awkwardness, the film claimed, was a gentle lovingness towards her curious partner, who eventually returned it. Following the acquisition of some anatomical knowledge imparted during the visit of Antoinette's brother, the Holy Roman Emperor Joseph II, their first child was duly born.

Once students have been led to appreciate the film's deep, and deeply psychoanalytic, deployment of the fantasies of learning, they are then at liberty to evaluate its possible contribution, or lack thereof, to their own experiences and existing structures of knowledge acquisition as they wish. This is not pedagogical diffidence, for the operative notion here is indeed 'to be freed', as in 'to deliver from something troublesome or oppressive', and the film becomes relevant on a level very different from that of fashion and its attendant historical facticity. It is, I would argue, 'liberation relevance' which stages the scenario of learning itself, and positions the students to evaluate for themselves whether or not this scenario is occluded or revealed in their own encounters with the object of study. What is then achieved is discontent, the discontent of the questioner, and that can only be good for the study of history.

However, its content may well be specific to the study of history as such. Coppola's film is certainly not the first or the only filmed representation of the early modern period to have irked and fascinated historians. From *The Return of Martin Guerre* to *Vatel* to *Tous les matins du monde* to *Ridicule* to *La Reine Margot*, the filmography of the period has challenged teachers to set aside what they most love and what they think they have gained, in many cases, through hard archival graft: a memory, perhaps precisely a screen memory, of what never existed as such, but which lives largely through their work and careers, that is, a credo of the past.[23] 'We believe' that Marie Antoinette did not wear Jimmy Choos, did not patronize Ladurée and certainly did not say that thing about cake. And yet the reference to the screen memory is no idle pun. Freud was theoretically wary of all memory. In a series of writings beginning in 1899, he developed the notion of the screen memory (*Deckerinnerung*), which could be any memory, to the extent that that memory screens out something unacceptable to the ego.[24]

There are two aspects of screen memory theory that map onto the problematic of film of the early modern period. Firstly, in some cases, the tip-off to the existence of a screen memory was precisely the representability or the intense nature of the memory, its presentation as vivid and gripping history, something, we might say, apt to be filmed. Secondly, in his account of the famous 'Rat Man' case, Freud pointed out in a long footnote that this process of what he called 'remodelling' of the past is precisely analogous to the process by which a nation constructs legends about its own history.[25] This leaves 'historical reality' in a precarious position. Even within the living 'memory' of many, the Watergate scandal has enjoyed a big screen version as Ron Howard's *Frost/Nixon*, a film based on Peter Morgan's 2006 play of the same name, which itself took up Richard Nixon's strangely therapeutic 1977 memorialization in televised interviews with David Frost of the events which culminated in his resignation in 1974. The facts almost certainly are not, and perhaps cannot be, the film's paramount concern; instead, the process of national legend construction is ongoing on its screen. And so it is with the more distant past: we as historians and as citizens flit from screen to screen, sometimes bothering to deny the vulnerability of the screen from our anchorages in the factual, sometimes not, while the Coppola film, in all of its exuberant prettiness and amusing shoe fetishism, swallows the past whole, and embraces it, in a precisely instructive way.

The conclusions for the teaching of the early modern period form part of a larger problematic of the teaching of history. Unless the structure, funding and global ambitions of the disciplines of history and modern languages change unexpectedly and beyond recognition, it is safe to say that the philology which is so fundamental a concern of historians will remain the province of a small group of specialists. Furthermore, eros and the affections will not come under the control of any of us any time soon, and it is this situation, well documented for the teaching of early modern literature in both France and the United States, which will surely remain unresponsive to purely pedagogical initiatives.[26] Attempts to engineer relevance of the affective variety, or to rail against it when its object is a popular culture success, are quite beside the point. Equally, the magic of the charismatic teacher will remain just that. From Guarino Guarini to Paul de Man, inspiration, with its profound abilities to uplift and heal, has been in the gift of some and not of others and has, perhaps rightly, remained resistant to appropriation by institutions, be their goals those of learning or of worship. A teacher of the early modern period, like many another, may succeed in inspiring students to undertake a life of scholarship or a life of productive citizenship through charismatic teaching, but such charisma is a quality apart.

Marie Antoinette had her head chopped off, and the rhetoric of the cut has lately been much in the air with respect to the work undertaken by teachers of the early modern period in universities.[27] I have argued here that the Coppola film succeeds in depicting Marie Antoinette as a learner. Through powerful images of eating and loving, it shows that desire to learn about a foreign country, in her case, or about the past as a foreign country, in the case of teachers of the early modern period, is a project deeply embedded in fundamental structures of desire and identity construction, both on the part of individuals and on the part of nations. However, we could also say that what the French beheaded was a failed learner. On this point the film spectacularly fails to follow through its own premises, ending as it does with a dawn carriage ride taking the royal family, captive but still very much alive, away from Versailles. What fails to be implied is that it was precisely a failure to learn that was the condition of possibility for the founding of the French republic; it is this that the film refuses to show. Teaching, typically, bears the brunt of the vicissitudes of nation formation and dissolution. This was the case for the fifteenth- and sixteenth-century humanists studied by Jardine and Grafton; it was the case in France in 1870, when the universities were blamed for the French defeat;[28] it was the case in 1918, when Lloyd George claimed that

The most formidable institution we had to fight in Germany was not the arsenals of the Krupps or the yards in which they turned out submarines, but the schools of Germany. They were our most formidable competitors in business and our most terrible opponents in war. An educated man is a better worker, a more formidable warrior, and a better citizen. That was only half-comprehended before the war.[29]

And it is the case in 2010, when Joe Moran's blog has observed that

If you were wondering who was responsible for the worst economic crisis since the war, I can now reveal that it wasn't those evil bankers after all, or indeed the sleepwalking politicians in hock to market fundamentalism who let them get away with it. No – and bear with me on this one because it's a bit counter-intuitive – it turns out it was university lecturers. Which is presumably why we are the first (although we certainly won't be the last) to be punished with budget cuts aimed at plugging the financial hole left by the billions used to rescue the banks eighteen months ago.[30]

Teachers of the early modern period, I would say, should profit from the popularity and attractiveness of the Coppola film. But students must be led on to the ending of the story, to the deep mysteries of liberation: the processes of projection, scapegoating, tragedy, rebirth and profound discontent, that history and literature can teach.

Notes

1. http://www.mla.org/flreport [accessed 4 March 2010].
2. Anthony Grafton and Lisa Jardine, *From Humanism to the Humanities: Education and the Liberal Arts in Fifteenth- and Sixteenth-Century Europe* (London: Duckworth, 1986).
3. *Ibid.*, pp. xiii–xiv.
4. Chris Baldick, *The Social Mission of English Criticism, 1842–1932* (Oxford: Clarendon Press, 1983), p. 73.
5. Grafton and Jardine, *From Humanism to the Humanities*, p. xv.
6. *Ibid.*, p. 27.
7. http://www.youtube.com/edu [accessed 4 March 2010].
8. *Oxford English Dictionary*, 2nd edn, 1989, http://dictionary.oed.com, s.v. 'relieve' [accessed 8 January 2009].
9. *Ibid.*, s.v. 'relate' [accessed 8 January 2009].
10. Sigmund Freud, *Civilization and its Discontents*, in *The Standard Edition of the Complete Psychological Works of Sigmund Freud*, ed. and trans. James Strachey, 24 vols (London: Hogarth Press and Institute of Psycho-analysis, 1953–74), XXI, pp. 57–146.

262 *Teaching Sofia Coppola's* Marie Antoinette

11. *OED*, s.v. 'relevance', 'relevancy', 'relevant' [accessed 9 January 2009].
12. https://lists.uakron.edu/sympa/arc/h-france/2005–6 [accessed 28 April 2008].
13. Antonia Fraser, *Marie Antoinette: The Journey* (New York: N.A. Talese and Doubleday, 2001).
14. Lori Gottlier, 'Settle for Less', *Sunday Times Style*, 11 May 2008, pp. 16–19.
15. Norbert Elias, *The Court Society*, ed. S. Mennell, trans. E. Jephcott (University College Dublin Press, 2006 [1969]), pp. 49–51.
16. Graham Robb, *The Discovery of France: A Historical Geography from the Revolution to the First World War* (New York and London: Norton, 2007).
17. https://lists.uakron.edu/sympa/arc/h-france/2007–8 [accessed 28 April 2008].
18. David A. Bell, 'Bicycle History', *The New Republic* (13 February 2008), pp. 43–6, http://powells.com/reviews/2008_02_07.html [accessed 9 January 2009].
19. https://lists.uakron.edu/sympa/arc/h-france/2008-04/msg00111.html [accessed 27 August 2010].
20. Waldemar Januszczak, 'Why is the Imperial War Museum Celebrating James Bond?' *Sunday Times Culture* (27 April 2008), pp. 6–7, http://entertainment. timesonline.co.uk/tol/arts_and_entertainment/visual_arts/article3805217. ece [accessed 9 January 2009].
21. See *The Ship of Thought: Essays on Psychoanalysis and Learning* (London: Karnac, 2002), ed. Duncan Barford, and particularly Duncan Barford, 'Is Anything More Interesting than Sex? The Freudian Perspective on Learning and Teaching', pp. 41–63.
22. Jacques Lacan, *The Seminar of Jacques Lacan, Book XX: On Feminine Sexuality, The Limits of Love and Knowledge*, ed. J.-A. Miller, trans. B. Fink (London: Norton, 1999), p. 144.
23. For an introduction to the necessary bibliography, see http://www.early-modernweb.org.uk [accessed 16 January 2009].
24. Freud, 'Screen Memories', in *The Standard Edition*, III, pp. 299–322. A useful overview of this theoretical strand can be found at F. Richard, 'Screen Memory', http://www.enotes.com/psychoanalysis-encyclopedia/screen-memory [accessed 18 January 2009].
25. Freud, 'Notes Upon a Case of Obsessional Neurosis', *The Standard Edition*, X, pp. 151–318 (p. 206n).
26. See John Campbell, '"Enseigner Racine", mission impossible?' in *Racine et/ou le classicisme*, ed. Ronald W. Tobin, coll. Biblio 17, No 129 (Tübingen: Gunter Narr Verlag, 2001), pp. 249–60 (pp. 250–3), and, in the same volume, Michael S. Koppisch, '"Tout fuit, tout se refuse à mes embrassements": Can We Continue to Teach Racine?' pp. 309–19 (p. 319).
27. W. Rees-Mogg, 'We Ignore the Lessons of History at Our Peril. In a Game of Brinksmanship over Swingeing University Cuts, Cherished Faculties Could be Obliterated – It Has Happened Before', http://www.timesonline.co.uk/ tol/comment/columnists/william_rees_mogg/article7026836.ece [accessed 10 March 2010].
28. Koppisch, 'Tout fuit', p. 312.
29. Baldick, *The Social Mission of English Criticism*, p. 93.
30. J. Moran, 'Britain's got "Talent"', http://joemoransblog.blogspot.com/ [accessed 10 March 2010].

23
Presence, Performance and Critical Pleasure: Play and Prerequisites in Research and Teaching

Christian Biet

As will be seen from what follows, my teaching and research have been shaped by French and North American academic practices which readers will no doubt find familiar. They developed gradually, untroubled by educational theories or teaching methodologies, in the course of my experiences, seminars and classes at the École Normale Supérieure in Fontenay-Saint-Cloud, at the Université Paris Ouest-Nanterre, and at New York University in particular. I would listen, whether out of good manners or interest, to comments and contributions; I was sparing in my use of didactic assertions and persuasive remarks (but did not forego them); I would keep discussions going (but not eternally) while stubbornly refusing to engage in debates founded on value judgements; I encouraged original critical ideas, if only to test them out; but I would always come back to history, to rigour, to critical distance and to the need to produce a coherent view of the past that makes itself felt in the *present*. I shall add to these one further practice: a systematic questioning of the ideas of the majority, accompanied by a decided taste for diversions from the well-trodden highways of scholarship, taking an interest in whatever *deviates*, in the *heterodox*, in whatever is, or makes one, *curious*. It is here, in working with alternative corpuses, in asking the questions which have escaped mainstream research, but also in the pleasure of and need for discovery and shared engagement, that the interest of teaching lies. I have now been teaching literature and theatre, in particular that of the seventeenth century, for 30 or so years, first in secondary school and later at university level, and it seems to me that none of this could have happened without a sense of play.

Playing at *what if*, transporting oneself into the past in a rigorous game of make-believe, while maintaining awareness that it is only a game.

But also *introducing play* between the jigsaw pieces, the descriptions and interpretations, introducing it into well-constructed critical edifices and solid academic certainties leading, possibly, to the discovery of other realities more (or less) in tune with our own times. Playing the writing game, of course, playing and writing, but also *being there in the game*, developing a presence, a voice, the spoken word, being there in the company of other living, feeling beings. Preserving one's distance, again, rigorously so, reflecting that our current knowledge of the past, of past corpuses, of the methods we use to analyse and interpret such corpuses, is there to be grasped in our own space and time, and must be thought of as transient because, inevitably, it will soon be subjected to criticism, to revision, and renewal both in the field of theory and through creative practice. Adopting the premise that we consciously produce, in the here-and-now, an interpretable and present reality out of a past for which we are the self-appointed guardians. But we must be careful to achieve this without compromise. We must refuse to allow critical distance to result in the misapprehension that all things are equal, that all analyses and interpretations are as good or as bad as each other, and that no idea is worth a fight. Playing at *what if* and preserving one's distance are in fact perfectly compatible with the production of vigorous defences and hardy challenges because all things are so very *un*equal, because there is such a need for us to assert the validity of our interpretations, however impermanent their truths may be. Play, distance and humour are necessary to our arguments, absolutely, but the latter must also be strong enough to meet the various demands that arise in the teaching of early modern literature and theatre.

'Literary' teaching and research call, then, for an approach combining rigour with play. But they also require a very real practice of writing. Here is the first prerequisite: the need to produce a discourse, a text and a voice, by means of a practice. Not just the practice of academic writing, nor even the specific requirements of the written essay or formal spoken presentation, with their painstaking attention to the manner, protocols and methods of commentary, but also the practice of a form of writing situated *in* the space of the corpus; a practice which itself puts into practice the ability we all have to imitate, to parody, to pastiche and to rewrite earlier texts. For, while description, analysis and commentary are certainly significant practices in a work *on* literature, insinuating ourselves into its words and phrases, behaving *as if* we were (the) authors, imagining that we can be absorbed into the place, the time and the realities that were theirs, playing at writing a source text and, finally, rewriting the texts of the past (with or without distance), are practices – indeed, very ancient practices – which are absolutely essential to any discipline concerned with the arts and literature. Learning to write like Madame de Lafayette, Molière and La Rochefoucauld, rewriting Corneille just as Corneille rewrote Sophocles in his *Œdipe*, as Voltaire rewrote Corneille, and so on. Indeed, it has always been traditional practice to imitate and rewrite the fictions, fables and proofs of earlier writers, to plunder them, borrowing, with or without permission, overtly or covertly, their styles, their words, their thoughts and their minds. And in this, the legal and moral concept of intellectual property, written into law by the French (bourgeois) Revolution, but in no way set in stone, should not hold us back: the notion of literary ownership is open to a whole range of interpretations, subject, like ourselves, to historical processes, and every author, unless he is either naïve or a liar, knows full well that he has purloined the property of his predecessors and his rivals in order to become what he is. We are therefore fully authorized to do likewise. To be authors, to play at being authors, or to understand what they are and do, we must practise fictional writing, know how to be textual thieves, rewriters of fables and borrowers of ideas.

However, to avoid confusion between those activities associated with the individual and artistic freedom of writing (rewriting and imitating as we choose, quoting or not quoting according to our mood) and reading (attributing our own meanings to a text without being answerable for them, responding subjectively and emotionally throughout, having the right to judge or not, whether out of commitment or caprice) and those pertaining to social practice (taking account of literary ownership, adopting the ethics of a profession or a discipline), we should be careful to distinguish between creation and criticism. From this necessity we arrive at the second prerequisite: training in critical discourse.

In order to avoid exercises in pure subjectivity, that can be neither communicated nor shared, that are unscientific and unbounded by any discipline, it is absolutely essential that the processes of description, analysis, commentary and interpretation should be subjected to contractual protocols. Such protocols evolve over time, but are intended to bring together, through shared practice, all those involved in a discipline, profession or pursuit. Ground rules, therefore, need to be defined so that all practitioners of the discipline (writers, critics, academics) can understand them and share in the general code of practice, acknowledging its validity, but also so that the community in question may criticize and revise the code according to agreed procedures. For example, each element of a text drawn from the work of another author must be accurately quoted, referenced and, where appropriate, glossed, so that every reader-scholar can position himself as much in relation to the arguments under discussion as to the new critical argument set out in the text. And in the age of constant 'cut and paste', of unattributed web quotations, and of uncontrolled universal twitters and tweets, it is not at all obvious that this should be the case. In order to become academic critics, or to aspire to that status, we have therefore to steal nothing, to reference our sources, to take account, *ideally* and cumulatively, of all of our peers, so as to commentate legitimately on the texts we appropriate, all the while providing justifications for our practice and motives in interpreting the corpus we have assigned ourselves.

Divided between a practice of writing which assumes that we steal from others in order to create our own individual and original art (a practice of artistic borrowing generally shared by the authors in our corpus of study), and a rigorous scholarship governed by respect for academic practices which allows us to provide a series of original (we hope!) interpretations in acceptable form that are themselves also open to criticism, we in the 'literary' professions find ourselves in the position of double-agents: on the one hand, when reading, imitating and rewriting our reference corpuses, or when being inspired by them in the creation of other texts, we can enjoy the traditional pleasure of freedom from any convention or constraint other than those we set ourselves; on the other, when, in our capacity as academics or critics, we apply ourselves to our corpuses, we are subjected to the scientific, ethical, even legal and moral protocols, which turn our profession into a particular shared social practice within the framework of a discipline.

As a consequence, it is necessary for us as literary specialists – teachers and students, amateurs and professionals – to move constantly and consciously between these two apparently contradictory practices, to play with them, anticipating that one might lead to an understanding and vision of the other, in short, to know how to adopt the role of either the artist or the critic, while allowing ourselves, on occasion, the pleasure of confusing the two. Furthermore, when working on early corpuses, 'literary scholars' must also become 'historians' to a certain extent. This is the third prerequisite — the historical prerequisite. And in order to do so, we must first know how to understand the realities, the languages and the tastes of earlier times, not because they provide evidence of a period which can be claimed to be admirable, detestable, savage, exotic, distant or very close to our own, but because they correspond to a specific moment, when social practices, realities and thoughts were *different*. Not *radically different*, but *conceivable as different*, viewed within a different temporal, social, political and sociological framework, a different system of historicity. When we achieve an understanding of earlier times, and thence of an earlier corpus, in order to imitate it, to critique it or to shed light on previously unconsidered aspects of it, we are always setting out to *consider and contrast* those times in relation to our own present, to express the bonds which unite the two periods and to highlight the differences between them, but in doing so we must never forget that our words, thoughts and interpretations all have our own present as their starting point. Once we have consciously sought to *understand the past from the standpoint of our present*, we can study it as freely as we imitate it. We can now *play at what if*. As if we were in (or from) the seventeenth century. We can imitate the characteristics and behaviours of the past, without necessarily thinking of recreating them, *except in play* – we all know what happens when attempts at revival such as Viollet-le-Duc's architectural restorations in the nineteenth century, or the twenty-first-century historically informed performances of theatre and music, suffused with the earnest idealism of their authors, fail to engage in play ...

Another obvious way of introducing play between past and present in the course of analysis and interpretation is to adopt a synchronic and/or diachronic approach to the critical apparatuses we ourselves employ. It is entirely possible, when engaging with a seventeenth-century text, to develop a taste for the exclusive use of rhetorical tools available to Racine's contemporaries, but it is also possible, and perhaps more relevant, to engage with such a text using a post-Perelmanian system of modern rhetoric; we can, for example, interpret texts featuring women through reference to the opinions on the sexes expressed in contemporary casuistic legal and religious debate, but we can also, and rightly so, re-contextualize this synchronic historical analysis by adopting a gender perspective and so on. There is most certainly a benefit to be had in taking synchronic analyses, grounded in the period studied, and system-atically re-contextualizing them through a series of analyses employing modern concepts, ideas and systems, provided that the internal coher-ence of each historicized system is carefully preserved, and the shifts from one system to another are always flagged. In addition, by making synchronic and diachronic approaches compatible with each other, we can focus on the current relevance of the subject matter while ensuring that our reading of the corpus is not thereby impoverished. Further, this combined approach, which is by no means new (every period has similarly brought the modern analytical concepts at its disposal to bear on its analysis of the past), enables us to justify our critical act, in as far as it is required, at whatever juncture, to both ourselves and our audience, to demonstrate the axiological and contemporary relevance of a piece of teaching or research. Finally, this type of interplay allows us to be adventurous in our interpretations, to avoid rehearsing well-worn arguments, to question, to reflect, sometimes even to produce new ideas and, in due course, to change our view of the corpus we are studying ... otherwise what is the point of teaching and research?

Grasping the past in order to improve our understanding of the links between an earlier corpus and our own present; comparing different systems of historicity; creating a complementary relationship between past and current concepts and systems of analysis (or setting them in opposition should the need arise); always being able to understand how criticism functions within its own historical moment; and, last, knowing how to justify the content of our research or teaching, not because it features on a syllabus, because its authority is accepted or because it is part of the canon, but because it is contemporary, relevant and original; these are the practices which are key, in my view, to a profitable study of the past. I am not suggesting that we should treat the seventeenth century as our own, or that it is particularly relevant to our own times, quite the contrary, but I do believe that, across the distance that separates us, there is a *link*, and this link is formed by History. It is not that there is anything inherently laudable or deplorable about the seventeenth century, but rather that it is perceived as the object, over the centuries, of the admirations and hatreds of successive periods; in this respect, it is of interest not only for itself, but also because it gives us an understanding of those other periods which have taken it as a reference point, providing insights into the nature of each period's interpretation of the past in the name of its own present.

Where theatre is concerned, the situation is both more complicated and more interesting. While the above considerations can easily be applied to teaching and research on the aesthetics and history of theatre, it is even more important to approach the latter through praxis, or through reference to aesthetic and social practices. In order to teach theatre, we must indeed engage in a practice of writing and criticism, but we must also draw on the practices of actors, technicians, playwrights and directors, and systematically explore, visualize and experience the heterogeneous, hyper-democratic practice of the audience. It is far from immaterial, when considering the urban theatre of the seventeenth and eighteenth centuries, for us to know that the great majority of audience members (more than 60 per cent) would be standing in the pit, or that, from 1637 to 1759, a significant number of spectators (between about 40 and 150) would be seated on the stage itself, while a general 'hubbub' reigned throughout the theatre. It is not without interest, either, to know that in principle it was the actors who controlled the production, and that their power was reduced gradually through the efforts of authors, that there were attempts by theorists of theatre to exert an influence they did not yet have, or, again, that traditions of performance and delivery have evolved, as have costumes, scenery, special effects and so on. And here, once again, we must transport ourselves into the past while maintaining our position in the present, if only to look on theatre as a series of 'events', 'sessions' or 'performances', depending on whatever critical framework we are using. Likewise, while we should in no way renounce the canon which represents great moments of French dramatic literature and always demands our attention (Racine, Molière, Corneille, Marivaux, Beaumarchais), a glance away from the mainstream may reveal a few surprises: a blood and thunder French theatre, very similar to Elizabethan theatre, and dating from the beginning of the seventeenth century; comedies written between 1680 and 1715 describing a world where love, money, marriage and inheritance are intertwined in such a way that fictional power, self-interest and morals become shamelessly interchangeable; comedies and pastorals portraying female homosexuality (*Iphis et Iante* by Benserade), or male homosexuality (*Le Beau Berger* by Fonteny) and so on. In this process, the type of theatre we call early modern, once it has divested itself of the traditions of admiration and respect established by French twentieth-century theatre, may appear, if not more modern, at least more engaged with contemporary views relating to the theatrical arts.

As a result, I have found it impossible when teaching theatre (even more so than in the teaching of narrative, poetry or theoretical writing) to separate historical and theoretical research from practices, whether they are those of the spectator or those associated with the stagecraft of the practitioner (dramaturgy, production and, occasionally, acting). By exerting its presence in the present, the theatre of the past remains, above all, a live performance. And it is perhaps these two words which sum up the essence of my teaching practice, one perpetually and vigorously inspired by research and by a curiosity about what might change our views on early corpuses: we must contrive to maintain a relationship between teacher and students that is as filled with surprises as that maintained by actors with their audience in the theatre. Teaching is a live performance, built out of enthusiasm, exchanges and vigorous critical debates, out of what are, in sum, *pleasures*.

Translated by Teresa Bridgeman

Index